The White Man's Burden

The White Man's Burden

HISTORICAL ORIGINS OF RACISM IN THE UNITED STATES

WINTHROP D. JORDAN

OXFORD UNIVERSITY PRESS
London   Oxford   New York
1974

OXFORD UNIVERSITY PRESS

Oxford   London   New York
Glasgow   Toronto   Melbourne   Wellington
Cape Town   Salisbury   Ibadan   Nairobi   Lusaka   Addis Ababa
Bombay   Calcutta   Madras   Karachi   Lahore   Dacca
Kuala Lumpur   Hong Kong   Tokyo

First published by Oxford University Press, New York, 1974
First issued as an Oxford University Press paperback, 1974

Printed in the United States of America

To Phyllis

Preface

This study deals with the historical origins of racism in the United States. I use the term *racism* with some reluctance, since it is very easy, and dangerous, to read present conditions into the past. Racial attitudes in this country are very different now from what they were three hundred years ago, and it is very important that we deal with our past, insofar as possible, on its own terms.

The relevance, if any, of this study to the present is left principally to the reader to determine, though I confess to having written several sentences on the subject. My assumptions about the value of historical study are similar to those of most historians. A comprehension of the past seems to have two opposite advantages in the present: it makes us aware of how different people have been in other ages and accordingly enlarges our awareness of the possibilities of human experience, and at the same time it impresses upon us those tendencies in human beings which have *not* changed and which accordingly are unlikely to, at least in the immediate future. Viewed from a slightly different vantage point, an understanding of the history of our own culture gives some inkling of the categories of possibilities within which for the time being we are born to live.

To say this is, I suppose, to make something of a claim for the value of studying current racial attitudes by taking, as they say, "the historical approach." What an historian contributes, inevitably, is a sense and appreciation of the important effect—perhaps even the great weight—of prior upon ensuing experience.

A word about the provenance of this book. It is a quite drastic abridgement with minor modifications of my *White Over Black: American Attitudes toward the Negro, 1550-1812* (Chapel Hill: University of North Carolina Press, 1968). Since publication of that work, it has become apparent, not altogether to my astonishment, that many people do not find themselves entirely comfortable wading through six hundred and fifty pages on a single subject. It has become obvious, too, that many college and school instructors are insufficiently merciless when contemplating inflicting a book of that length upon their students. In addition, I will admit to having something of a missionary urge about the subject with which this book deals. *The White Man's Burden* results from these factors.

It may appear rather a large claim to say that a book concerning attitudes toward Negroes is also a book about the origins of American racism. Let me say two things by way of explanation. First of all, when I began work on what became *White Over Black* I started by analyzing white American attitudes toward blacks *and* Indians. It soon became obvious, as I then thought, that I could not attempt both, so I dropped Indians. But in continuing with attitudes toward Negroes, Indians kept creeping (to use the prevailing stereotype) back in. So in fact there is considerable discussion about attitudes toward Indians in this book. Secondly, I remain convinced that white American attitudes toward blacks have done a great deal to shape and condition American responses to other racial minorities. To prove this contention would require another book, a project which lassitude leads me to leave generously to someone else.

Some, but by no means all, readers schooled in the behavioral sciences will discover a disgraceful lack of system in the approach taken here toward the way societies are held together and toward the way men think, act, and feel. There is, however, a certain sloppiness in the available evidence. If it were possible to poll the inhabitants of Virginia concerning their reactions to those famous first "twenty Negars" who arrived in 1619 I would be among the first at the foot of the gangplank, questionnaire in hand. Lacking this opportunity, I have operated with certain working assumptions which some readers will detect as drawing upon some "psychologies"—the assumptions about how people operate—of the twentieth century and upon some of the psychological imagery of the eighteenth. I have taken "attitudes" to be discrete entities susceptible of historical analysis. This term seems to me to possess a desirable combination of precision and embraciveness. It suggests thoughts and feelings (as opposed to actions) directed toward some specific object (as opposed to generalized faiths and beliefs). At the same time it suggests a wide range in consciousness, intensity, and saliency in the response to the object. We are all aware that our "attitude toward" sex is not of precisely the same order as our "attitude toward" Medicare, and the same may be said of our attitudes toward the neighbor's cat or Red China or acid-rock or the Ku Klux Klan—not, of course, that it is right to suppose that our various attitudes toward these objects are altogether unconnected with another. This book treats attitudes as existing not only at various levels of intensity but at various levels of consciousness and unconsciousness; it is written on the assumption that there is no clear dividing line between "thought" and "feeling," between conscious and unconscious mental processes. The book therefore deals with "attitudes" toward blacks and Indians which range from highly articulated ideas about the church or natural rights or the structure of the human skin, through off-hand notions and traditional beliefs about climate or savages or the duties of Christian ministers, through myths about Africa or Noah or the properties of chimpanzees, down to expressions of the most profound human urges— to the coded languages of our strivings for death and life and self-identification.

To deal with the roots of American racism in this way is not to ignore the crucial matters of economic exploitation and social degradation. Without those factors we would have no racism as we know it. But to say, as many have done, that racism is merely the rationalizing ideology of the oppressor, is to advance a grievous error. To rest the analysis there is to close one's eyes to the complexity of human oppression.

NOTE ON THE CONCEPT OF RACE

Since the presently difficult terms *race* and *racial* are used throughout this book, it seems desirable that their meaning be clear. It is notorious that *race* has been defined in a great variety of (usually unfortunate) ways, but it is less widely known that in recent years race as a scientific concept has undergone a virtual revolution. Since about 1950 scientists have made notable advances in the study of human races and have dispelled much confusion on the subject. Though there remain broad areas of disagreement and many unanswered questions, most reputable investigators now share certain fundamental suppositions and modes of approach.

Increasingly the tendency has been to study human races within the context of human evolution and genetics. At first some scientists directed their attention to physical features which seemed obviously susceptible to modification by natural selection. Attempts were made to link the more gross and obvious physiognomic characteristics with climate factors: thus the typical Mongolian face and stature were declared admirably adapted to extreme cold. Partly because such characteristics are difficult to analyze genetically, other scientists set out to investigate certain characteristics, such as blood types, which are governed not by many genes but by one. Initially it was supposed that blood types of the major series A-B-O were selectively neutral (that is, that individuals were neither advantaged nor disadvantaged by having a given type of blood); but it now seems almost certain that some of these types are connected with susceptibility to certain diseases. More strikingly, it has been established that a gene responsible for sickle-cell hemoglobin (which is especially common in Africa) often causes fatal anemia in those individuals with two parents contributing the gene but affords protection against malaria to individuals inheriting the sickle-cell gene from one parent only and who do not develop the anemia. In malarial areas the frequency of the gene remains roughly constant in the population as a whole: for while the sickling gene makes for a fatal disease in some persons, it saves others from death by malaria but itself does no harm, and it is thereby passed on to the next generation. In non-malarial areas, of course, the gene is entirely disadvantageous. Discovery of these facts has served to highlight man's plasticity under pressure of environmental change: elimination of mosquitoes may result eventually in elimination of a racial characteristic.

The sickling gene and indeed genes as such are not commonly thought of as racial characteristics. Obviously, however, human groups which differ markedly in appearance also differ genetically. One of the most important recent breakthroughs has been the conception of *race* as a group of individuals sharing a common gene pool. Such a definition emphasizes the fact that racial characteristics such as skin color are unlikely to remain stable over long periods of time. It underlines the fact that the continued existence of races is dependent upon geographical or social separation. It places in proper perspective the biological differences among human beings: all mankind shares a vast number of genes in common, yet at the same time various populations differ as to frequency of certain genes. With this in mind, racial characteristics may be defined as biological traits which various populations possess in varying frequencies. By this definition, arms and legs are not racial characteristics; on the other hand, blue eyes do constitute a racial characteristic, but blue-eyed people do not constitute a race. Finally, the genetic approach to race makes clear that permanent isolation of any group of individuals from the common gene pool of the species *Homo sapiens* would result eventually in development of a new species which would be incapable of genetic intermingling with its progenitor. In this sense, races are incipient species. Obviously, however, the biocultural attributes of *Homo sapiens* make the prospect of permanent reproductive isolation very unlikely.

There are several important, broad emphases implicit in this evolutionary view of race which run somewhat counter to widely held popular notions. It is now clear that mankind is a single biological species; that races are neither discrete nor stable units but rather that they are plastic, changing, integral parts of a whole which is itself changing. It is clear, furthermore, that races are best studied as products of a process; and, finally, that racial differences involve the relative frequency of genes and characteristics rather than absolute and mutually exclusive distinctions. It is also true, however, that the process of human raciation remains imperfectly understood. The evolutionary history of human races is still a subject of dispute, though at this writing a majority of investigators think that present races derived from a single progenitor who had already developed into *Homo sapiens*.

Unfortunately, recent advances in the study of race have done little to settle certain important questions concerning racial differences in physiology and anatomy—let alone the slippery problem of mental abilities. It remains hazardous, for instance, to offer summary findings as to skeletal differences between whites and blacks, except to say that such differences do exist, have often been exaggerated, required discussion in terms of frequency, and need further investigation. It is perhaps more surprising that the facts concerning skin color remain in doubt. It is clear that the complex structure of the skin consists of three basic layers, that differences in skin color are quantitative in the sense that all peoples (except albinos) possess in varying measure a granulated pigment known as melanin in the middle layer, and that melanin in greater or less degree largely governs external complexion. The most convincing of recent suggestions is that a light complexion protects the body against a deficiency of vitamin D and that a dark complexion prevents too much absorbtion of that vitamin. It is well established that either too little or too much vitamin D results in injury to the body. But this suggestion still remains only a best-possibility. The medical and evolutionary value of light or dark skin has not been fully and unquestionably established. It is arresting that a scientific problem which has been grappled with for centuries by Western culture still remains largely unsolved. It is one of the points of this book that the "problem" is a problem at all.

August 1973   W.D.J.

Contents

I

Genesis
1550–1700

1

First Impressions
Initial English Confrontation with Africans

When the Atlantic nations of Europe began expanding overseas in the sixteenth century, Portugal led the way to Africa and to the east while Spain founded a great empire in America. It was not until the reign of Queen Elizabeth that Englishmen came to realize that overseas exploration and plantations could bring home wealth, power, glory, and fascinating information. By the early years of the seventeenth century Englishmen had developed a taste for empire and for tales of adventure and discovery. More than is usual in human affairs, one man, the great chronicler Richard Hakluyt, had roused enthusiasm for western planting and had stirred the nation with his monumental compilation, *The Principal Navigations, Voyages, Traffiques and Discoveries of the English Nation.* Here was a work to widen a people's horizons. Its exhilarating accounts of voyages to all quarters of the globe constituted a national hymn, a scientific treatise, a sermon, and an adventure story.

English voyagers did not touch upon the shores of West Africa until after 1550, nearly a century after Prince Henry the Navigator had mounted the sustained Portuguese thrust southward for a water passage to the Orient. Usually Englishmen came to Africa to trade goods *with* the natives. The earliest English descriptions of West Africa were written by adventurous traders, men who had no special interest in converting the natives or, except for the famous Hawkins voyages in the 1560's, in otherwise laying hands on them. Extensive English participation in the slave trade did not develop until well into the seventeenth century. Initially English contact with Africans did not take place primarily in a context which prejudged the Negro as a slave, at least not as a slave of Englishmen. Rather, Englishmen met Africans merely as another sort of men.

Englishmen found the peoples of Africa very different from themselves. "Negroes" looked different to Englishmen; their religion was un-Christian; their manner of living was anything but English; they seemed to be a particularly libidinous sort of people. All these clusters of perceptions were related to each other, though they may be spread apart for inspection, and they were related also to the circumstances of contact in Africa, to previously accumulated traditions concerning that strange and distant continent, and to certain special qualities of English society on the eve of its expansion into the New World.

THE BLACKNESS WITHOUT

For Englishmen, the most arresting characteristic of the newly discovered African was his color. Travelers rarely failed to comment upon it; indeed when describing Africans they frequently began with complexion and then moved on to dress (or, as they saw, lack of it) and manners. At Cape Verde, "These people are all blacke, and are called Negroes, without any apparell, saving before their privities." Robert Baker's narrative poem recounting his two voyages to the West African coast in 1562 and 1563 introduced the people he saw with these engaging lines:

> And entering in [a river], we see
>   a number of blacke soules,
> Whose likelinesse seem'd men to be,
>   but all as blacke as coles.
> Their Captain comes to me
>   as naked as my naile,
> Not having witte or honestie
>   to cover once his taile.

Englishmen actually described Negroes as *black*—an exaggerated term which in itself suggests that the Negro's complexion had powerful impact upon their perceptions. Even the peoples of northern Africa seemed so dark that Englishmen tended to call them "black" and let further refinements go by the board. In Shakespeare's day, the Moors, including Othello, were commonly portrayed as pitchy black and the terms *Moor* and *Negro* were used almost interchangeably. With curious inconsistency, however, Englishmen recognized that Africans south of the Sahara were not at all the same people as the much more familiar Moors. Sometimes they referred to West Africans as "black Moors" to distinguish them from the peoples of North Africa.

The powerful impact which the Negro's color made upon Englishmen must have been partly owing to suddenness of contact. Though the Bible as well as the arts and literature of antiquity and the Middle Ages offered some slight introduction to the "Ethiope," England's immediate acquaintance with "black"-skinned peoples came with relative rapidity. People much darker than Englishmen were not entirely unfamiliar, but really "black" men were virtually unknown except as vaguely referred to in the hazy literature about the sub-Sahara which had filtered down from antiquity. Native West Africans probably first appeared in London in 1554; in that year five "Negroes," as one trader reported, were taken to England, "kept till they could speake the language," and then brought back again "to be a helpe to Englishmen" who were engaged in trade with Africans on the coast. Hakluyt's later discussion of these Africans suggests that these "blacke Moores" were a novelty to Englishmen. In this respect the English experience was markedly different from that of the Spanish and Portuguese who for centuries had been in close contact with North Africa and had actually been invaded and subjected by people both darker and more "highly civilized" than themselves. The impact of the Negro's color was the more powerful upon Englishmen, moreover, because England's principal contact with Africans came in West Africa and the Congo, which meant that one of the lightest-skinned of the earth's peoples suddenly came face to face with one of the darkest.

In England perhaps more than in southern Europe, the concept of blackness was loaded with intense meaning. Long before

—they found that some men were black, Englishmen found in the idea of blackness a way of expressing some of their most ingrained values. No other color except white conveyed so much emotional impact. As described by the *Oxford English Dictionary*, the meaning of *black* before the sixteenth century included, "Deeply stained with dirt; soiled, dirty, foul. . . . Having dark or deadly purposes, malignant; pertaining to or involving death, deadly; baneful, disastrous, sinister. . . . Foul, iniquitous, atrocious, horrible, wicked. . . . Indicating disgrace, censure, liability to punishment, etc." Black was an emotionally partisan color, the handmaid and symbol of baseness and evil, a sign of danger and repulsion.

Embedded in the concept of blackness was its direct opposite—whiteness. No other colors so clearly implied opposition, "beinge coloures utterlye contrary":

> Everye white will have its blacke,
> And everye sweete its sowre.

White and black connoted purity and filthiness, virginity and sin, virtue and baseness, beauty and ugliness, beneficence and evil, God and the devil. Whiteness, moreover, carried a special significance for Elizabethan Englishmen: it was, particularly when complemented by red, the color of perfect human beauty, especially *female* beauty. This ideal was already centuries old in Elizabeth's time, and their fair Queen was its very embodiment: her cheeks were "roses in a bed of lillies." (Elizabeth was naturally pale but like many ladies then and since she freshened her "lillies" at the cosmetic table.) An adoring nation knew precisely what a beautiful Queen looked like.

> Her cheeke, her chinne, her neck, her nose,
> This was a lillye, that was a rose;
> Her bosome, sleeke as Paris plaster,
> Held upp twoo bowles of Alabaster.

By contrast, the Negro was ugly, by reason of his color and also his "horrid Curles" and "disfigured" lips and nose. A century later blackness still required apology: one of the earliest attempts to delineate the West African as a heroic character, the popular story *Oroonoko* (1688), presented Negroes as capable of blushing and turning pale. It was important, if incalculably so, that English discovery of black Africans came at a time when the accepted English standard of ideal beauty was a fair complexion of rose and white. Negroes seemed the very picture of perverse negation.

From the first, however, many English observers displayed a certain sophistication about the Negro's color. Despite an ethnocentric tendency to find blackness repulsive, many writers were fully aware that Africans themselves might have different tastes. As early as 1621 one writer told of the "Jetty coloured" Negroes, "Who in their native beauty most delight,/And in contempt doe paint the Divell white"; this assertion became almost a commonplace. Many accounts of Africa reported explicitly that the Negro's preference in colors was inverse to the European's. Even the Negro's features were conceded to be appealing to Negroes.

THE CAUSES OF COMPLEXION

Black human beings were not only startling but extremely puzzling. The complexion of Africans posed problems about its nature, especially its permanence and utility, its cause and origin, and its significance. Although these were rather separate questions, there was a pronounced tendency among Englishmen and other Europeans to formulate the problem in terms of causation alone. If the cause of human blackness could be explained, then its nature and significance would follow.

Not that the problem was completely novel. The ancient Greeks had touched upon it. The story of Phaëton's driving the chariot sun wildly through the heavens apparently served as an explanation for the Ethiopian's blackness even before written records, and traces of this ancient fable were still drifting about during the seventeenth century. Ptolemy had made the important suggestion that the Negro's blackness and woolly hair were caused by exposure to the hot sun and had pointed out that people in northern climates were white and those in temperate areas an intermediate color. Before the sixteenth century, though, the question of the Negro's color can hardly be said to have drawn the attention of Englishmen or indeed of Europeans generally.

The discovery of West Africa and the development of Negro slavery made the question far more urgent. The range of possible answers was rigidly restricted, however, by the virtually universal assumption, dictated by church and Scripture, that all mankind stemmed from a single source. Indeed it is impossible fully to understand the various efforts at explaining the Negro's complexion without bearing in mind the strength of the tradition which in 1614 made the chronicler, the Reverend Samuel Purchas, proclaim vehemently: "the tawney Moore, blacke Negro, duskie Libyan, ash-coloured Indian, olive-coloured American, should with the whiter European become one *sheep-fold,* under *one great Sheepheard* . . . without any more distinction of Colour, Nation, Language, Sexe, Condition, all may bee *One* in him that is One. . . ."

In general, the most satisfactory answer to the problem was some sort of reference to the action of the sun, whether the sun was assumed to have scorched the skin, drawn the bile, or blackened the blood. People living on the Line had obviously been getting too much of it; after all, even Englishmen were darkened by a little exposure. How much more, then, with the Negroes who were "so scorched and vexed with the heat of the sunne, that in many places they curse it when it riseth." This association of the Negro's color with the sun became a commonplace in Elizabethan literature; as Shakespeare's Prince of Morocco apologized, "Mislike me not for my complexion,/ The shadow'd livery of the burnish'd sun,/ To whom I am a neighbour and near bred."

Unfortunately this theory ran headlong into a stubborn fact of nature which simply could not be overridden: if the equatorial inhabitants of Africa were blackened by the sun, why not the people living on the same Line in America? Logic required them to be the same color. Yet by the middle of the sixteenth century it was becoming perfectly apparent that the Indians living in the hottest regions of the New World could by no stretch of the imagination be described as black. They were "olive" or "tawny," and moreover they had long hair rather than the curious "wool" of Negroes. Clearly the method of accounting for human complexion by latitude just did not work. The worst of it was that the formula did not seem altogether wrong, since it was apparent that in general men in hot climates tended to be darker than in cold ones.

Another difficulty with the climatic explanation of skin color arose as lengthening experience provided more knowledge about Negroes. If the heat of the sun caused the Negro's blackness, then his removal to cold northerly countries ought to result in his losing it; even if he did not himself surrender his peculiar color, surely his descendants must. By mid-seventeenth century it was becoming increasingly apparent that this expectation was ill founded: Negroes in Europe and northern America were simply not whitening up very noticeably.

From the beginning, in fact, some Englishmen were certain that the Negro's blackness was permanent and innate and that no amount of cold was going to alter it. There was good authority in Jeremiah 13:23; "Can the Ethiopian change his skin/ or the leopard his spots?" Elizabethan dramatists used the stock expression "to wash in Ethiop white" as indicating sheer impossibility. In 1578 a voyager and speculative geographer, George Best, announced that the blackness of Negroes "proceedeth of some naturall infection of the first inhabitants of that country, and so all the whole progenie of them descended, are still polluted with the same blot of infection." An essayist in 1695 declared firmly, "A negroe will always be a negroe, carry him to Greenland, give him chalk, feed and manage him never so many ways."

There was an alternative to the naturalistic explanations of the Negro's blackness. Some writers felt that God's curse on Ham (Cham), or upon his son Canaan, and all their descendants was entirely sufficient to account for the color of Negroes. This could be an appealing explanation, especially for men like George Best who wished to stress the "natural infection" of blackness and for those who hoped to incorporate the Negro's complexion securely within the accepted history of mankind. The original story in Genesis 9 and 10 was that after the Flood, Ham had looked upon his father's "nakedness" as Noah lay drunk in his tent, but the other two sons, Shem and Japheth, had covered their father without looking upon him; when Noah awoke he cursed Canaan, son of Ham, saying that he would be a "servant of servants" unto his brothers. Given this text, the question becomes why a tale which logically implied slavery but absolutely nothing about skin color should have become a popular explanation of the Negro's blackness. The matter is puzzling, but probably, over the very long run, the story was supported by the ancient association of heat with sensuality and by the fact that some sub-Saharan Africans had been enslaved by Europeans since ancient times. In addition, the extraordinary persistence of the tale in the face of centuries of constant refutation was probably sustained by a feeling that blackness could scarcely be anything *but* a curse and by the common need to confirm the facts of nature by specific reference to Scripture. In contrast to the climatic theory, God's curse provided a satisfying purposiveness which the sun's scorching heat could not match until the eighteenth century.

In the long run, of course, the Negro's color attained greatest significance not as a scientific problem but as a social fact. Englishmen found blackness in human beings a peculiar and important point of difference. The African's color set him radically *apart* from Englishmen. But then, distant Africa had been known to Christians for ages as a land of men radically different in religion.

DEFECTIVE RELIGION

While distinctive appearance set Africans apart in a novel way, their religious condition distinguished them in a more familiar manner. Englishmen and Christians everywhere were sufficiently acquainted with the concept of heathenism that they confronted its living representatives without puzzlement. Certainly the rather sudden discovery that the world was teeming with heathen people made for heightened vividness and urgency in a long-standing problem; but it was the fact that this problem was already well formulated long before contact with Africa which proved important in shaping English reaction to the Negro's defective religious condition.

In one sense heathenism was less a "problem" for Christians than an exercise in self-definition: the heathen condition defined by negation the proper Christian life. In another sense, the presence of heathenism in the world constituted an imperative to intensification of religious commitment. From its origin Christianity was a universalist, proselytizing religion, and the sacred and secular histories of Christianity made manifest the necessity of bringing non-Christians into the fold. For Englishmen, then, the heathenism of Negroes was at once a counter-image of their own religion and a summons to eradicate an important distinction between the two peoples. Yet the interaction of these two facets of the concept of heathenism made for a peculiar difficulty: On the one hand, to act upon the felt necessity of converting Africans would have been to eradicate the point of distinction which Englishmen found most familiar and most readily comprehensible. Yet if they did not act upon this necessity, continued heathenism among Negroes would remain an unwelcome reminder to Englishmen that they were not meeting their obligations to their own faith—nor to the benighted Negroes. Englishmen resolved this implicit dilemma by doing nothing.

Considering the strength of the Christian tradition, it is almost startling that Englishmen failed to respond to the discovery of heathenism in Africa with at least the rudiments of a campaign for conversion. Although the impulse to spread Christianity seems to have been weaker in Englishmen than, say, in the Catholic Portuguese, it cannot be said that Englishmen were indifferent to the obligation imposed upon them by the overseas discoveries of the sixteenth century. While they were badly out of practice at the business of conversion (again in contrast to the Portuguese) and while they had never before been faced with the practical difficulties involved in Christianizing entire continents, they nonetheless were able to contemplate with equanimity and even eagerness the prospect of converting the heathen. Indeed they went so far as to conclude that converting the natives in America was sufficiently important to demand English settlement there. As it turned out, the well-publicized English program for converting Indians produced very meager results, but the avowed intentions certainly were genuine. It was in marked contrast, therefore, that Englishmen did not avow similar intentions concerning Africans until the late eighteenth century. Fully as much as with skin color, though less consciously, Englishmen distinguished between the heathenisms of Indians and of Negroes.

It is not easy to account for the distinction which Englishmen made. On the basis of the travelers' reports there was no reason for Englishmen to suppose Indians inherently superior to Negroes as candidates for conversion. But America was not Africa. Englishmen contemplated settling in America, where voyagers had established the King's claim and where supposedly the climate was temperate; in contrast, Englishmen did not envision settlement in Africa, which had quickly gained notoriety as a graveyard for Europeans and where the Portuguese had been first on the scene. Certainly these very different circumstances meant that Englishmen confronted Negroes and Indians in radically different social contexts and that Englishmen would find it far easier to contemplate converting Indians than Negroes. Yet it remains difficult to see why Negroes were not included, at least as a secondary target. The fact that English contact with Africans so frequently occurred in a context of slave dealing does not entirely explain the omission of Negroes, since in that same context the Portuguese and Spanish did sometimes attempt to minister to the souls of Africans and since Englishmen in America enslaved Indians when good occasion arose. Given these circumstances, it is hard to escape the conclusion that the distinction which Englishmen made as to conversion was at least in some small measure modeled after the difference they saw in skin color.

The most important aspect of English reaction to African heathenism was that Englishmen evidently did not regard it as separable from the Negro's other attributes. Heathenism was treated not so much as a specifically religious defect but as one manifestation of a general refusal to measure up to proper standards, as a failure to be English or even civilized. There was every reason for Englishmen to fuse the various attributes they found in Africans. During the first century of English contact with Africa, Protestant Christianity was an important element in English patriotism; especially during the struggle against Spain the Elizabethan's special Christianity was interwoven into his conception of his own nationality, and he was therefore inclined to regard the Negroes' lack of true religion as part of theirs. Being a Christian was not merely a matter of subscribing to certain doctrines; it was a quality inherent in oneself and in one's society. It was interconnected with all the other attributes of normal and proper men: as one of the earliest English travelers described Africans, they were "a people of beastly living, without a God, lawe, religion, or common wealth"—which was to say that Negroes were not Englishmen. Far from isolating African heathenism as a separate characteristic, English travelers sometimes linked it explicitly with blackness and savagery.

SAVAGE BEHAVIOR

The condition of savagery—the failure to be civilized—set Negroes apart from Englishmen in an ill-defined but crucial fashion. Africans were *different* from Englishmen in so many ways: in their clothing, housing, farming, warfare, language, government, morals, and (not least important) in their table manners. To judge from the comments of voyagers, Englishmen had an unquenchable thirst for the details of savage life. Englishmen were, indeed, enormously curious about their rapidly expanding world, and it is scarcely surprising that they should have taken an interest in reports about cosmetic mutilation, polygamy, infanticide, ritual murder, and the like. In addition, reports about "savages" began arriving at a time when Englishmen very much needed to be able to translate their apprehensive interest in an uncontrollable world out of medieval religious terms. The discovery of savages overseas enabled them to make this translation easily, to move from miracles to verifiable monstrosities, from heaven to earth.

As with skin color, English reporting of African customs was partly an exercise in self-inspection by means of comparison. The necessity of continuously measuring African practices with an English yardstick of course tended to emphasize the differences between the two groups, but it also made for heightened sensitivity to instances of similarity. Thus the Englishman's ethnocentrism tended to distort his perception of African culture in two opposite directions. While it led him to emphasize differences and to condemn deviations from the English norm, it led him also to seek out similarities. Particularly, Englishmen were inclined to see the structures of African societies as analogous to their own, complete with kings, counselors, gentlemen, and the baser sort.

Here especially they found Africans like themselves, partly because they know no other way to describe any society and partly
because there was actually good basis for such a view of the social
organization of West African communities.

Despite the fascination and self-instruction Englishmen derived
from discussing the savage behavior of Africans, they never felt
that savagery was as important a quality in Africans as it was in
the American Indians. As was the case with heathenism, contrasting social contexts played an important role in shaping the English response to savagery in the two peoples. Inevitably, the savagery of the Indians assumed a special significance in the minds of
those actively engaged in a program of planting civilization in
the American wilderness. The case with the African was different;
the English errand into Africa was not a new or a perfect community but a business trip. No hope was entertained for civilizing the Negro's steaming continent, and Englishmen therefore
lacked compelling reason to develop a program for remodeling the
African natives.

From the beginning, also, the importance of the Negro's savagery was muted by the Negro's color. Englishmen could go a long
way toward expressing their sense of being different from Africans
merely by calling them "black." By contrast, the aboriginals in
America did not have the appearance of being radically distinct
from Europeans except in religion and savage behavior. English
voyagers placed much less emphasis upon the Indian's color than
upon the Negro's, and they never permitted the Indian's physiognomy to distract their attention from what they regarded as his
essential quality, his savagery.

It would be a mistake, however, to slight the importance of
what was seen as the African's savagery, since it fascinated Englishmen from the very first. English observers in West Africa were
sometimes so profoundly impressed by the Negro's behavior that
they resorted to a powerful metaphor with which to express their
own sense of difference from him. They knew perfectly well that
Negroes were men, yet they frequently described the Africans as
"brutish" or "bestial" or "beastly." The supposed hideous tortures,
cannibalism, rapacious warfare, revolting diet (and so forth page
after page) seemed somehow to place the Negro among the beasts.

The eventual circumstances of the Englishman's contact with Africans served to strengthen this feeling. *Slave* traders in Africa necessarily handled Negroes the same way men in England handled beasts, herding and examining and buying, as with any other animals which were products of commerce.

THE APES OF AFRICA

If Negroes were likened to beasts, there was in Africa a beast which was likened to men. It was a strange and eventually tragic happenstance of nature that Africa was the habitat of the animal which in appearance most resembles man. The animal called "orang-outang" by contemporaries (actually the chimpanzee) was native to those parts of western Africa where the early slave trade was heavily concentrated. Though Englishmen were acquainted (for the most part vicariously) with monkeys and baboons, they were unfamiliar with tail-less apes who walked about like men. Accordingly, it happened that Englishmen were introduced to the anthropoid apes and to Negroes at the same time and in the same place. The startlingly human appearance and movements of the "ape"—a generic term though often used as a synonym for the "orang-outang"—aroused some curious speculations.

In large measure these speculations derived from traditions which had been accumulating in Western culture since ancient times. Medieval books on animals contained rosters of strange creatures who in one way or another seemed disturbingly to resemble men. There were the *simia* and the *cynocephali* and the *satyri* and the others, all variously described and related to one another, all jumbled in a characteristic blend of ancient reports and medieval morality. The confusion was not easily nor rapidly dispelled, and many of the traditions established by this literature were very much alive during the seventeenth century.

The section on apes in Edward Topsell's *Historie of Foure-Footed Beastes* (1607) serves to illustrate how certain seemingly trivial traditions and associations persisted in such form that they were bound to affect the way in which Englishmen would perceive the inhabitants of Africa. Above all, according to Topsell, "apes," were venerous. The red apes were "so venerous that they will ravish their Women." Baboons were "as lustful and venerous as goats"; a baboon which had been "brought to the French king . . . above all loved the companie of women, and young maidens; his genitall member was greater than might match the quantity of his other parts." Pictures of two varieties of apes, a "Satyre" and an "Ægopithecus," graphically emphasized the "virile member."

In addition to stressing the "lustful disposition" of the ape kind, Topsell's compilation contained suggestions concerning the character of simian facial features. "Men that have low and flat nostrils," readers were told in the section on apes, "are Libidinous as Apes that attempt women. . . ." There also seemed to be some connection between apes and devils. In a not altogether successful attempt to distinguish the "Satyre-apes" from the mythical creatures of that name, Topsell straightened everything out by explaining that it was "probable, that Devils take not any dænomination or shape from Satyres, but rather the Apes themselves from Devils whome they resemble, for there are many things common to the Satyre-apes and devilish Satyres." Association of apes and/or satyrs with devils was common in England: the inner logic of this association derived from uneasiness concerning the ape's "indecent likenesse and imitation of man"; it revolved around evil and sexual sin; and, rather tenuously, it connected apes with blackness.

Given this tradition and the coincidence of contact, it was virtually inevitable that Englishmen should discern similarity between the manlike beasts and the beastlike men of Africa. A few commentators went so far as to suggest that Negroes had sprung from the generation of ape-kind or that apes were themselves the offspring of Negroes and some unknown African beast. These contentions were squarely in line with the ancient tradition that Africa was a land "bringing dailie foorth newe monsters" because, as Aristotle himself had suggested, many different species came into proximity at the scarce watering places. Jean Bodin, the famous sixteenth-century French political theorist, summarized this wisdom of the ages with the categorical remark that "promiscuous coition of men and animals took place, wherefore the regions of Africa produce for us so many monsters." Despite all these monsters out of Africa, the notion that Negroes stemmed from beasts in a literal sense was not widely believed. It simply floated about, available, later, for anyone who wanted it.

Far more common and persistent was the notion that there sometimes occurred "a beastly copulation or conjuncture" between apes and Negroes, and especially that apes were inclined wantonly to attack Negro women. The very explicit idea that apes assaulted female human beings was not new; Africans were merely being asked to demonstrate what Europeans had known for centuries. As late as the 1730's a well-traveled, well-educated, and intelligent naval surgeon, John Atkins, was not at all certain that the stories were false: "At some Places the *Negroes* have been suspected of Bestiality with them [apes and monkeys], and by the Boldness and Affection they are known under some Circumstances to express to our Females; the Ignorance and Stupidity on the other side, to guide or control Lust; but more from the near resemblance [of apes] . . . to the Human Species would tempt one to suspect the Fact."

By the time Atkins addressed himself to this evidently fascinating problem, some of the confusion arising from the resemblance of apes to men had been dispelled. In 1699 the web of legend and unverified fact was disentangled by Edward Tyson, whose comparative study of a young "orang-outang" was a masterwork of critical scientific investigation. Throughout his dissection of the chimpanzee, Tyson meticulously compared the animal with human beings in every anatomical detail, and he established beyond question both the close relationship and the non-identity of ape and man. Here was a step forward; the question of the ape's proper place in nature was now grounded upon much firmer knowledge of the facts. Despite their scientific importance, Tyson's conclusions did nothing to weaken the vigorous tradition which linked the Negro with the ape. The supposed affinity between apes and men had as frequently been expressed in sexual as in anatomical terms, and his findings did not effectively rule out the possibility of unnatural sexual unions. Tyson himself remarked that orangs were especially given to venery.

The sexual association of apes with Negroes had an inner logic which kept it alive: sexual union seemed to prove a certain affinity without going so far as to indicate actual identity—which was what Englishmen really thought was the case. By forging a sexual link between Negroes and apes, furthermore, Englishmen were able to give vent to their feeling that Negroes were a lewd, lascivious, and wanton people.

LIBIDINOUS MEN

Undertones of sexuality run throughout many English accounts of West Africa. To liken Africans—any human beings—to beasts was to stress the animal within the man. Indeed the sexual connotations embodied in the terms *bestial* and *beastly* were considerably stronger in Elizabethan English than they are today, and when the Elizabethan traveler pinned these epithets upon the behavior of Africans he was more frequently registering a sense of sexual shock than describing swinish manners.

Lecherousness among Africans was at times for Englishmen merely another attribute which one would expect to find among heathen, savage, beastlike men. One commentator's remarks made evident how closely interrelated all these attributes were in the minds of Englishmen: "They have no knowledge of God . . . they are very greedie eaters, and no lesse drinkers, and very lecherous, and theevish, and much addicted to uncleanenesse: one man hath as many wives as hee is able to keepe and maintaine." Sexuality was what one expected of savages.

Clearly, however, the association of Africans with potent sexuality represented more than an incidental appendage to the concept of savagery. Long before first English contact with West Africa, the inhabitants of virtually the entire continent stood confirmed in European literature as lustful and venerous. About 1526 Leo Africanus (a Spanish Moroccan Moor converted to Christianity) supplied an influential description of the little-known lands of "Barbary," "Libya," "Numedia," and "Land of Negroes"; and Leo was as explicit as he was imaginative. In the English translation (1600) readers were informed concerning the "Negros" that "there is no Nation under Heaven more prone to Venery." Leo disclosed that "the Negroes . . . leade a beastly kind of life, being utterly destitute of the use of reason, of dexteritie of wit, and of all arts. Yea, they so behave themselves, as if

they had continually lived in a Forrest among wild beasts. They
have great swarmes of Harlots among them; whereupon a man
may easily conjecture their manner of living." Nor was Leo Africanus the only scholar to elaborate upon the ancient classical
sources concerning Africa. In a highly eclectic work first published
in 1566, Jean Bodin sifted the writings of ancient authorities and
concluded that heat and lust went hand in hand and that "in
Ethiopia . . . the race of men is very keen and lustful." Bodin
announced in a thoroughly characteristic sentence, "Ptolemy reported that on account of southern sensuality Venus chiefly is
worshiped in Africa and that the constellation of Scorpion, which
pertains to the pudenda, dominates that continent."

Depiction of the Negro as a lustful creature was not radically
new, therefore, when Englishmen first met Africans face to face.
Seizing upon and reconfirming these long-standing and apparently
common notions, Elizabethan travelers and literati dwelt explicitly with ease upon the especial sexuality of Africans. Othello's
embraces were "the gross clasps of a lascivious Moor." Francis
Bacon's *New Atlantis* (1624) referred to "an holy hermit" who
"desired to see the Spirit of Fornication; and there appeared to
him a little foul ugly Æthiop." Negro men, reported a seventeenth-century traveler, sported "large Propagators." In 1623
Richard Jobson, a sympathetic observer, reported that Mandingo
men were "furnisht with such members as are after a sort bur-
thensome unto them." Another commentator thought Negroes
"very lustful and impudent, especially, when they come to hide
their nakedness, (for a *Negroes* hiding his Members, their extraordinary greatness) is a token of their Lust, and therefore much
troubled with the Pox." By the eighteenth century a report on the
sexual aggressiveness of African women was virtually required of
European commentators. By then, of course, with many Englishmen actively participating in the slave trade, there were pressures
making for descriptions of "hot constitution'd Ladies" possessed
of a "temper hot and lascivious, making no scruple to prostitute
themselves to the *Europeans* for a very slender profit, so great is
their inclination to white men."

While the animus underlying these and similar remarks becomes sufficiently obvious once Englishmen began active partici-

pation in the slave trade, it is less easy to see why Englishmen
should have fastened upon Negroes a pronounced sexuality virtually upon first sight. The ancient notions distilled by Bodin and
Leo Africanus must have helped pattern initial English perceptions. Yet clearly there was something in English culture working
in this direction. It is certain that the presumption of powerful
sexuality in black men was far from being an incidental or casual
association in the minds of Englishmen. How very deeply this
association operated is obvious in *Othello,* a drama which loses
most of its power and several of its central points if it is read with
the assumption that because the black man was the hero English
audiences were indifferent to his blackness. Shakespeare was writing both *about* and *to* his countrymen's feelings concerning physical distinctions between peoples; the play is shot through with the
language of blackness and sex. Iago goes out of his way to talk
about his own motives: "I hate the Moor,/ And it is thought
abroad that 'twixt my sheets/ He has done my office." Later, he
becomes more direct, "For that I do suspect the lusty Moor hath
leaped into my seat." It was upon this so obviously absurd
suspicion that Iago based his resolve to "turn her virtue into
pitch." Such was his success, of course, that Othello finally rushes
off "to furnish me with some means of death for the fair devil."
With this contorted denomination of Desdemona, Othello unwittingly revealed how deeply Iago's promptings about Desdemona's
"own clime, complexion, and degree" had eaten into his consciousness. Othello was driven into accepting the premise that
the physical distinction *matters:* "For she had eyes," he has to
reassure himself, "and chose me." Then, as his suspicions give way
to certainty, he equates her character with his own complexion:

> Her name, that was as fresh,
> As Dian's visage, is now begrim'd and black
> As mine own face.

This important aspect of Iago's triumph over the noble Moor
was a subtly inverted reflection of the propositions which Iago,
hidden in darkness, worked upon the fair lady's father. No one
knew better than Iago how to play upon hidden strings of emo-

tion. Not content with the straightforward crudity that "your daughter and the Moor are now making the beast with two backs," Iago told the agitated Brabantio that "an old black ram/ Is tupping your white ewe" and alluded politely to "your daughter cover'd with a Barbary horse." This was not merely the language of (as we say) a "dirty" mind: it was the integrated imagery of blackness and whiteness, of Africa, of the sexuality of beasts and the bestiality of sex. And of course Iago was entirely successful in persuading Brabantio, who had initially welcomed Othello into his house, that the marriage was "against all rules of nature." Eventually Brabantio came to demand of Othello what could have brought a girl "so tender, fair, and happy"

> To incur a general mock
> Run from her guardage to the sooty bosom
> Of such a thing as thou.

Altogether a curious way for a senator to address a successful general.

These and similar remarks in the play *Othello* suggest that Shakespeare and his audiences were not totally indifferent to the sexual union of "black" men and "white" women. Shakespeare did not condemn such union; rather, he played upon an inner theme of black and white sexuality, showing how the poisonous mind of a white man perverted and destroyed the noblest of loves by means of bringing to the surface (from the darkness, whence Iago spoke) the lurking shadows of animal sex to assault the whiteness of chastity. Never did "dirty" words more dramatically "blacken" a "fair" name. At the play's climax, standing stunned by the realization that the wife he has murdered was innocent, Othello groans to Emilia, " 'Twas I that killed her"; and Emilia responds with a torrent of condemnation: "O! the more angel she,/ And you the blacker devil." Of Desdemona: "She was too fond of her filthy bargain." To Othello: "O gull! O dolt!/ As ignorant as dirt!" Shakespeare's genius lay precisely in juxtaposing these two pairs: inner blackness and inner whiteness. The drama meant little if his audiences had felt no response to this cross-inversion and to the deeply turbulent double meaning of black *over* white.

It required a very great dramatist to expose some of the more inward biocultural values which led—or drove—Englishmen to accept readily the notion that Negroes were peculiarly sexual men. Probably these values and the ancient reputation of Africa upon which they built were of primary importance in determing the response of Englishmen to Africans. Whatever the importance of biologic elements in these values—whatever the effects of long northern nights, of living in a cool climate, of possessing light-colored bodies which excreted contrasting lumps of darkness— these values by Shakespeare's time were interlocked with English history and culture and, more immediately, with the circumstances of contact with Africans and the social upheaval of Tudor England.

THE BLACKNESS WITHIN

The Protestant Reformation in England was a complex development, but certainly it may be said that during the sixteenth and early seventeenth century the content and tone of English Christianity were altered in the direction of Biblicism, personal piety, individual judgment, and more intense self-scrutiny and internalized control. Many pious Englishmen, not all of them "Puritans," came to approach life as if conducting an examination and to approach Scripture as if peering in a mirror. As a result, their inner energies were brought unusually close to the surface, more frequently than before into the almost rational world of legend, myth, and literature. The taut Puritan and the bawdy Elizabethan were not so much enemies as partners in this adventure which we usually think of in terms of great literature—of Milton and Shakespeare—and social conflict—of Saints and Cavaliers. The age was driven by the twin spirits of adventure and control, and while "adventurous Elizabethans" embarked upon voyages of discovery overseas, many others embarked upon inward voyages of discovery. Some men, like William Bradford and John Winthrop, were to do both. Given this charged atmosphere of (self-)discovery, it is scarcely surprising that Englishmen should have used peoples overseas as social mirrors and that they were especially inclined to discover attributes in savages which they found first, but could not speak of, in themselves.

Nowhere is the way in which certain of these cultural attributes came to bear upon Negroes more clearly illustrated than in a discourse by George Best, an Elizabethan adventurer who sailed in 1577 in search of the Northwest Passage. In the course of demonstrating the habitability of all parts of the world, George Best veered off to the problem of the color of Negroes. The cause of their blackness, he decided, was explained in Scripture. Noah and his sons and their wives were "white" and "by course of nature should have begotten . . . white children. But the envie of our great and continuall enemie the wicked Spirite is such, that as hee coulde not suffer our olde father Adam to live in the felicitie and Angelike state wherein he was first created . . . so againe, finding at this flood none but a father and three sons living, hee so caused one of them to disobey his fathers commandment, that after him all his posteritie should bee accursed." The "fact" of this "disobedience," Best continued, was this: Noah "commanded" his sons and their wives to behold God "with reverence and feare," and that "while they remained in the Arke, they should use continencie, and abstaine from carnall copulation with their wives . . . which good instructions and exhortations notwithstanding his wicked sonne Cham disobeyed, and being perswaded that the first childe borne after the flood . . . should inherite . . . all the dominions of the earth, hee . . . used company with his wife, and craftily went about thereby to dis-inherite the off-spring of his other two brethren." To punish this "wicked and detestable fact," God willed that "a sonne should bee born whose name was Chus, who not onely it selfe, but all his posteritie after him should bee so blacke and lothsome, that it might remain a spectacle of disobedience to all the worlde. And of this blacke and cursed Chus came all these blacke Moores which are in Africa."

The inner themes running throughout this extraordinary exegesis testify eloquently to the completeness with which English perceptions could integrate sexuality with blackness, the devil, and the judgment of a God who had originally created man not only "Angelike" but "white." These running equations lay em-

bedded at a deep and almost inaccessible level of Elizabethan culture; only occasionally did they appear in complete clarity, as
when evil dreams

> . . . hale me from my sleepe like forked Devils,
> Midnight, thou Æthiope, Empresse of Black Soules, Thou general
> Bawde to the whole world.

But what is still more arresting about George Best's discourse is
the shaft of light it throws upon the dark mood of strain and control in Elizabethan culture. In an important sense, Best's remarks
are not about Negroes; rather they play upon a theme of external
discipline exercised upon the man who fails to discipline himself.
The linkages he established—"disobedience" with "carnall copulation" with something "black and lothsome"—were not his alone.
The term *dirt* first began to acquire its meaning of moral impur-
ity, of smuttiness, at the very end of the sixteenth century. Perhaps
the key term, though, is "disobedience"—to God and parents—and
perhaps therefore, the passage echoes one of the central concerns
of Englishmen of the sixteenth and early seventeenth century.
Tudor England was undergoing social ferment, caused in large
part by an increasingly commercialized economy and reflected in
such legislative monuments as the Statute of Apprentices and the
Elizabethan vagrancy and poor laws. Overseas mercantile expansion brought profits and adventure but also a sense, in some men,
of disquietude. One commentator declared that the merchants,
"whose number is so increased in these our daies," had "in times
past" traded chiefly with European countries but "now . . . as
men not contented with these journies, they have sought out the
east and west Indies, and made now and then suspicious voiages."
Literate Englishmen generally (again not merely the Puritans)
were concerned with the apparent disintegration of social and
moral controls at home; they fretted endlessly over the "masterless
men" who had once had a proper place in the social order but
who were now wandering about, begging, robbing, raping. They
fretted also about the absence of a spirit of due subordination—of
children to parents and servants to masters. They assailed what
seemed a growing spirit of avariciousness, a spirit which one
social critic described revealingly as "a barbarous or slavish desire

to turne the [penny]." They denounced the laborers who demanded too high wages, the masters who squeezed their servants, and the landed gentlemen who valued sheep more than men—in short, the spirit of George Best's Cham, who aimed to have his son "inherite and possessè all the dominions of the earth."

It was the case with English confrontation with Africans, then, that a society in a state of rapid flux, undergoing important changes in religious values, and comprised of men who were energetically on the make and acutely and often uncomfortably self-conscious of being so, came upon a people less technologically advanced, markedly different in appearance and culture. From the first, Englishmen tended to set Africans over against themselves, to stress what they conceived to be radically contrasting qualities of color, religion, and style of life, as well as animality and a peculiarly potent sexuality. What Englishmen did not at first fully realize was that Africans were potentially subjects for a special kind of obedience and subordination which was to arise as adventurous Englishmen sought to possess for themselves and their children one of the most bountiful dominions of the earth. When they came to plant themselves in the New World, they were to find that they had not entirely left behind the spirit of avarice and insubordination. Nor does it appear, in light of attitudes that developed during their first two centuries in America, that they left behind all the impressions initially gathered of the *Negro* before he became pre-eminently the *slave*.

2

Unthinking Decision
Enslavement of Africans in America to 1700

At the start of English settlement in America, no one had in mind to establish the institution of Negro slavery. Yet in less than a century the foundations of a peculiar institution had been laid. The first Africans landed in Virginia in 1619, though very little is known about their precise status during the next twenty years. Between 1640 and 1660 there is evidence of enslavement, and after 1660 slavery crystallized on the statute books of Maryland, Virginia, and other colonies. By 1700, when Africans began flooding into English America, they were treated as somehow deserving a life and status radically different from English and other European settlers. Englishmen in America had created a new legal status which ran counter to English law.

Unfortunately the details of this process can never be completely reconstructed; there is simply not enough evidence to show precisely when and how and why Negroes came to be treated so differently from white men. Concerning the first years of contact especially we have very little information as to what impression Negroes made upon English settlers: accordingly, we are left knowing less about the formative years than about later periods of American slavery. That those early years were crucial is obvious, for it was then that the cycle of Negro debasement began; once the African became fully the slave it is not hard to see why Englishmen looked down upon him. Yet precisely because understanding the dynamics of these early years is so important to understanding the centuries which followed, it is necessary to bear with the less than satisfactory data and to attempt to reconstruct the course of debasement undergone by Africans in seventeenth-century America.

THE NECESSITIES OF A NEW WORLD

When Englishmen crossed the Atlantic to settle in America, they were immediately subject to novel strains. A large proportion of migrants were dead within a year. The survivors were isolated from the world as they had known it, cut off from friends and family and the familiar sights and sounds and smells which have always told men who and where they are. A similar sense of isolation and disorientation was inevitable even in the settlements that did not suffer through a starving time. English settlers had undergone the shock of detachment from home in order to set forth upon a dangerous voyage of from ten to thirteen weeks that ranged from unpleasant to fatal and that seared into every passenger's memory the ceaselessly tossing distance that separated him from his old way of life.

Life in America put great pressure upon the traditional social and economic controls that Englishmen assumed were to be exercised by civil and often ecclesiastical authority. Somehow the empty woods seemed to lead much more toward license than restraint. At the same time, by reaction, this unfettering resulted in an almost pathetic social conservatism, a yearning for the forms and symbols of the old familiar social order. When in 1618, for example, the Virginia Company wangled a knighthood for a newly appointed governor of the colony the objection from the settlers was not that this artificial elevation was inappropriate to wilderness conditions but that it did not go far enough to meet them. English social forms were transplanted to America not simply because they were nice to have around but because without them the new settlements would have fallen apart and English settlers would have become men of the forest, savage men devoid of civilization.

For the same reason, the communal goals and values that animated the settlement of the colonies acquired great functional importance in the wilderness; they served as antidotes to social and individual disintegration. For Englishmen planting in America, it was of the utmost importance to know that they were Englishmen, which was to say that they were educated (to a degree suitable to their station), Christian (of an appropriate Protestant variety), civilized, and (again to an appropriate degree) free men.

It was with personal freedom, of course, that wilderness conditions most suddenly reshaped English laws, assumptions, and practices. In America land was plentiful, labor scarce, and, as in all new colonies, a cash crop desperately needed. These economic conditions were to remain crucial for many years; in general they tended to encourage greater geographical mobility, less specialization, higher rewards, and fewer restraints on the processes and products of labor. In general men who invested capital in agriculture in America came under fewer customary and legal restraints than in England concerning what they did with their land and with the people who worked on it. On the other hand their activities were restricted by the economic necessity of producing cash crops for export. Men without capital could obtain land relatively easily: hence the shortage of labor and the notably blurred line between men who had capital and men who did not.

Three major systems of labor emerged amid the interplay of these social and economic conditions in America. One, which was present from the beginning, was free wage labor. Another, which was the last to appear, was chattel slavery. The third, which virtually coincided with first settlement in America, was temporary servitude, in which contractual arrangements gave shape to the entire system. It was this third system, indentured servitude, which permitted so many English settlers to cross the Atlantic barrier. Indentured servitude was linked to the development of chattel slavery in America, and its operation deserves closer examination.

A very sizable proportion of settlers in the English colonies came as indentured servants bound by contract to serve a master for a specified number of years, usually from four to seven or until age twenty-one, as repayment for their ocean passage. The time of service to which the servant bound himself was negotiable property, and he might be sold or conveyed from one master to another at any time up to the expiration of his indenture, at which point he became a free man. (Actually it was his *labor* which was owned and sold, not his *person,* though this distinction was neither important nor obvious at the time.) Custom and statute law regulated the relationship between servant and master. Obligation was reciprocal: the master undertook to feed and clothe and sometimes to educate his servant and to refrain from abusing him, while the servant was obliged to perform such work as his master set him and to obey his master in all things.

FREEDOM AND BONDAGE IN THE ENGLISH TRADITION

While in retrospect we can readily see these three distinct categories, thinking about freedom and bondage in Tudor England was in fact confused and self-contradictory. In a period of social dislocation there was considerable disagreement among contemporary observers as to what actually was going on and even as to what ought to be. *Ideas* about personal freedom tended to run both ahead of and behind actual social conditions. Both statute and common law were sometimes considerably more than a century out of phase with actual practice and with commonly held notions about servitude. Finally, both ideas and practices were changing rapidly. It is possible, however, to identify certain important tenets of social thought that served as anchor points amid this chaos.

Englishmen lacked accurate methods of ascertaining what actually was happening to their social institutions, but they were not wrong in supposing that villeage, or "bondage" as they more often called it, had virtually disappeared in England. In the middle ages, being a villein had meant dependence upon the will of a feudal lord but by no means deprivation of all social and legal rights. By the fourteenth century villenage had decayed markedly, and it no longer existed as a viable social institution in the second half of the sixteenth century. Personal freedom had become the normal status of Englishmen. Most contemporaries welcomed this fact; indeed it was after about 1550 that there began to develop in England that preening consciousness of the peculiar glories of

English liberties. This consciousness was to flower in America as well.

How had it all happened? Among those observers who tried to explain, there was agreement that Christianity was primarily responsible. They thought of villenage as a mitigation of ancient bond slavery and that the continuing trend to liberty was animated, as Sir Thomas Smith said in a famous passage, by the "perswasion . . . of Christians not to make nor keepe his brother in Christ, servile, bond and underling for ever unto him, as a beast rather than as a man." They agreed also that the trend had been forwarded by the common law, in which the disposition was always, as the phrase went, "in favor of liberty."

At the same time there were in English society people who seemed badly out of control. From at least the 1530's the countryside swarmed with vagrants, sturdy beggars, rogues, and vagabonds, with men who *could* (it was thought) but *would not* work. They committed all manner of crimes, the worst of which was remaining idle. It was an article of faith among Tudor commentators that idleness was the mother of all vice and the chief danger to a well-ordered state. Tudor statesmen valiantly attempted to suppress idleness by means of the famous vagrancy laws which provided for houses of correction and (finally) for whipping the vagrant from constable to constable until he reached his home parish. They assumed that everyone belonged in a specific niche and that anyone failing to labor in the niche assigned to him by Providence must be compelled to do so by authority.

In response, Tudor authorities gradually hammered out the legal framework of a labor system which permitted compulsion but which did *not* permit so total a loss of freedom as lifetime hereditary slavery. And as things turned out, it was indentured servitude which best met the requirements for settling in America. Of course there were other forms of bound labor which contributed to the process of settlement: many convicts were sent and many children abducted. Yet among all the numerous varieties and degrees of non-freedom which existed in England, there was none which could have served as a well-formed model for the chattel slavery which developed in America. This is not to say, though, that slavery was an unheard-of novelty in Tudor England.

On the contrary, "bond slavery" was a memory trace of long standing. Vague and confused as the concept of slavery was in the minds of Englishmen, it possessed certain fairly consistent connotations which were to help shape English perceptions of the way Europeans should properly treat the newly discovered peoples overseas.

THE CONCEPT OF SLAVERY

At first glance, one is likely to see merely a fog of inconsistency and vagueness enveloping the terms *servant* and *slave* as they were used both in England and in seventeenth-century America. When Hamlet declaims "O what a rogue and peasant slave am I," the term seems to have a certain elasticity. When Peter Heylyn defines it in 1627 as "that ignominious word, *Slave;* whereby we use to call ignoble fellowes, and the more base sort of people," the term seems useless as a key to a specific social status.

In one sense it was, since the concept embodied in the terms *servitude, service,* and *servant* was widely embracive. *Servant* was more a generic term than *slave*. Slaves could be "servants," but servants *should not* be "slaves." This principle, which was common in England, suggests a measure of precision in the concept of slavery. In fact there was a large measure which merits closer inspection.

First of all, the "slave's" loss of freedom was complete. "Of all men which be destitute of libertie or freedome," explained one commentator in 1590, "the slave is in greatest subjection, for a slave is that person which is in servitude or bondage to an other, even against nature." "Even his children," moreover, ". . . are infected with the Leprosie of his father's bondage." At law, much more closely than in literary usage, "bond slavery" implied utter deprivation of liberty.

Slavery was also thought of as a perpetual condition. While it had not yet come invariably to mean lifetime labor, it was frequently thought of in those terms. Except sometimes in instances of punishment for crime, slavery was open ended; in contrast to servitude, it did not involve a definite term of years. Slavery was perpetual also in the sense that it was often thought of as hereditary. It was these dual aspects of perpetuity which were to assume such importance in America.

So much was slavery a complete loss of liberty that it seemed to Englishmen somehow akin to loss of humanity. No theme was more persistent than the claim that to treat a man as a slave was to treat him as a beast. Almost half a century after Sir Thomas Smith had made this connection a Puritan divine was condemning masters who used "their servants as slaves, or rather as beasts." No analogy could have better demonstrated how strongly Englishmen felt about total loss of personal freedom.

Certain prevalent assumptions about the origins of slavery paralleled this analogy at a different level of intellectual construction. Lawyers and divines alike assumed that slavery was impossible before the Fall, that it violated natural law, that it was instituted by positive human laws, and, more generally, that in various ways it was connected with sin. These ideas were as old as the church fathers and the Roman writers on natural law. Sir Edward Coke, the great jurist, spelled out what was perhaps the most important and widely acknowledged attribute of slavery: ". . . it was ordained by Constitution of Nations . . . that he that was taken in Battle should remain Bond to his taker for ever, and he to do with him, all that should come of him, his Will and Pleasure, as with his Beast, or any other Cattle, to give, or to sell, or to kill." This final power, Coke noted, had since been taken away (owing to "the Cruelty of some Lords") and placed in the hands only of kings. The animating rationale here was that captivity in war meant an end to a person's claim to life as a human being; by sparing the captive's life, the captor acquired virtually absolute power over the life of the man who had lost the power to control his own.

More than any other single quality, *captivity* differentiated slavery from servitude. Although there were other, subsidiary ways of becoming a slave, such as being born of slave parents, selling oneself into slavery, or being adjudged to slavery for crime, none of these was considered to explain the way slavery had originated. Slavery was a power relationship; servitude was a relationship of service. Men were "slaves" to the devil but "servants" of God. Men were "galley-slaves," not galley servants.

This tendency to equate slavery with captivity had important ramifications. Warfare was usually waged against another people; captives were usually foreigners—"strangers" as they were termed. Until the emergence of nation-states in Europe, by far the most important category of strangers was the non-Christian. International warfare seemed above all a ceaseless struggle between Christians and Muslims. In the sixteenth and seventeenth centuries Englishmen at home could read scores of accounts concerning the miserable fate of Englishmen and other Christians taken into "captivity" by Turks and Moors and oppressed by the "verie worst manner of bondmanship and slaverie." Clearly slavery was tinged by the spirit of religious difference.

It is clear, therefore, that Englishmen did possess a *concept* of slavery, formed by the clustering of several rough but not illogical equations. The slave was treated like a beast. Slavery was inseparable from the evil in men; it was God's punishment upon Ham's prurient disobedience. Enslavement was captivity, the loser's lot in a contest of power. Slaves were infidels or heathens.

On every count, Negroes qualified.

THE PRACTICES OF PORTINGALS AND SPANYARDS

Which is not to say that Englishmen were casting about for a people to enslave. What happened was that they found thrust before them not only instances of Negroes being taken into slavery but attractive opportunities for joining in that business. Englishmen actually were rather slow to seize these opportunities; on most of the sixteenth-century English voyages to West Africa there was no dealing in slaves. The notion that it was appropriate to do so seems to have been drawn chiefly from the example set by the Spanish and Portuguese.

Without inquiring into the reasons, it can be said that slavery had persisted since ancient times in Spain and Portugal, that prior to the discoveries it was primarily a function of the religious wars against the Moors, that Portuguese explorers pressing down the coast in the fifteenth century captured thousands of Negroes whom they carried back to Portugal as slaves, and that after 1500, Portuguese ships began supplying the Spanish and Portuguese settlements in America with Negro slaves. By 1500 European enslavement of Negroes had become a fixture of the New World.

There is no need to inquire into the precise nature of this slavery except to point out that in actual practice it did fit the English concept of bond slavery. The question which needs answering pertains to contemporary English knowledge of what was going on. And the answer may be given concisely: Englishmen had easily at hand a great deal of not very precise information.

The news that Africans were being carried off to forced labor in America was broadcast across the pages of the widely read Hakluyt and Purchas collections. While only one account stated explicitly that Negroes "be their slaves during their life," it was clear that the Portuguese and Spaniards treated Negroes and frequently the Indians as "slaves." This was the term customarily used by English voyagers and by translators of foreign documents. William Towrson was told by an African in 1556 "that the Portingals were bad men, and that they made them slaves, if they could take them, and would put yrons upon their legges." There were "rich trades" on that coast in Negroes "which be caried continually to the West Indies." The Portuguese in the Congo "have divers rich Commodities from this Kingdome, but the most important is every yeere about five thousand Slaves, which they transport from thence, and sell them at good round prices in . . . the West Indies."

Some Englishmen decided that there might be profit in supplying the Spanish with Negroes, despite the somewhat theoretical prohibition of foreigners from the Spanish dominions in the New World. John Hawkins was first; in the 1560's he made three voyages to Africa, the Caribbean, and home. The first two were successful; the third met disaster when the Spanish attacked his ships, took most of them, and turned the captured English seamen over to the Inquisition. This famous incident helped discourage English slave trading in favor of other maritime activities. English vessels were not again active frequently in the slave trade until the seventeenth century. But Englishmen learned, from the accounts published by Richard Hakluyt, that Hawkins had taken Africans in Africa and sold them as "marchandise" in the West Indies.

By the end of the first quarter of the seventeenth century it had become abundantly evident in England that Negroes were being enslaved on an international scale. Clearly an equation had developed between Africans and slavery. Primarily, the associations were with the Portuguese and Spanish, with captivity, with buying and selling in Guinea and in America. Yet there is no reason to suppose Englishmen especially eager to enslave Negroes, nor even to regard the traveler Richard Jobson eccentric in his response to an African chief's offer to buy some "slaves": "I made answer, We were a people, who did not deale in any such commodities, neither did wee buy or sell one another, or any that had our owne shapes." By the seventeenth century, after all, English prejudices as well as English law were "in favor of liberty."

When they came to settle in America, Englishmen found that things happened to liberty, some favorable, some not. Negroes became slaves, partly because there were economic necessities in America which called for some sort of bound, controlled labor. The Portuguese and Spanish had set an example, which, however rough in outline, proved to be, at very least, suggestive to Englishmen. It would be surprising if there had been a clear-cut line of influence from Latin to English slavery. Elizabethans were not in the business of modeling themselves after Spaniards. Yet from about 1550, Englishmen were in such continual contact with the Spanish that they could hardly have failed to acquire the notion that Negroes could be enslaved. The terms *negro* and *mulatto* were incorporated into English from the Hispanic languages. This is the more striking because a perfectly adequate term, identical in meaning to *negro,* already existed in English; of course *black* was used also, though not so commonly in the sixteenth century as later.

By 1640 it was becoming apparent that in many of their new colonies overseas English settlers had bought Negroes and were holding them, frequently, as hereditary slaves for life. In considering this development, it is important to remember that the status of slave was at first distinguished from servitude more by duration than by onerousness; the key term in many early descriptions of the Negro's condition was *perpetual.* Negroes served "for ever" and so would their children. Englishmen did not do so.

Servitude, no matter how long, brutal, and involuntary, was not the same thing as perpetual slavery. Servitude comprehended alike the young apprentice, the orphan, the indentured servant, the convicted debtor or criminal, the political prisoner, and, even, the Scottish and Irish captive of war who was sold as a "slave" to New England or Barbados. None of these persons, no matter how miserably treated, served for life in the colonies, though of course many died before their term ended. Hereditary lifetime service was restricted to Indians and Africans. Among the various English colonies in the New World, this service known as "slavery" seems first to have developed in the international cockpit known as the Caribbean.

ENSLAVEMENT: THE WEST INDIES

The Englishmen who settled the Caribbean colonies were not very different from those who went to Virginia, Bermuda, Maryland, or even New England. Their experience in the islands, however, was very different indeed. By 1640 there were roughly as many English (and Irish and Scots) in the little islands as on the American continent. A half-century after the first settlements were established in the 1620's, many of the major islands—Barbados, and the Leeward Islands—were overcrowded. Thousands of whites who had been squeezed off the land by sugar plantations migrated to other English colonies, including much larger Jamaica which had been captured from the Spanish in 1655. Their places were taken by African slaves who had been shipped to the islands, particularly after 1640, to meet an insatiable demand for labor which was cheap to maintain, easy to dragoon, and simple to replace when worked to death. Negroes outnumbered whites in Barbados as early as 1660.

In that colony, at least, this helpful idea that Negroes served for life seems to have existed even before they were purchased in large numbers. Any doubt which may have existed as to the appropriate status of Africans was dispelled in 1636 when the Governor and Council resolved "that *Negroes* and *Indians,* that came here to be sold, should serve for life, unless a Contract was before made to the contrary." Europeans were not treated in this manner. In the 1650's several observers referred to the lifetime slavery of Negroes as if it were a matter of common knowledge. "It's the Custome for a Christian servant to serve foure yeares," one wrote at the beginning of the decade, "and then enjoy his freedome . . . the Negroes and Indians (of which latter there are but few here) they and the generation are Slaves to their owners to perpetuity." As another visitor described the people of the island in 1655:

> The genterey heare doth live far better than ours doue in England: thay have most of them 100 or 2 or 3 of slaves apes whou they command as they pleas. . . . This Island is inhabited with all sortes: with English, french, Duch, Scotes, Irish, Spaniards thay being Jues: with Ingones and miserabell Negors borne to perpetuall slavery thay and thayer seed . . . some planters will have 30 more or les about 4 or 5 years ould: they sele them from one to the other as we doue shepe. This Illand is the Dunghill wharone England doth cast forth its rubidg: Rodgs — and hors and such like peopel are those which are gennerally Broght heare.

Dunghill or no dunghill, Barbados was treating its Negroes as slaves for life.

ENSLAVEMENT: NEW ENGLAND

It was ironic that slavery in the West Indies should have influenced, of all places, New England. The question with slavery in New England is not why it was weakly rooted, but why it existed at all. No staple crop demanded regiments of raw labor. That there was no compelling economic demand for Negroes is evident in the numbers actually imported: there could have been no need for a distinct status for only 3 per cent of the labor force. Indentured servitude was completely adequate to New England's needs. Why, then, did New Englanders enslave Negroes, probably as early as 1638? Why was it that the Puritans rather mindlessly (which was not their way) accepted slavery for blacks and Indians but not for whites?

The early appearance of slavery in New England may in part

be explained by the fact that the first Negroes were imported in the ship *Desire* in 1638 from an island colony where Negroes were already being held perpetually. After 1640 a brisk trade got under way between New England and the English Caribbean islands. These strange Negroes from the West Indies must surely have brought with them to New England prevailing notions about their usual status. Ship masters who purchased perpetual service in Barbados would not have been likely to sell service for term in Boston.

No amount of contact with the West Indies could have by itself created Negro slavery in New England; settlers there had to be willing to accept the proposition. Because they were Englishmen, they were so prepared—and at the same time they were not. Characteristically, as Puritans, they officially codified this ambivalence in 1641 as follows: ". . . there shall never be any bond-slavery, villenage or captivitie amongst us; unlesse it be lawfull captives taken in just warrs, and such strangers as willingly sell themselves, or are solde to us. . . ." Thus as early as 1641 the Puritan settlers were seeking to guarantee their own liberty without closing off the opportunity of taking it from others whom they identified with the Biblical term, "strangers."

It would be wrong to suppose, though, that all the Puritans' preconceived ideas about freedom and bondage worked in the same direction. While the concepts of difference in religion and of captivity worked against Indians and Negroes, certain Scriptural injunctions and English pride in liberty told in the opposite direction. In Massachusetts the magistrates demonstrated that they were not about to tolerate glaring breaches of "the Law of God established in Israel" even when the victims were Africans. In 1646 the authorities arrested two mariners who had carried two Negroes directly from Africa and sold them in Massachusetts. What distressed the General Court was that the Negroes had been obtained during a raid on an African village and that this "haynos and crying sinn of man stealing" had taken place on the Lord's Day. The General Court decided to free the unfortunate victims and ship them back to Africa, though the death penalty for the crime (clearly mandatory in Scripture) was not imposed. More quietly than in this dramatic incident, Puritan authorities extended the same protections against maltreatment to Negroes and Indians as to white servants.

From the first, however, there were scattered signs in New England that Negroes were regarded as different from English people not merely in their status as slaves. In 1652, for example, the Massachusetts General Court ordered that Scotsmen, Indians, and Negroes should train with the English in the militia, but four years later abruptly excluded Negroes, as did Connecticut in 1660. Evidently Negroes, even free Negroes, were regarded as distinct from the English. They were, in New England where economic necessities were not sufficiently pressing to determine the decision, treated differently from other men.

ENSLAVEMENT: VIRGINIA AND MARYLAND

In Virginia and Maryland the development of Negro slavery followed a very different course, for several reasons. Most obviously, geographic conditions and the intentions of the settlers quickly combined to produce a successful agricultural staple. Ten years after settlers first landed at Jamestown they were on the way to proving, in the face of assertions to the contrary, that it was possible "to found an empire upon smoke." More than the miscellaneous productions of New England, tobacco required labor which was cheap but not temporary, mobile but not independent, and tireless rather than skilled. In the Chesapeake area more than anywhere to the northward, the shortage of labor and the abundance of land—the "frontier"—placed a premium on involuntary labor.

This need for labor played more directly upon these settlers' ideas about freedom and bondage than it did either in the West Indies or in New England. Perhaps it would be more accurate to say that settlers in Virginia (and in Maryland after settlement in 1634) made their decisions concerning Negroes while relatively virginal, relatively free from external influences and from firm preconceptions. Of all the important early English settlements, Virginia had the least contact with the Spanish, Portuguese, Dutch, and other English colonies. At the same time, the settlers of Virginia did not possess either the legal or Scriptural learning of the New England Puritans whose conception of the just war had opened the way to the enslavement of Indians. Slavery in the tobacco colonies did not begin as an adjunct of captivity; in marked contrast to the Puritan response to the Pequot War, the settlers of Virginia did not react to the Indian massacre of 1622 with propositions for taking captives and selling them as "slaves."

In the absence, then, of these influences in other English colonies, slavery as it developed in Virginia and Maryland assumes a special interest and importance over and above the fact that Negro slavery was to become a vitally important institution there and, later, to the southwards. In the tobacco colonies it is possible to watch Negro slavery *develop,* not pop up full-grown overnight, and it is therefore possible to trace, very imperfectly, the development of the shadowy, unexamined rationale which supported it. The concept of Negro slavery there was neither borrowed from foreigners, nor extracted from books, nor invented out of whole cloth, nor extrapolated from servitude, nor generated by English reaction to Negroes as such, nor necessitated by the exigencies of the New World. Not any one of these made the Negro a slave, but all.

In rough outline, slavery's development in the tobacco colonies seems to have undergone three stages. Africans first arrived in 1619, an event Captain John Smith referred to with the utmost unconcern: "About the last of August came in a dutch man of warre that sold us twenty Negars." Africans trickled in slowly for the next half-century; one report in 1649 estimated that there were three hundred among Virginia's population of fifteen thousand—about 2 per cent. Long before there were more appreciable numbers, the development of slavery had, so far as we can tell, shifted gears. Prior to about 1640 there is very little evidence to show how Negroes were treated. After 1640 there is mounting evidence that some Negroes were in fact being treated as slaves. This is to say that the twin essences of slavery—lifetime service and inherited status—first became evident during the twenty years prior to the beginning of legal formulation. After 1660 slavery was written into statute law.

Concerning the first of these stages, there is only one major historical certainty. There simply is not enough evidence to indicate whether Negroes were treated like white servants or not. At least we can be confident, therefore, that the two most common assertions about the first Negroes—that they were slaves and that they were servants—are *unfounded,* though not necessarily incorrect. And what of the positive evidence?

Some of the first group bore Spanish names and presumably had been baptized, which would mean they were at least nominally Christian, though of the Papist sort. They had been "sold" to the English; so had other Englishmen but not by the Dutch. Probably these Negroes were not fully free, but many Englishmen were not. It can be said, though, that from the first in Virginia Negroes were set apart from white men by the word *Negroes.* The earliest Virginia census reports plainly distinguished Negroes from white men; often Negroes were listed as such with no personal names—a critical distinction. It seems logical to suppose that this perception of the Negro as being distinct from the Englishman must have operated to debase his status rather than to raise it, for in the absence of countervailing social factors the need for labor in the colonies usually told in the direction of non-freedom. There were few countervailing factors present, surely, in such instances as in 1629 when a group of Negroes were brought to Virginia freshly captured from a Portuguese ship which had snatched them from Angola a few weeks earlier. Given the context of English thought and experience sketched in this chapter, it seems probable that the Negro's status was not ever the same as that accorded the white servant. But we do not know for sure.

When the first fragmentary evidence appears about 1640 it becomes clear that *some* Negroes in both Virginia and Maryland were serving for life and some Negro children inheriting the same obligation. Not all blacks, certainly, for after the mid-1640's the court records show that some Negroes were incontestably free and were accumulating property of their own. At least one black freeman, Anthony Johnson, himself owned a slave. Some blacks served only terms of usual length, but others were held for terms far longer than custom and statute permitted with white servants. The first fairly clear indication that slavery was practiced in the tobacco colonies appears in 1639, when a Maryland statute declared that "all the Inhabitants of this Province being Christians

(Slaves excepted) Shall have and enjoy all such rights liberties immunities priviledges and free customs within this Province as any
naturall born subject of England." Another Maryland law passed
the same year provided that "all persons being Christians (Slaves
excepted)" over eighteen who were imported without indentures
would serve for four years. These laws make very little sense unless the term *slaves* meant Negroes and perhaps Indians.

The next year, 1640, the first definite indication of outright enslavement appears in Virginia. The General Court pronounced
sentence on three servants who had been retaken after absconding
to Maryland. Two of them, both white, were ordered to serve
their masters for one additional year and then the colony for
three more, but "the third being a negro named John Punch shall
serve his said master or his assigns for the time of his natural life
here or else where." No white servant in any English colony, so
far as is known, ever received a like sentence.

After 1640, when surviving Virginia county court records began
to mention Negroes, sales for life, often including any future
progeny, were recorded in unmistakable language. In 1646 Francis Pott sold a Negro woman and boy to Stephen Charlton "to the
use of him . . . forever." Similarly, six years later William Whit-
tington sold to John Pott "one Negro girle named Jowan; aged
about Ten yeares and with her Issue and produce duringe her (or
either of them) for their Life tyme. And their Successors forever";
and a Maryland man in 1649 deeded two Negro men and a
woman "and all their issue both male and Female." The ex-
ecutors of a York County estate in 1647 disposed of eight Negroes
—four men, two women, and two children—to Captain John Chis-
man "to have hold occupy posesse and injoy and every one of the
afforementioned Negroes forever."

Further evidence that some Negroes were serving for life in
this period lies in the prices paid for them. In many instances the
valuations placed on Negroes (in estate inventories and bills of
sale) were far higher than for white servants, even those servants
with full terms yet to serve. Higher prices must have meant that
Negroes were more highly valued because of their greater length
of service. The labor owned by James Stone in 1648, for example,
was evaluated as follows:

	lb tobo
Thomas Groves, 4 yeares to serve	1300
Francis Bomley for 6 yeares	1500
John Thackstone for 3 yeares	1300
Susan Davis for 3 yeares	1000
Emaniell a Negro man	2000
Roger Stone 3 yeares	1300
Mingo a Negro man	2000

Besides setting a higher value on Negroes, these inventories failed to indicate a last name and the number of years they had still to serve, presumably because their service was for an unlimited time.

Where Negro women were involved, higher valuations probably reflected the facts that their issue were valuable and that they could be used for field work while white women generally were not. This latter discrimination between black and white women did not necessarily involve perpetual service, but it meant that blacks were set apart in a way clearly not to their advantage. This was not the only instance in which Negroes were subjected to degrading distinctions not immediately and necessarily attached to the concept of slavery. Blacks were singled out for special treatment in several ways which suggest a generalized debasement of blacks as a group. Significantly, the first indications of this debasement appeared at about the same time as the first indications of actual enslavement.

The distinction concerning field work is a case in point. A law of 1643 provided that *all* adult men were taxable and, in addition, *Negro* women. The same distinction was made twice again before 1660. Maryland adopted a similar policy beginning in 1654. This official discrimination between black women and other women was made by white men who were accustomed to thinking of field work as being ordinarily the work of men exclusively. The essentially racial character of this discrimination stood out clearly in a law passed in 1668 at the time slavery was taking shape in the statute books:

> Whereas some doubts, have arisen whether negro women set free were still to be accompted tithable according to a former act, *It is declared by this grand assembly* that negro women, though permitted to enjoy their Freedome yet ought not in all

respects to be admitted to a full fruition of the exemptions and impunities of the English, and are still lyable to payment of taxes.

Virginia law set blacks apart from all other groups in a second way by denying them the important right and obligation to bear arms. Few restraints could indicate more clearly the denial to Africans of membership in the English community. This first foreshadowing of the slave codes came in 1640, at just the time when other indications first appeared that blacks were subject to special treatment.

Finally, an even more compelling sense of the separateness of Negroes was revealed in early reactions to sexual union between the races. Prior to 1660 the evidence concerning these reactions is equivocal, and it is not possible to tell whether repugnance for intermixture preceded legislative enactment of slavery. In the early 1660's, however, when slavery was gaining statutory recognition, the assemblies acted with full-throated indignation against miscegenation. These acts aimed at more than merely avoiding confusion of status. In 1662 Virginia declared that "if any christian shall committ Fornication with a negro man or woman, hee or shee soe offending" should pay double the usual fine. Two years later Maryland regulated interracial marriages: "forasmuch as divers freeborne English women forgettfull of their free Condicion and to the disgrace of our Nation doe intermarry with Negro Slaves by which alsoe divers suites may arise touching the issue of such woemen and a great damage doth befall the Masters of such Negros for prevention whereof for deterring such freeborne women from such shameful Matches," strong language indeed if "divers suites" had been the only problem. A Maryland act of 1681 described marriages of white women with Negroes as, among other things, "always to the Satisfaccion of theire Lascivious and Lustfull desires, and to the disgrace not only of the English butt allso of many other Christian Nations." When Virginia finally prohibited all interracial liaisons in 1691, the Assembly vigorously denounced miscegenation and its fruits as "that abominable mixture and spurious issue."

From the surviving evidence it appears that outright enslavement and these other forms of debasement appeared at about the

same time in Maryland and Virginia. Indications of perpetual
service, the very nub of slavery, coincided with indications that
English settlers discriminated against Negro women, withheld
arms from Negroes, and—though the timing is far less certain—
reacted unfavorably to interracial sexual union. The coincidence
suggests a mutual relationship between slavery and unfavorable
assessment of blacks. Rather than slavery causing "prejudice," or
vice versa, they seem rather to have generated each other. Both
were, after all, twin aspects of a general debasement of the Negro.
Slavery and "prejudice" may have been equally cause and effect,
continuously reacting upon each other, dynamically joining hands
to hustle the Negro down the road to complete degradation.
Much more than with the other English colonies, where the enslavement of Africans was to some extent a borrowed practice, the
available evidence for Maryland and Virginia points to less bor-
rowing and to this kind of process: a mutually interactive growth
of slavery and unfavorable assessment, with no cause for either
which did not cause the other as well. If slavery caused prejudice,
then invidious distinctions concerning working in the fields, bearing arms, and sexual union should have appeared *after* slavery's
firm establishment. If prejudice caused slavery, then one would
expect to find these lesser discriminations preceding the greater
discrimination of outright enslavement. Taken as a whole, the
evidence reveals a process of debasement of which hereditary lifetime service, while important, was not the only part.

Certainly it was the case in Maryland and Virginia that the legal enactment of Negro slavery followed social practice, rather
than vice versa. In 1661 the Virginia Assembly indirectly provided
statutory recognition that some Negroes served for life: "That in
case any English servant shall run away in company with any negroes who are incapable of makeing satisfaction by addition of
time," he must serve for the Negroes' lost time as well as his own.
Maryland enacted a similar law in 1663, and in the following
year came out with the categorical declaration that Negroes were
to serve "Durante Vita"—for life. During the next twenty-odd
years a succession of acts in both colonies defined with increasing
precision what sorts of persons might be treated as slaves.

By about 1700 the slave ships began spilling forth their black cargoes in greater and greater numbers. By that time racial slavery and the necessary police powers had been written into law. By that time, too, slavery had lost all resemblance to a perpetual and hereditary version of English servitude, though service for life still seemed to contemporaries its most essential feature. In the last quarter of the seventeenth century the trend was to treat Negroes more like property and less like people, to send them to the fields at younger ages, to deny them automatic existence as inherent members of the community, to tighten the bonds on their personal and civil freedom, and correspondingly to loosen the traditional restraints on the master's freedom to deal with his human property as he saw fit. In 1705 Virginia gathered up the random statutes of a whole generation and baled them into a "slave code" which would not have been out of place in the nineteenth century.

THE UN-ENGLISH: SCOTS, IRISH, AND INDIANS

In the minds of overseas Englishmen, slavery, the new tyranny, did not apply to any Europeans. Something about Africans, and to lesser extent Indians, set them apart for drastic exploitation, oppression, and degradation. In order to discover why, it is useful to turn the problem inside out, to inquire why Englishmen in America did not treat any other peoples as they did Negroes. It is especially revealing to see how English settlers looked upon the Scotch (as they frequently called them) and the Irish, whom they often had opportunity and "reason" to enslave, and upon the Indians, whom they enslaved, though only, as it were, casually.

In the early years Englishmen treated the increasingly numerous settlers from other European countries, especially Scottish and Irish servants, with condescension and frequently with exploitive brutality. Englishmen seemed to regard their colonies as exclusively *English* preserves and to wish to protect English persons especially from the exploitation which inevitably accompanied settlement in the New World. In Barbados, for example, the assembly in 1661 denounced the kidnapping of youngsters for service in the colony in a law which applied only to "Children of the *English* Nation."

While Englishmen distinguished themselves from other peoples, they also distinguished *among* those different peoples who failed to be English. It seems almost as if Englishmen possessed a view of other peoples which placed the English nation at the center of widening concentric circles, each of which contained a people more alien than the one inside it. On occasion these social distances felt by Englishmen may be gauged with considerable precision, as in the sequence employed by the Committee for Trade and Foreign Plantations in a query to the governor of Connecticut in 1680: "What number of English, Scotch, Irish or Foreigners have . . . come yearly to . . . your Corporation. And also, what Blacks and Slaves have been brought in." Sometimes the English sense of distance seems to have been based upon a scale of values which would be thought of today in terms of nationality. At other times, though, the sense of foreignness seems to have been explicitly religious, as instanced by a letter from Barbados in 1667: "We have more than a good many Irish amongst us, therefore I am for the down right Scott, who I am certain will fight without a crucifix about his neck." It is scarcely surprising that hostility toward the numerous Irish servants should have been especially strong, for they were doubly damned as foreign and papist. Already, for Englishmen in the seventeenth century the Irish were a special case, and it required more than an ocean voyage to alter this perception.

As time went on Englishmen began to absorb the idea that their settlements in America were not going to remain exclusively English preserves. In 1671 Virginia began encouraging naturalization of legal aliens, so that they might enjoy "all such liberties, priviledges, immunities whatsoever, as a naturall borne Englishman is capable of," and Maryland accomplished the same end with private naturalization acts.

The necessity of peopling the colonies transformed the longstanding urge to discriminate among non-English peoples into a necessity. Which of the non-English were sufficiently different and foreign to warrant treating as "perpetual servants"? The need to answer this question did not mean, of course, that upon arrival in America the colonists immediately jettisoned their sense of distance from those persons they did not actually enslave. They discriminated against Welshmen and Scotsmen who, while admittedly "the best servants," were typically the servants of Englishmen. There was a considerably stronger tendency to discriminate against papist Irishmen, those "worst" servants, but never to make slaves of them. And here lay the crucial difference. Even the Scottish prisoners taken by Cromwell during the English Civil Wars—captives in a just war!—were never treated as slaves in England or the colonies.

Indians too seemed radically different from Englishmen, far more so than any Europeans. They were enslaved, like Africans, and so fell on the losing side of a crucial dividing line. It is easy to see why: whether considered in terms of religion, nationality, savagery, or geographical location, Indians seemed more like Negroes than like Englishmen. Given this resemblance the essential problem becomes why Indian slavery never became an important institution in the colonies. Why did Indian slavery remain numerically insignificant and typically incidental in character? Why were Indian slaves valued at much lower prices than Negroes? Why were Indians, as a kind of people, treated like Negroes and yet at the same time very differently?

Certain obvious factors made for important differentiations in the minds of the English colonists. As was the case with first confrontations in America and Africa, the different contexts of confrontation made Englishmen more interested in converting and civilizing Indians than Negroes. That this campaign in America too frequently degenerated into military campaigns of extermination did nothing to eradicate the initial distinction. Entirely apart from English intentions, the culture of the eastern American Indians probably meant that they were less readily enslavable than Africans. By comparison, they were less used to settled agriculture, and their own variety of slavery was probably even less similar to the chattel slavery which Englishmen practiced in America than was the domestic and political slavery of the various West African cultures. But it was the transformation of English intentions in the wilderness which counted most heavily in the long run. The Bible and the treaty so often gave way to the clash of flintlock and tomahawk. The colonists' perceptions of the Indians came to be organized not only in pulpits and printshops but at the bloody cutting edge of the English thrust into the Indians' lands. Thus the most pressing and mundane circumstances worked to make Indians seem very different from Negroes. In the early years especially, Indians were in a position to mount murderous reprisals upon the English settlers, while the few scattered Africans were not. When English-Indian relations did not turn upon sheer power they rested on diplomacy. In many instances the colonists took careful precautions to prevent abuse of Indians belonging to friendly tribes. Most of the Indians enslaved by the English had their own tribal enemies to thank. It became common practice to ship Indian slaves to the West Indies where they could be exchanged for slaves who had no compatriots lurking on the outskirts of English settlements. In contrast, Negroes presented much less of a threat—at first.

Equally important, Negroes had to be dealt with as individuals —with supremely impartial anonymity, to be sure—rather than as nations. Englishmen wanted and had to live with "their" Negroes, as it were, side by side. Accordingly their impressions of blacks were forged in the heat of continual, inescapable personal contacts. There were few pressures urging Englishmen to treat Indians as integral constituents in their society, which Negroes were whether Englishmen liked or not. At a distance the Indian could be viewed with greater detachment and his characteristics acknowledged and approached more cooly and more rationally. At a distance too, Indians could retain the quality of nationality, a quality which Englishmen admired in themselves and expected in other peoples. Under contrasting circumstances in America, the Negro nations tended to become Negro people.

Here lay the rudiments of certain shadowy but persistent themes in what turned out to be a multi-racial nation. Americans came to impute to the braves of the Indian "nations" an ungovernable individuality and at the same time to impart to Africans all the qualities of an eminently governable sub-nation, in which African tribal distinctions were assumed to be of no consequence. More immediately, Indians and Africans rapidly came to serve as two fixed points from which English settlers could triangulate their own position in America; the separate meanings of *Indian* and *Negro* helped define the meaning of living in America. The In-

dian became for Americans a symbol of their American experience; it was no mere luck of the toss that placed the profile of an
American Indian rather than an American Negro on the famous
old five-cent piece. Confronting the Indian in America was a test-
ing experience, common to all the colonies. Conquering the Indian symbolized and personified the conquest of the American
difficulties, the surmounting of the wilderness. To push back the
Indian was to prove the worth of one's own mission, to make
straight in the desert a highway for civilization. With the Negro
it was utterly different.

RACIAL SLAVERY: FROM REASONS TO RATIONALE

And *difference,* surely, was the indispensable key to the degradation of Africans in English America. In scanning the problem of
why Negroes were enslaved in America, certain constant elements
in a complex situation can be readily, if roughly, identified. *It
may be taken as given* that there would have been no enslavement
without economic need, that is, without persistent demand for labor in underpopulated colonies. Of crucial importance, too, was
the fact that Africans in America were relatively powerless. In
themselves, however, these two elements will not explain the enslavement of Indians and Negroes. The pressing need in America
was labor, and Irish, Scottish, and English servants were available.
Most of them would have been helpless to ward off outright enslavement if their masters had thought themselves privileged to
enslave them. As a group, though, masters did not think themselves so empowered. Only with Indians and Africans did Englishmen attempt so radical a deprivation of liberty—which brings the
matter abruptly to the most difficult and imponderable question
of all: what was it about Indians and Negroes which set them
apart from Englishmen, which rendered them *different,* which
made them special candidates for degradation?

To ask such questions is to inquire into the *content* of English
attitudes, and unfortunately there is little evidence with which to
build an answer. It may be said, however, that the heathen condition of Negroes seemed of considerable importance to English
settlers in America—more so than to English voyagers upon the
coasts of Africa—and that heathenism was associated in some set-

tlers' minds with the condition of slavery. Clearly, though, this is not to say that English colonists enslaved Africans merely because of religious difference. In the early years, the English settlers most frequently contrasted themselves with Negroes by the term *Christian,* though they also sometimes described themselves as *English.* Yet the concept embodied by the term *Christian* embraced so much more meaning than was contained in specific doctrinal affirmations that it is scarcely possible to assume on this basis that Englishmen set Negroes apart because they were heathen. The historical experience of the English people in the sixteenth century had made for fusion of religion and nationality; the qualities of being English and Christian had become so inseparably blended that it seemed perfectly consistent to the Virginia Assembly in 1670 to declare that "noe negroe or Indian though baptised and enjoyned their owne Freedome shall be capable of any such purchase of christians, but yet not debarred from buying any of their owne nation."

From the first, then, the concept embedded in the term *Christian* seems to have conveyed much of the idea and feeling of *we* as against *they:* to be Christian was to be civilized rather than barbarous, English rather than African, white rather than black. The term *Christian* itself proved to have remarkable elasticity, for by the end of the seventeenth century it was being used to define a kind of slavery which had altogether lost any connection with explicit religious difference. In the Virginia code of 1705, for example, the term sounded much more like a definition of race than of religion: "And for a further christian care and usage of all christian servants, *Be it also enacted* . . . That no negroes, mulattos, or Indians, although christians, or Jews, Moors, Mahometans, or other infidels, shall, at any time, purchase any christian servant, nor any other, except of their own complexion, or such as are declared slaves by this act." By this time "Christianity" had somehow become intimately and explicitly linked with "complexion." The 1705 statute declared "That all servants imported and brought into this country, by sea or land, who were not christians in their native country . . . shall be accounted and be slaves, and as such be here bought and sold notwithstanding a conversion to christianity afterwards." As late as 1753 the Vir-

ginia slave code anachronistically defined slavery in terms of religion when everyone knew that slavery had for generations been
based on the racial and not the religious difference.

It is worth making still closer scrutiny of the terminology which
Englishmen employed when referring both to themselves and to
the two peoples they enslaved, for this terminology affords the
best single means of probing the content of their sense of difference. The terms *Indian* and *Negro* were both borrowed from the
Hispanic languages, the one originally deriving from (mistaken)
geographical locality and the other from human complexion.
When referring to the Indians the English colonists either used
that proper name or called them *savages,* a term which reflected
primarily their view of Indians as uncivilized. In significant contrast, the colonists referred to *negroes,* and by the eighteenth century to *blacks* and to *Africans,* but almost never to African *heathens* or *pagans* or *savages.* Most suggestive of all, there seems to
have been something of a shift during the seventeenth century in
the terminology which Englishmen in the colonies applied to
themselves. From the initially most common term *Christian,* at
mid-century there was a marked shift toward the terms *English*
and *free.* After about 1680, taking the colonies as a whole, a new
term of self-identification appeared—*white.*

So far as the weight of analysis may be imposed upon such
terms, diminishing reliance upon *Christian* suggests a gradual
muting of the specifically religious elements in the Christian-
Negro distinction in favor of secular nationality: Negroes were,
in 1667, "not in all respects to be admitted to a full fruition of
the exemptions and impunities of the English." As time went on,
as some Negroes became assimilated to the English colonial culture, as more "raw Africans" arrived, and as increasing numbers
of non-English Europeans were attracted to the colonies, English
colonists turned increasingly to what they saw as the striking
physiognomic difference. In Maryland a revised law prohibiting
miscegenation (1692) retained *white* and *English* but dropped the
term *Christian*—a symptomatic modification. By the end of the
seventeenth century dark complexion had become an independent rationale for enslavement: in 1709 Samuel Sewall noted in his
diary that a "Spaniard" had petitioned the Massachusetts Coun-

cil for freedom but that "Capt. Teat alledg'd that all of that Color were Slaves." Here was a barrier between "we" and "they" which was visible and permanent: the black man could not become a white man. Not, at least, as yet.

What had occurred was not a change in the justification of slavery from religion to race. No such justifications were made. There seems to have been, within the unarticulated concept of the Negro as a different sort of person, a subtle but highly significant shift in emphasis. A perception of Negro heathenism remained through the eighteenth and into the nineteenth and even the twentieth century, and an awareness, at very least, of the African's different appearance was present from the beginning. The shift was an alteration in emphasis within a single concept of difference rather than a development of a novel conceptualization. Throughout the colonies the terms *Christian, free, English,* and *white* were for many years employed indiscriminately as synonyms. A Maryland law of 1681 used all four terms in one short paragraph.

Whatever the limitations of terminology as an index to thought and feeling, it seems likely that the English colonists' initial sense of difference from Africans was founded not on a single characteristic but on a cluster of qualities which, taken as a whole, seemed to set the Negro apart. Virtually every quality in "the Negro" invited pejorative feelings. What may have been his two most striking characteristics, his heathenism and his appearance, were probably prerequisite to his complete debasement. His heathenism alone could not have led to permanent enslavement since conversion easily wiped out that failing. If his appearance, his racial characteristics, meant nothing to the English settler, it is difficult to see how slavery based on race ever emerged, how the concept of complexion as the mark of slavery ever entered the colonists' minds. Even if the English colonists were most unfavorably struck by the Negro's color, though, blackness itself did not urge the complete debasement of slavery. Other cultural qualities —the strangeness of his language, gestures, eating habits, and so on—certainly must have contributed to the English colonists' sense that he was very different, perhaps disturbingly so. In Africa these qualities had for Englishmen added up to *savagery;*

they were major components in that sense of *difference* which
provided the mental margin absolutely requisite for placing the
European on the deck of the slave ship and the African in the
hold.

The available evidence (what little there is) suggests that for
Englishmen settling in America, the specific religious difference
was initially of greater importance than color, certainly of much
greater relative importance than for the Englishmen who confronted Negroes in their African homeland. Perhaps Englishmen
in Virginia, tanning seasonally under a hot sun and in almost
daily contact with tawny Indians, found the Negro's color less arresting than they might have in other circumstances. Perhaps, too,
these first Virginians sensed how inadequately they had reconstructed the institutions and practices of Christian piety in the
wilderness; they would perhaps appear less as failures to themselves in this respect if compared to persons who as Christians
were *totally* defective. Perhaps, though, the Jamestown settlers
were told in 1619 by the Dutch shipmaster that these "negars" were
heathens and could be treated as such. We do not know. The
available data will not bear all the weight that the really crucial
questions impose.

Of course once the cycle of degradation was fully under way,
once slavery and racial discrimination were completely linked together, once the engine of oppression was in full operation, then
there is no need to plead lack of knowledge. By the end of the
seventeenth century in all the colonies of the English empire
there was chattel racial slavery of a kind which would have
seemed familiar to men living in the nineteenth century. No Elizabethan Englishman would have found it familiar, though certain strands of thought and feeling in Elizabethan England had
intertwined with reports about the Spanish and Portuguese to en-
gender a willingness on the part of English settlers in the New
World to treat some men as suitable for private exploitation. During the seventeenth century New World conditions had enlarged
this predisposition, so much so that English colonials of the eighteenth century were faced with full-blown slavery—something they
thought of not as an institution but as a host of ever present problems, dangers, and opportunities.

II

Provincial Decades

1700–1755

3
Anxious Oppressors
Freedom and Control in a Slave Society

During the first quarter of the eighteenth century African slaves arrived in the English colonies on the American continent in unprecedented numbers. This sudden growth of the slave population meant for white men a thoroughgoing commitment to slavery; the institution rapidly thrust its roots deeply into a maturing American society. For roughly the first sixty years of the eighteenth century slavery itself grew without appreciable opposition, or even comprehension, gradually becoming barnacled with traditions, folkways, and a whole style of life. Most important for the future, unthinking acquiescence in the existence of slavery resulted in unthinking acceptance of the presuppositions upon which slavery rested. Slavery seemed a necessary response to conditions, a submission to the decrees of life in America.

DEMOGRAPHIC CONFIGURATIONS IN THE COLONIES

The influx of Negroes into the American colonies was part of a more general development, the arrival of large numbers of non-English peoples. The trend toward variety in Britain's colonial peoples accelerated rapidly in the early years of the eighteenth century. Three groups contributed most heavily to this novel diversity. The Scotch-Irish (the lowland Scots who migrated to and then from Ulster, now Northern Ireland) tended to push through to frontier regions. The Germans came especially to Pennsylvania, where by mid-century they constituted a third of the population.

By far the most numerous of the three major non-English groups were the Africans. From about 1730 almost until the Revolution Negroes comprised at least one-third the total population within the line of English settlement from Maryland to South Carolina (and to Georgia after its firm establishment in mid-century). Within this area there were significant variations from colony to colony: North Carolina had only about 25 per cent blacks, Maryland had over 30 per cent, Virginia about 40, and South Carolina probably 60 per cent. The concentration of blacks varied greatly within each colony, too, since usually the movement of slaves onto new lands lagged markedly behind the pace of western settlement. A similar lag occurred in representation of the white population in the assemblies, so that the areas with the heaviest slave populations were usually over-represented in the legislatures, a fact of some but probably not overriding importance concerning legal regulation of slavery. From Pennsylvania northwards there were spots of black concentration in the bustling port cities. The colony of New York contained the highest proportion of Negroes north of the plantations (14 per cent), with Rhode Island having slightly fewer although far more than the 3 per cent for New England as a whole. New Jersey and Pennsylvania had about 8 per cent.

These figures are important only insofar as they made for important, even crucial differences in social atmosphere among various regions of the colonies. The tone and rhythm of life in an inland Connecticut village, where the only black to be seen was the minister's house servant, must have been rather different, to say the least, from that on a rice plantation in South Carolina where within a five-mile radius there were ten blacks for every white person, man, woman, and child. In the middle of the eighteenth century perhaps 200,000 white persons in the continental colonies lived in neighborhoods where blacks outnumbered them. And the population of the colonies which later became the United States, taken as a whole, contained a higher proportion of Afro-Americans in the period 1730–65 than at any other time in the nation's history.

SLAVERY AND THE SENSES OF THE LAWS

As slavery rapidly entrenched itself in the plantation colonies during the early years of the eighteenth century, it forced English colonists to come to grips with novel problems which arose from the very nature of the institution. Plainly, Negro slaves were property in a sense not thoroughly comprehended by traditional English concepts and legal categories. Sometimes this novelty produced legal confusion: Could a slaveowner will or deed Negroes not yet conceived, property which did not yet exist? Should slaves be taxed by head or by value? These were vexing if not crucial problems. Chattel slavery required, in common with other manifestations of the commercialization of society, decisions as to how the account books were to be kept.

Considered as men, slaves raised much more difficult problems. The most pressing necessity was maintenance of discipline: hence the famous slave codes. The older plantation colonies at first adopted brief laws aimed at specific problems and later codified them during the early years of the eighteenth century. The newer colonies plunged in more directly: Georgia formulated in 1755 a full-scale code based on South Carolina's. The process of revision and recapitulation continued throughout the eighteenth century, but alterations in the statutory framework of slavery were in most cases minor until the time of the Revolution. No English colony remained without laws dealing specifically with the governance of Negroes, though in England itself there were no such statutes.

In the northern colonies, laws concerning Negroes were less detailed, more haphazard, and generally less harsh than to the southwards. Except on occasions of panic, the punishments prescribed for Negro offenders in the North were considerably lighter than in the southern colonies, where the traditional thirty-nine lashes (a number derived from Hebraic law) was the usual rule but by no means the limit of chastisement. Contemporaries recognized this progression of severity from northern to southern to West Indian colonies; as the famous lawyer Daniel Dulany of Maryland explained, "In proportion of the jealousy entertained of them [the slaves], or as they are considered to be formidable, the rigours and severities to which they are exposed, seem to rise, and the power of the magistrate or of the master, is more easily admitted."

Unharnessed personal power characterized the slave codes of the southern colonies, codes which varied in detail from one colony to another but displayed underlying similarities. Slaves were forbidden to wander off their plantation without a "ticket" from their master or overseer. They were never to be allowed to congregate in large numbers, carry clubs or arms, or strike a white person. Masters were given immunity from legal prosecution should their slave die under "moderate" correction. All white persons were authorized to apprehend any Negro unable to give a satisfactory account of himself. In areas of heavy slave concentration white men were required to serve in the slave "patrols" which were supposed to protect the community especially at night and on Sundays, though except in periods of special alarm the patrols were probably far more impressive on paper than in actuality. In addition, slaves committing felonies were tried in specially constituted courts which typically consisted of a justice of the peace and two (other) slaveowners. Official punishments ranged from a specific number of stripes "well laid on," all the way, occasionally, to burning at the stake.

The codes devoted much attention to the most persistent and potentially dangerous problem of slave control—running away. Probably more time, money, and energy were expended on this problem by white slaveowners, legislators, constables, jailers, and newspaper printers than on any other aspect of administering the slave system. Getting the slaves to work efficiently was the owner's problem, but runaways affected the safety of everyone, the security of all movable property, and the very discipline upon which slavery rested.

Running away was of course not confined in America to Negro slaves; it reflected the inherent difficulty of binding any sort of labor when labor was in short supply. Virtually every issue of every newspaper published in the colonies contained advertisements of servants or slaves "run away" or "taken up" at the public jail. Indeed, the problem was as old as bound labor in America. As one writer summarized the situation in 1708, " 'Tis supposed by the Planters, that all unknown Persons are run away from some Master."

Africans represented something of an answer to the problem of identification. Their distinctive appearance was one attribute which might initially have led masters to prefer Negroes as such to white servants, though this factor undoubtedly was of minor relevance to the growth of slave importations. Still, the Negro was readily identifiable as such; he was born branded. His appearance was not without its disadvantages as an identifying mark, however, for the very distinctiveness of his features tended to overwhelm the white man's ability to discriminate among individuals: some descriptions of the faces of plantation Negroes in runaway advertisements sound as if they might well have fitted every fifth Negro in the region. Much more drastic, there were leaks in a system which logically should have been watertight; not all black men were slaves, a fact which badly weakened the practical effectiveness of blackness as the badge of slavery, as the constantly reiterated phrase "he may try to pass for a free man" so cogently indicated.

While the colonial slave codes seem at first sight to have been intended to discipline Negroes, a very slight shift in perspective shows the codes in a different light: they aimed, paradoxically, at disciplining white men. Principally, the law told the white man, not the Negro, what he must do. It was the white man who was *required* to punish his runaways, prevent assemblages of slaves, enforce the curfews, sit on the special courts, and ride the patrols. Members of the assemblies, most of whom owned slaves, were attempting to enforce slave-discipline by the only means available, by forcing owners, individually and collectively, to exercise it. This surely was a novel situation. The slaveholding gentry were coerced as individuals by the popularly elected legislatures toward maintenance of a private tyranny which was conceived to be in the community interest. In the community at large, effective maintenance of slavery depended to considerable degree on vigilance and force, and colonial governments had at their direct command precious little force with which to be vigilant. The militia was available in emergency but the effectiveness of the militia depended on the spirit of the populace. Thus the maintenance of slavery depended on mass consent among the white population, on widespread agreement that every master should, indeed had to maintain effective control. This situation, sensed but not thought out by white men, tended to highlight in the white slaveowner's mind the necessity and the nakedness of his personal power. The slave codes played a vital role in this process, for they were, in an important sense, public dialogues among masters and among white men generally, intended to confirm their sense of mastery over their black slaves—and over themselves. Here were the makings of a lockstep discipline.

The slave codes served white men in still another way by furnishing indirect justification for the severities of slavery. Even in the seventeenth century, a period not distinguished by public agonizing over human misery, it is possible to detect a slight sense of uneasiness over the rigorous restraints which Negroes seemed to require and over the complete absence of restraints on the individual master's power. In 1692 the Maryland legislature freed a mulatto girl whose master and mistress had cut off her ears; the master's claim was, significantly, that the girl was a thief and a runaway and that he had punished her "thinking that as his Slave, he might do with her as he pleased." Probably this sense of uneasiness was somewhat alleviated by spelling out the necessities of slavery on paper; a slaveowner might lash his slaves unmercifully, in full confidence that he was carrying out an obligation to society—and he had the written law to prove it.

SLAVE REBELLIOUSNESS AND WHITE MASTERY

Fear of slave rebellion, expressed as early as 1672 in Virginia, was ever-present in the West Indies, the plantation colonies on the continent, and even, with less good reason, in some areas in the North. In many areas it was a gnawing, gut-wringing fear, intermittently heightened by undeniable instances of servile discontent. Every planter knew that *the* fundamental purpose of the slave laws was prevention and deterrence of slave insurrection. In pleading for a strengthened law in 1710 Governor Alexander Spotswood reminded the Virginia Assembly that constant vigilance was the price of continued mastery: "the Tryals of Last *Aprill* Court may shew that we are not to Depend on Either their Stupidity, or that Babel of Languages among 'em; freedom Wears a Cap which Can Without a Tongue, Call Togather all Those who Long to Shake of the fetters of Slavery. . . ." Freedom wore the red cap of bloody rebellion, and the colonists never doubted for a moment that their slaves might suddenly clap it to their heads.

Actual slave revolts were not common, but they did occur— often enough to confirm beyond question the horrifying conviction that they would occur again. A rumor of a poisoning in the next county, an outbreak of unexplained conflagrations, the cluster of furtive blacks discovered on some lonely road, the vivid memory of the wooly head spiked on a pole at the nearby crossroads (stark punctuation closing the last conspiracy), the image of sullen looks of black defiance which scudded across the impassive faces at today's whipping—only the blind could be free from fear, a chilling fear which even the rhythmic tedium of daily life could never entirely smother.

Whenever slaves offered violent resistance to the authority of white persons, the reaction was likely to be swift and often vicious even by eighteenth-century standards. The bodies of offenders were sometimes hanged in chains, or the severed head impaled upon a pole in some public place as a gruesome reminder to all passers-by that black hands must never be raised against white. These instructive tableaux were not invented by the colonists, for they had been common enough in England; the colonists thought of them as warnings to slaves, though of course they were also warning and counseling themselves by erecting tangible monuments to their own fears.

Presumably the principal reason for the colonists' fear of slave insurrections was an understandable distaste for having their throats cut. Plainly, however, their fears were exaggerated far beyond the proportions of the danger and were in part a response to more complicated anxieties. The spectre of Negro rebellion presented an appalling world turned upside down, a crazy nonsense world of black over white, an anti-community which was the direct negation of the community as white men knew it. This picture of the Negro as a potential insurrectionary was of course most vivid in the plantation colonies, though it was present in the North as well. Significantly, it cut two ways in its implications about blacks in general. While it implied that the Negro shared with other men a common desire for freedom, it also underlined his difference from the white man by presupposing his natural antagonism: as one report said of a supposed conspirator in Charleston, he looked "upon every white Man he should meet as his declared Enemy." Thus every insurrection reinforced both a sense of identity with the Negro and a sense of the gulf between him and his master.

FREE NEGROES AND FEARS OF FREEDOM

A chief source of danger, the colonists often felt, was the Negro who was not a slave. Most of the laws restricting free Negroes claimed merely that they were given to receiving goods stolen by slaves and to harboring runaways. Yet Governor William Gooch of Virginia thought he detected a far more serious danger: as he said, "there had been a Conspiracy discovered amongst the Negros to Cutt off the English, wherin the Free-Negros and Mullatos were much Suspected to have been Concerned, (which will forever be the Case)." While there may have been good grounds for the charges of theft and harboring runaways, there certainly were not for thinking that free Negroes encouraged slave conspiracies. *No* free Negro—with one possible exception—was clearly implicated in any conspiracy in the United States until 1822. Plainly the fear of free Negroes rested on something more than the realities of the situation.

The colonists' claim was grounded on a revealing assumption: that free blacks were essentially more black than free, that in any contest between oppressed and oppressors free blacks would side not with their brethren in legal status but with their brethren in color. The flowering of racial slavery had crowded out the possibility, which had once been perhaps close to an actuality, that some free blacks would think of themselves as full members of the white community. Paralleling this assumption was the assured feeling that all white men would stand together in any final crisis.

Many colonies made efforts in the first half of the eighteenth century to prevent too many Negroes from becoming free. In every colony, though, there was a steady trickle of private manumissions and in the southern colonies an occasional dramatic bestowal of freedom by the legislature upon a Negro who had revealed a conspiracy or compounded a remedy for syphilis or rattlesnake bite. No one suggested, as men were to do in the waning days of slavery, that free Negroes be re-enslaved.

Once free, whether born so or manumitted, Negroes were in many instances subjected to humiliating restrictions, though no colony worked out a well-considered policy. In the southern colonies free blacks were barred from testifying against white persons—a disability which gave carte blanche to any unscrupulous white man—but were themselves often the legitimate objects of testimony by slaves, who under no circumstances could testify against whites. By contrast, free Negroes in New York were immune from testimony by slaves, and in New England slaves themselves could testify against anyone. In many colonies, north and south, free Negroes were sometimes cavalierly included in certain provisions of the slave codes.

RACIAL SLAVERY IN A FREE SOCIETY

These legal restrictions on free Negroes suggest a trend toward exclusion of all blacks from full participation in the white community. The trend was least obvious in the arena of human activity within which the relation between the two races was most completely rationalized—work. Slavery itself operated on an exclusionary principle, so that when the Negro was considered in his role as a laboring machine he appeared sufficiently separated from the white community. As a laborer in the colonies, the Negro slave did not arouse widespread hostility among white men. This fact attains additional importance in light of the widespread use of slaves not merely as agricultural laborers but as seamen and porters, as coachmen and house servants; a considerable number were trained to skilled trades, everything from cooper and carpenter to baker and blacksmith, both in towns and on the plantations. There were, however, some expressions of resentment against the use of slaves in certain areas and occupations. Protests against slave competition were slanted principally at the employment of Negroes as skilled craftsmen, porters, and boat pilots; these protests cropped up particularly in urban centers, where competition was most obvious and protest most easily organized.

Absence of widespread resentment against Negro competition reflected the prevailing shortage of all kinds of labor in America. Employers wanted blacks because they were cheaper to buy and keep than whites and perhaps, as one contemporary claimed, because blacks of both sexes could be put to work in the fields while white women could not. Then, too, a white craftsman could never tell when he might want to hire or buy a Negro of his own. For men on the make, Negroes afforded additional leverage for pulling oneself up by the bootstraps.

Apart from the sphere of work, though, slavery did much less to structure the Negro's role in the white man's mind, and accordingly white men were under greater pressure to elaborate upon their sense of distinctness from Negroes. This pressure operated with all blacks, slave almost as much as free. On occasion slaves were criticized for dressing too finely, though on this score gentlemen had been having trouble with all their inferiors ever since landing in America. In 1745, Massachusetts expressly prohibited Negroes from participating in a government lottery, presumably to preclude the off-chance that some Negro might win it. More revealing was Delaware's law of 1770 which forbade employing blacks to administer corporal punishment to white offenders.

This tendency to hold Negroes at arm's length amounted to something very different from modern "segregation." Much later, something resembling the twentieth-century practice developed in the ante-bellum North, but in the South segregation did not come into general existence with legal support until after the Civil War. "Segregation," as a mechanism for maintaining social distance and control, was for the most part unnecessary and almost meaningless in the period when most Negroes were slaves, for slavery was very effective segregation—at least in the mind, where it counted. Until the latter part of the eighteenth century, moreover, there was no explicit doctrine in existence which could have served as rationale for separate public water pumps. Then, too, life in the colonies was characterized by much less travel, schooling, and urban concentration, that is, by few of the focal points of twentieth-century controversy. Indeed there were only two or three points at which whites and blacks were likely to come together in a social context which might have implied equality and hence have threatened the white man's security. Specifically these were the church and the burying ground and to less extent the schools.

It may be said generally that *some* blacks attended regular church services, were occasionally accepted into full membership, and that a few were even invited to address largely white congregations. They were usually seated in a distinct section of the church, a seemingly flagrant instance of "segregation" which was actually in large measure an expression of eighteenth-century ideas about people in general rather than blacks in particular. The pattern of seating in most colonial churches was partly governed (whether formally or not) by accepted social distinctions; the meaner sort of people accepted seats at the back or in the gallery, and Negroes, even Negroes who owned some property, were patently of the meaner sort. Here lay the makings but not the actuality of a radical separation.

Occasionally one or two Negroes attended school with a group of white children, but the vast majority of blacks, slave and free, grew old and died with no education at all. What little schooling was available to blacks came by way of the churches. More often than not blacks were catechized in exclusively black groups at an hour appointed by the catechist, though there were many exceptions to this practice. The Reverend Adam Dickie reported in Virginia, for instance, that he had to conduct separate catechizing sessions "because White People thought it a Mighty Scandal to have their Children repeat the Catechism with Negroes."

Mightily scandalized or not, white colonials in general seemed wary of opening their society to blacks, even to those who were legally free and whose ancestors may have been free (by 1760) for three or four generations. This exclusionary trend, if not principle, stood out all the more sharply in a society which by European standards was wide open to all comers. In committing themselves to a slavery whose logic rested, in the final analysis, on racial differences, the colonists may in fact have enhanced the fluidity of the American social structure *above* the racial line. For the firmness of black exclusion may have served as a bedrock of assured but inexpressible confidence that the structure of the entire community was indeed as firmly ordered as it should be, thus permitting the revolutionary new social mobility among white persons to develop without crippling apprehensiveness that proper social ordering was going entirely by the board.

Yet the development of biracial slavery in America, with its accompanying themes of license and discipline, did nothing to quiet among colonial Englishmen the mood of taut adventurousness and control which had done so much to make England a restless navigating, discovering, trafficking, planting nation. Rather, the new freedom and the new slavery in America acted together to vivify this mood, to raise practical problems which agitated it, and to rake toward the surface certain of its energies which had somehow to be dealt with. For intimately related with economic exploitation, exclusion of free blacks from the white community, slave unrest, and daily discipline in America was another kind of restlessness, discipline, exploitation, and exclusion.

4
Fruits of Passion
The Dynamics of Interracial Sex

When Europeans met Africans in America the result was slavery, revolt, the sociability of daily life, and, inevitably, sexual union. The blending of black and white began almost with the first contact of the two peoples and has far outlasted the institution of chattel slavery.

The tensions which arose may be viewed in several interrelated ways. The Englishmen who came to America brought with them not merely a prevalent social mood but also certain specific sexual standards and certain more or less definite ideas about African sexuality. Many of them came with more or less explicit intentions as to the proper character of the communities they wished to establish in the wilderness. These intentions were not always, or perhaps ever, fully realized; they were deflected—again sometimes more, sometimes less—by conditions in the New World. One of the most important deflectors was the development of a racial slavery which itself became one of the New World's "conditions," though of course the character of this condition was not everywhere the same. The Negro was encountered in very different contexts in the various English colonies. Particularly important in making for differences in the Englishman's reaction to interracial sex was the demographic pattern which developed during the first quarter of the eighteenth century; variations in the numbers of the races and of the sexes in the English colonies may be shown to be almost determinative in shaping certain attitudes.

REGIONAL STYLES IN RACIAL INTERMIXTURE

Miscegenation was extensive in all the English colonies, a fact made evident to contemporaries by the presence of large numbers of mulattoes. It is impossible to ascertain how much intermixture there actually was, though it seems likely there was more during the eighteenth century than at any time since. Although miscegenation was probably most common among the lower orders, white men of every social rank slept with black women. Almost everyone who wrote anything about America commented upon this fact of life.

No one thought intermixture was a good thing. Rather, English colonials were caught in the push and pull of an irreconcilable conflict between desire and aversion for interracial sexual union. The prerequisite for this conflict is so obvious as to be too easily overlooked: desire and aversion rested on the bedrock fact that white men perceived Negroes as being *both alike and different* from themselves. Without perception of similarity, no desire and no widespread gratification was possible. Without perception of difference, on the other hand, no aversion to miscegenation nor tension concerning it could have arisen. Without perception of difference, of course, the term *miscegenation* had no meaning. Given these simultaneous feelings of desire and aversion, it seems probable that of the two the latter is more demanding of explanation. The sexual drive of human beings has always, in the long run, overridden even the strongest sense of difference between two groups of human beings and, in some individuals, has even overridden the far stronger sense which men have of the difference between themselves and animals. What demands explanation, in short, is why there was *any* aversion among the white colonists to sexual union with blacks.

In most colonies virtually all the offspring of interracial unions were illegitimate, though legally sanctified interracial marriage did occur, especially though not exclusively in New England. Miscegenation in colonial America, as has been true since, typically involved fornication between white men and black women, though the inverse combination was common, far more so than is generally supposed. Probably a majority of interracial marriages in New England involved Negro men and white women of "the meaner sort." In the plantation colonies, although there were occasional instances of white women marrying black men, legitimization of this relationship was unusual.

Public feeling against miscegenation was strong enough to force itself over the hurdles of the legislative process into the statute books of many English continental colonies. As early as the 1660's the Maryland and Virginia assemblies had begun to lash out at miscegenation in language dripping with distaste and indignation. By the turn of the century it was clear in many continental colonies that the English settlers felt genuine revulsion for interracial sexual union, at least in principle. Two northern and all the plantation colonies legally prohibited miscegenation. Though there were exceptions, the weight of community opinion was set against the sexual union of white and black, as the long-standing statutory prohibitions indicated. In significant contrast, none of the British West Indian assemblies prohibited extramarital miscegenation.

In the West Indian colonies especially, and less markedly in South Carolina, the pattern of miscegenation was far more inflexible than in the other English settlements. White women in the islands did not sleep with black men, let alone marry them. Nor did white men actually marry Negroes or mulattoes. Yet white men commonly, almost customarily, took Negro women to bed with little pretense at concealing the fact. Edward Long of Jamaica described the situation: "He who should presume to shew any displeasure against such a thing as simple fornication, would for his pains be accounted a simple blockhead; since not one in twenty can be persuaded, that there is either sin; or shame in cohabiting with his slave." Negro concubinage was an integral part of island life, tightly interwoven into the social fabric.

It is scarcely necessary to resort to speculation about the influence of tropical climate in order to explain this situation, for life in the islands was in large degree shaped by the enormous disproportion of Negroes to white settlers and characterized by brutal nakedness of planter domination over the slaves. In the West Indian islands and to less extent South Carolina, racial slavery con-

sisted of unsheathed dominion by relatively small numbers of
white men over enormous numbers of Negroes, and it was in
these colonies that Negro men were most stringently barred from
sexual relations with white women. Sexually, as well as in every
other way, Negroes were utterly subordinated. White men extended their dominion over their Negroes to the bed, where the
sex act itself served as ritualistic re-enactment of the daily pattern
of social dominance.

Congruent to these regional differences in slavery and interracial relationships were the bedrock demographic facts which so
powerfully influenced, perhaps even determined, the kind of society which emerged in each colony. With blacks overwhelmingly
outnumbering whites in the various islands (ten to one in Jamaica), and with whites outnumbering Negroes everywhere on
the continent except South Carolina, it was inevitable that radically dissimilar social styles should have developed in the two
areas. As a French traveler perceptively characterized this dissimilarity in 1777: "In the colonies of the Antilles, most of the colonists are people who have left their homeland with the intention
of rebuilding their fortunes. Far from settling in the islands, they
look upon them merely as a land of exile, never as a place where
they plan to live, prosper, and die. On the other hand, the Anglo-
American colonists are permanent, born in the country and attached to it; they have no motherland save the one they live in;
and, although London formerly was so considered, they have
clearly proved that they held it in less esteem than they did the
prosperity, tranquility, and freedom of their own country." The
West Indian planters were lost not so much in the Caribbean as
in a sea of blacks. They found it impossible to re-create English
culture as they had known it. They were corrupted by living in a
police state, though not themselves the objects of its discipline.
The business of the islands was business, the production of agricultural staples; the islands were not where one really lived, but
where one made one's money. By contrast, the American colonists
on the continent maintained their hold upon their English back-
ground, modifying it less for accommodating slavery than for
winning the new land. Unlike the West Indian planters, they felt
no need to be constantly running back to England to reassure

themselves that they belonged to civilization. Because they were conscious of having attained a large measure of success in transplanting their own society, they vehemently rejected any trespass upon it by a people so alien as the Negroes. The islanders could hardly resent trespass on something which they did not have.

It was precisely this difference which made the Negro seem so much more alien on the continent than on the islands, and miscegenation accordingly less common. For a West Indian to have declared, with Judge Samuel Sewall of Boston, that Negroes "cannot mix with us and become members of society, . . . never embody with us and grow up into orderly Families, to the Peopling of the Land" would have been false by reason of the extensive blending of the races in the islands and meaningless because the "peopling" of the islands had already been accomplished—by Africans. Americans on the continent stood poised for a destiny of conquering a vast wilderness, while Englishmen in the little crowded islands looked forward down a precipice of slave rebellion, or at best a slippery slope of peaceful but inevitable defeat. Certainly the bustling communities on the continent had good reason to feel that they had successfully established a beachhead of English civilization in America. They possessed optimism, self-confidence, and a well-defined sense of Englishness, a sense which came automatically to bear when they were confronted with peoples who seemed appreciably dissimilar. When large numbers of very dissimilar people threatened the identity of the continental colonists, their response was rejection of those people in the mind and a tendency to perceive them as being more dissimilar than ever. For the sense of dissimilarity fed on itself: once the cycle was started, the differences between white Americans and "others," which first sparked anxiety and rejection, loomed progressively larger and generated further anxiety and rejection.

Certainly many Americans on the continent became convinced that the American people were not intended to be Negroes. Benjamin Franklin, who was as fully attuned to American destiny as anyone, nervously expressed the idea that the continent should belong to "White People." "I could wish their Numbers were increased. Why increase the Sons of Africa, by Planting them in America, where we have so fair an Opportunity, by excluding all

Blacks and Tawneys, of increasing the lovely White and Red? But perhaps I am partial to the Complexion of my Country," he concluded with his usual self-conscious good sense, "for such Kind of Partiality is natural to Mankind." Franklin was expressing an important feeling, one which a famous Virginian, William Byrd, expressed more directly: "They import so many Negros hither, that I fear this Colony will some time or other be confirmed by the Name of New Guinea."

It was more than a matter of colonial Americans not wanting to give their country over to Africans. Miscegenation probably did not seem so much a matter of long-term discoloration as an immediate failure to live up to immemorial standards. Here again, the intentions which drove English overseas expansion were of crucial importance. The colonists' conviction that they must sustain their civilized condition wherever they went rendered miscegenation a negation of the underlying plan of settlement in America. Simply because most blacks were chattel slaves, racial amalgamation was stamped as irredeemably illicit; it was irretrievably associated with loss of control over the baser passions, with weakening of traditional family ties, and with breakdown of proper social ordering. Judge Sewall's "orderly Families" were rendered a mockery by fathers taking slave wenches to bed.

At the same time it would be a mistake to suppose that the *status* of Negroes in itself aroused white aversion to intermixture; the physical difference was of crucial importance. Without that difference there could never have developed well-formulated conceptions about sexual relations between Africans and Europeans in America. Although perhaps there was some feeling that the laws which prevented racial intermingling helped prevent blacks, as one astute foreign observer put it, "from forming too great opinions of themselves," the underlying reason for their passage was that these mixtures were "disagreeable" to white men.

MASCULINE AND FEMININE MODES IN CAROLINA
AND AMERICA

On the face of things it seems paradoxical that the one region on the continent which had become demographically most like a new Guinea should have been the one in which white men seemed least anxious about interracial sexual activity. While permanent unions between persons of the two races normally were quiet or secretive affairs elsewhere on the continent, in South Carolina and particularly in Charleston they were not. It was the only city worthy of the name in the plantation colonies. It was an elegant, gay, extravagant city, where men took advantage of certain of their opportunities in more overt, more relaxed, and probably more enterprising fashion than in the colonies to the north. They possessed an abundance of black women. The result may best be described by a visiting merchant from Jamaica (where the atmosphere surrounding interracial sex was so utterly different from New England), who wrote from Charleston in 1773: "I know of but one Gentleman who professedly keeps a Mulatto Mistress and he is very much pointed at: There are swarms of Negroes about the Town and many Mulattoes, and by the Dress of the Girls, who mostly imitate their Mistresses, I have no doubt of their Conversations with the whites, but they are carried on with more privacy than in our W. India Islands." "As I travell'd further North," the Jamaican visitor continued concerning his trip from Charleston to North Carolina, "there were fewer Negroes about the Houses, and these taken less notice of, and before I finish'd my Journey North, I found an empty House, the late Tenant of which had been oblig'd by the Church Wardens to decamp on Account of his having kept a Black Woman. Dont suppose Fornication is out of Fashion here," he added reassuringly about North Carolina, "more than in other Places, No! the difference only is, that the White Girls monopolize it."

Here was an important regional difference in social "fashion." Charleston was the only English city on the continent where it was at all possible to jest publicly concerning miscegenation. In 1736 the *South-Carolina Gazette* published some frank advice to the bachelors and widowers of Charleston: "that if they are in a Strait for Women, to wait for the next Shipping from the Coast of Guinny. Those African Ladies are of a strong, robust Constitution: not easily jaded out, able to serve them by Night as well as Day. When they are Sick, they are not costly, when dead, their funeral Charges are but . . . an old Matt, one Bottle Rum, and a lb. Sugar [.] The cheapness of a Commo-di-ty becomes more tak-

ing when it fully Answers the end, or T_____l." Next week another writer replied in obvious determination not to be outdone
in indelicacy of expression: "In my Opinion, our Country-
Women are full as capable for Service either night or day as any
African Ladies whatsoever. . . . In all Companies wheresoever I
have been, my Country-Women have always the praise for their
Activity of Hipps and humoring a Jest to the Life in what Posture soever their Partners may fancy, which makes me still hope
that they'll have the Preference before the black Ladies in the
Esteem of the Widowers and Batchelors at C_____town." Next
week the *Gazette* published still another verse.

If these contributions to the *South-Carolina Gazette* were a
trifle raw by the standards of a modern family newspaper, they
reflected more than eighteenth-century literary frankness about
sex. Newspapers elsewhere on the continent did not publish similar discussions of interracial sex, though everywhere (including
Boston) they published some none-too-delicate pieces concerning
sexual matters. Only in Charleston was it possible to debate publicly, "Is sex with Negroes right?"

This distinctiveness was owing partly to South Carolina's distinctive economic and social history. The preponderance of slaves
in the low country tended to give white men a queasy sense that
perhaps they were marooned, a feeling that their society was ir-
revocably committed to Negro slavery and that somehow their
mere Englishness had lost its savor in the shuffle for plantation
prosperity. The effect of this uneasiness was to make men feel like
both fleeing and embracing Negro slavery all at once: hence the
common annual flights from the plantations to Charleston and
from South Carolina to northern cities and England, the negation
of cherished traditional liberties in the slave codes, the importation of more and more slaves, the continual efforts to encourage
white immigration, and not least, the simultaneous embracing
of Negro women and rejection of the ensuing offspring. Caught
as they were in powerful crosscurrents, it is no wonder that white
men in Charleston joked nervously about their sexual abandon.

For white women the situation was different, and here again
the Charleston area seems to have been characterized by attitudes
somewhere midway between those of the West Indies and further

north. In the islands, where English settlers were most thoroughly committed to a Negro slave society and where strenuous attempts to attract more white settlers had been unavailing, white women were, quite literally, the repositories of white civilization. White men tended to place them protectively upon a pedestal and then run off to gratify their passions elsewhere. For their part white women, though they might propagate children, inevitably held themselves aloof from the world of lust and passion, a world which reeked of infidelity and Negro slaves. Under no circumstances would they have attempted, any more than they would have been allowed, to clamber down from their pedestal to seek pleasures of their own across the racial line. In fact white women in the West Indies tended to adhere rigidly to the double sexual standard which characterized English sexual mores and to refrain more than in the continental colonies from infidelity with white men. The oppressive presence of slavery itself tended to inhibit the white woman's capacity for emotional, sexual, and intellectual commitment. She served principally an ornamentive function, for everything resembling work was done by Negro slaves. Visitors to the islands were almost universally agreed in describing her life as one of indolence and lassitude, though some were impressed by a formal, superficial gaiety. Her choices were to withdraw from the world or to create an unreal one of her own.

The white women of the Charleston area were less tightly hemmed in. Nevertheless, they rarely if ever established liaisons with Negro men, as happened in the South Carolina back country. Some visitors to the city were struck by their desiccated formality, which seems now to betray the strains imposed by the prevailing pattern of miscegenation. One traveler from Philadelphia, described his unfavorable impressions in Charleston by first lamenting that the "superabundance of Negroes" had "destroyed the activity of whites," who "stand with their hands in their pockets, overlooking their negroes." In his letter of 1809 (known only as published much later in the century with some Victorian censorship at the end), he went on to say,

> These, however, are not one tenth of the curses slavery has brought on the Southern States. Nothing has surprised me more than the cold, melancholy reserve of the females, of the

best families, in South Carolina and Georgia. Old and young,
single and married, all have that dull frigid insipidity, and reserve, which is attributed to solitary old maids. Even in their
own houses they scarce utter anything to a stranger but yes or
no, and one is perpetually puzzled to know whether it proceeds from awkwardness or dislike. Those who have been at
some of their Balls [in Charleston] say that the ladies hardly
even speak or smile, but dance with as much gravity, as if they
were performing some ceremony of devotion. On the contrary,
the negro wenches are all sprightliness and gayety; and if report
be not a defamer—

The dissipation of the white gentleman was as much a tragedy
for his white lady as for him. A biracial environment warped her
affective life in two directions at once, for she was made to feel
that sensual involvement with the opposite sex burned bright and
hot with unquenchable passion and at the same time that any
such involvement was utterly repulsive.

If women were particularly affected by the situation in South
Carolina, white persons of both sexes in *all* the English colonies
were affected in a more general way by the tensions involved in
miscegenation. Though these tensions operated in white men
rather differently than in white women, it seems almost self-
evident that the emergent attitudes toward Negroes possessed a
unity which transcended differences between the two sexes. Put
another way, out of a pattern of interracial sexual relationships
which normally placed white men and white women in very different roles, there arose a common core of belief and mythology
concerning the Negro which belonged to neither sex but to white
American culture as a whole. The emergence of common beliefs
out of divergent experiences was of course principally a function
of the homogenizing effect of culture upon individual experience,
but it is important to bear in mind that the *functional* significance of beliefs about the Negro may have been very different for
white women than for white men even when the beliefs themselves were identical. Since the English and colonial American
cultures were dominated by males, however, sexually-oriented beliefs about the Negro in America derived principally from the

psychological needs of men and were to a considerable extent shaped by specifically masculine modes of thought and behavior. This is not to say the American attitudes toward the Negro were *male* attitudes but merely that when one talks about *American* attitudes toward anything (the frontier, the city, money, freedom, the Negro) one is using a shorthand for attitudes common to both sexes but predominantly male in genesis and tone.

NEGRO SEXUALITY AND SLAVE INSURRECTION

As for these ideas or beliefs about the Negro, many seem startlingly modern. Least surprising, perhaps, was the common assumption that black women were especially passionate, an idea which found literary or at least literate expression especially in the *South-Carolina Gazette* and in West Indian books. The Negro woman was the sunkissed embodiment of ardency:

> Next comes a warmer race, from sable sprung,
> To love each thought, . . . to lust each nerve is strung;
>
>   .   .   .
>
> These sooty dames, well vers'd in Venus's school,
> Make love an art, and boast they kiss by rule.

If such amiable assessments found their way into public print, one can imagine what tavern bantering must have been like.

Plainly white men were doing more than reporting pleasant facts. For by calling the Negro woman passionate they were offering the best possible justification for their own passions. Not only did the black woman's warmth constitute a logical explanation for the white man's infidelity, but, much more important, it helped shift responsibility from himself to her. If she was *that* lascivious—well, a man could scarcely be blamed for succumbing against overwhelming odds.

Attitudes toward the Negro male were more complex and potentially far more explosive. The notion that black men were particularly virile, promiscuous, and lusty was of course not new in the eighteenth century, but the English colonists in America showed signs of adding a half-conscious and revealingly specific corollary: they sometimes suggested that black men lusted after

white women. There was probably some objective basis for the
charge, since sexual intercourse with a white woman must in part
have been for black men an act of retribution against the white
man. For different reasons there was also good basis for the common feeling that only the most depraved white woman would
consent to sleep with a Negro, since white women of the lowest
class had the least to lose in flouting the maxims of society and
the most reason to hate them. No matter how firmly based in fact,
however, the image of the sexually aggressive Negro was rooted
even more firmly in deep strata of irrationality. For it is apparent
that white men projected their own desires onto Negroes: their
own passion for black women was not fully acceptable to society
or the self and hence not readily admissible. Sexual desires could
be effectively denied and the accompanying anxiety and guilt in
some measure eased, however, by imputing them to others. It is
not we, but others, who are guilty. It is not we who lust, but they.
Not only this, but white men anxious over their own sexual in-
adequacy were touched by a racking fear and jealousy. Perhaps
the Negro better performed his nocturnal offices than the white
man. Perhaps, indeed, the white man's woman really wanted the
Negro more than she wanted him.

Significantly, these tensions tended to bubble to the surface especially at times of interracial crisis when the colonists' control
over their Negroes appeared in jeopardy. During many scares
over slave conspiracies, for instance, reports circulated that the
Negroes had plotted killing all white persons except the young
women, whom they "intended to reserve for themselves." In fact
these charges were ill-founded at best, for there is no evidence
that any Negroes in revolt ever seized any white women for their
"own use," even though rebellious slaves certainly had opportunity to do so during the successful insurrections in the West Indies and also at Stono in South Carolina.

From these indications it seems more than likely that fears of
Negro sexual aggression during periods of alarm over insurrection did not represent direct response to actual overt threat, but
rather a complex of reactions in the white man. Any group faced
with a real threat of serious proportions is inclined to sense, even
on a conscious level, a sexual element in the opponents' aggres-

siveness—as many have identified Communism with free love. Any black insurrection, furthermore, threatened the white man's dominance, including his valuable sexual dominance, and hence the awful prospect of being overthrown was bound to assume a sexual cast. And finally, white men anxious and guilty over their own sexual aggressiveness were quick to impute it to others, especially at a time of interracial crisis. One has only to imagine the emotions flooding through some planter who had been more or less regularly sleeping with some of his slave wenches when he suddenly learned of a conspiracy among their male counterparts; it was virtually inevitable that his thoughts turn in a torrent of guilt to the "safety" of his wife.

DISMEMBERMENT, PHYSIOLOGY, AND SEXUAL PERCEPTIONS

The white man's fears of Negro sexual aggression were equally apparent in the use of castration as a punishment in the colonies. This weapon of desperation was not employed by angry mobs in the manner which became familiar after Emancipation. Castration was dignified by specific legislative sanction as a lawful punishment in Antigua, the Carolinas, Bermuda, Virginia, Pennsylvania, and New Jersey. It was sometimes prescribed for such offenses as striking a white person or running away: employed in this way, castration was a not irrational method of slave control, closely akin to the Jamaica law which authorized severing one foot of a runaway. Yet castration was not simply another of the many brands of hideous cruelty which graced the colonial criminal codes: it was reserved for Negroes and occasionally Indians. In some colonies, laws authorizing castration were worded so as to apply to all blacks whether free or slave. As a legal punishment castration was a peculiarly American experiment, for there was no basis for it in English law. Indeed officials in England were shocked and outraged at the idea, calling castration "inhumane and contrary to all Christian Laws," "a punishment never inflicted by any Law [in any of] H.M. Dominions." Some Americans thought the practice necessary to restrain a lecherous and barbarous people; Englishmen thought the barbarity was on the other side.

Castration of blacks clearly indicated a need in white men to persuade themselves that they were really masters and in all ways masterful, and it illustrated dramatically the ease with which white men slipped over into treating their Negroes like their bulls and stallions whose "spirit" could be subdued by emasculation. In some colonies, moreover, the specifically sexual aspect of castration was so obvious as to underline how much of the white man's insecurity about blacks was fundamentally sexual. The Pennsylvania and New Jersey laws passed early in the eighteenth century (and quickly disallowed by authorities in England) prescribed castration of Negroes as punishment for one offense only, attempted rape of a white woman. Still more strikingly, Virginia's provision for castration of Negroes, which had been on the books for many years and permitted castration for a variety of serious offenses, was repealed in 1769 for humanitarian reasons, but the repealing statute specifically declared that it might still be inflicted for one particular offense—rape or attempted rape of a white woman.

The concept of the Negro's aggressive sexuality was reinforced by what was thought to be an anatomical peculiarity of the Negro male. He was said to possess an especially large penis. The idea was considerably older even than the exegesis on Ham's offense against his father offered by West African travelers. Indeed the idea without question predated the settlement of America and possibly even the Portuguese explorations of the West African coast. Several fifteenth-century map makers decorated parts of Africa with little naked figures which gave the idea graphic expression, and in due course, in the seventeenth century, English accounts of West Africa were carefully noting the "extraordinary greatness" of the Negroes' "members." By the final quarter of the eighteenth century the idea that the Negro's penis was larger than the white man's had become something of a commonplace in European scientific circles. Whether it was a commonplace in popular circles in the English colonies is more difficult to ascertain, since it was scarcely the sort of assertion likely to find its way into print even if a great many people talked about it. Certainly the idea was not unheard of, for as an officer in the First Pennsylvania Regiment commented pointedly in his journal about the Negro boys waiting on Virginia dinner tables: "I am surprized this does not hurt the feelings of this fair Sex to see these young boys of about Fourteen and Fifteen years Old to Attend them. these whole nakedness Expos'd and I can Assure you It would Surprize a person to see these d____d black boys how well they are hung."

Partly because their relationships with blacks were structured by daily contact, Negroes seemed more highly sexed to the colonists than did the American Indians. The magnitude of the differentiation they made between the two aboriginal peoples on this score was so great as to suggest that it reflected not merely the immediate circumstances in which the colonists found themselves but the entirety of English historical experience since the beginning of expansion overseas. Far from finding Indians lusty and lascivious, they discovered them to be notably deficient in ardor and virility. (Eventually and almost inevitably a European commentator announced that the Indian's penis was smaller than the European's.) And the colonists developed no image of the Indian as a potential rapist: their descriptions of Indian attacks did not include the Indians "reserving the young women for themselves." In fact the entire interracial sexual complex did not pertain to the Indian. In the more settled portions of the colonies, Englishmen did not normally take Indian women to bed, but neither did an aura of tension pervade the sexual union of red and white. Of the various laws which penalized illicit miscegenation, none applied to Indians, and only North Carolina's (and Virginia's for a very brief period) prohibited intermarriage. On the contrary, several colonists were willing to allow, even advocate, intermarriage with the Indians—an unheard of proposition concerning Negroes.

MULATTO OFFSPRING IN A BIRACIAL SOCIETY

Inevitably, miscegenation resulted in children. Somehow they had to be accommodated to a system of racial slavery whose strictest logic their existence violated. How were mulattoes to be treated? Were they to be free or slave, acknowledged or denied, white or black? The ways in which American colonials answered these questions are profoundly revealing. The question arose, of course, in the cultural matrix of purpose, accomplishment, self-conception, and social circumstances of settlement in the New World. Inevitably the fruits of interracial sex grew differently in different contexts of self-identification.

As far as the continental colonies were concerned, it is easy to detect a pattern which has since become so familiar to Americans that they rarely pause to think about it or to question its logic and inevitability. The word *mulatto* is not frequently used in the United States. For social purposes a mulatto is termed a "Negro." Americans lump together both socially and legally all persons with perceptible admixture of African ancestry, thus making social definition without regard to genetic logic; white blood becomes socially advantageous only in overwhelming proportion. This peculiar bifurcation seems to have existed almost from the beginning of English contact with Africans. The word *mulatto,* borrowed from the Spanish, was in English usage from about 1600 and was probably first used in Virginia records in 1666. Thereafter laws dealing with Negro slaves began to add "and mulattoes," presumably to make clear that mixed blood did not confer exemption from slavery. From the first, every English continental colony lumped mulattoes with Negroes in their slave codes and in statutes governing the conduct of free Negroes: the law was clear that mulattoes and Negroes were not to be distinguished for different treatment.

In addition to the statutory homogenization of all persons of African ancestry, mulattoes do not seem to have been accorded higher status than Negroes in actual practice. Whatever the case in other countries or in later centuries, mulattoes seem generally to have been treated no better than unmixed Africans. The diaries, letters, travel accounts, and newspapers of the period do not indicate any pronounced tendency to distinguish mulattoes from Negroes, any feeling that their status was higher and demanded different treatment. These sources give no indication, for instance, that mulattoes were preferred as house servants or concubines. There was a relatively high proportion of mulattoes among manumitted slaves, but probably this was owing to the desire of some masters to liberate their own offspring.

The existence of a rigid barrier between whites and those of African ancestry necessarily required a means by which the barrier could on occasion be passed. Some accommodation had to be made for those persons with so little African blood that they appeared to be white, for one simply could not go around calling apparently white persons Negroes. Once the stain was washed out visibly it was useless as a means of identification. Thus there developed the silent mechanism of "passing." Such a device would have been unnecessary if those of mixed ancestry and appearance had been regarded as midway between white and black. It was the existence of a broad chasm which necessitated the sudden leap which passing represented.

It is possible to find direct evidence of successful passing, but unfortunately there is no way of telling how *many* blacks were effectively transformed into whites. Passing was difficult but not impossible, and it stood as a veiled, unrecognized, and ironic monument to the American ideal of a society open to all comers. But the problem of evidence is insurmountable. The success of the passing mechanism depended upon its operating in silence. Passing was a conspiracy of silence not only for the individual but for a biracial society which had drawn a rigid color line based on visibility. Unless a white man was a white man, the gates were open to endless slander and confusion.

That the existence of such a line in the continental colonies was not predominantly the effect of the English cultural heritage is suggested by even a glance at the English colonies in the Caribbean. The social accommodation of mixed offspring in the islands followed a very different pattern from that on the continent. It was regarded as improper, for example, to work mulattoes in the fields—a fundamental distinction. One observer wrote that mulatto slaves "fetch a lower price than blacks, unless they are tradesmen, because the purchasers cannot employ them in the druggeries to which negroes are put too; the colored [i.e. mulatto] men, are therefore mostly brought up to trades or employed as house slaves, and the women of this description are generally prostitutes." Though the English in the Caribbean thought of their society in terms of white, colored, and black, they employed a complicated battery of names to distinguish persons of various

racial mixtures. This terminology was borrowed from the neighboring Spanish, but words are never acquired unless they fulfill
a need. While the English settlers on the continent borrowed one
Spanish word to describe all mixtures of black and white, the islanders borrowed at least four—*mulatto, sambo, quadroon,* and
mestize—to describe differing degrees of intermixture.

The connection between the status of mulattoes and the prevailing pattern of miscegenation is obvious. Mulattoes in the
West Indies were products of accepted practice, something they
assuredly were not in the continental colonies. In the one area,
they were the fruits of a desire which society tolerated and almost
institutionalized; in the other, they represented an illicit passion
which public morality unhesitatingly condemned. On the continent, unlike the West Indies, mulattoes represented a practice
about which men could only feel guilty.

The colonist on the American continent, therefore, remained
firm in his categorization of mixed-bloods as belonging to the
lower caste. It was an unconscious decision dictated perhaps in
large part by the weight of Negroes on his community, heavy
enough to be a burden, yet not so heavy as to make him abandon
all hope of maintaining his own identity, physically and cultur-
ally. Interracial propagation was a constant reproach that he
was failing to be true to himself. Sexual intimacy strikingly symbolized a union he wished to avoid. If he could not restrain his
sexual nature, he could at least reject its fruits and thus solace
himself that he had done no harm. Perhaps he sensed as well that
continued racial intermixture would eventually undermine the
logic of the racial slavery upon which his society was based. For
the separation of slaves from free men depended on a clear de-
marcation of the races, and the presence of mulattoes blurred this
essential distinction. Accordingly he made every effort to nullify
the effects of racial intermixture. By classifying the mulatto as a
Negro he was in effect denying that intermixture had occurred
at all.

5

The Souls of Men
The Negro's Spiritual Nature

Despite their intimate contacts with Negroes, Anglo-American colonists generally made little conscious effort to assess the nature of the people they enslaved and took to bed. They felt no pressing need for assessment because both the Negro and slavery were, by and large, self-explanatory. Negroes were people from Africa bought for the purpose of performing labor. What fact could be more obvious and less demanding of explanation?

There were strains, of course, beneath the surface of this placid acceptance. The colonists felt the tug of two opposing ways of looking at the Negro's essential nature. One view derived from his uniquely base status in the colonies. In all societies men tend to extrapolate from status to inherent character, to impute to individuals characteristics suited to their social roles. As one member of a much older slave society put it, some men were "slaves by nature." In the face of Aristole's contention, the societies in the Western tradition have minimized this tendency and have emphasized the contrary idea that all individuals possess inherently the same fundamental nature. This emphasis originally drew much of its strength from the doctrines of Christianity, and still in the seventeenth century any assertion of human unity was bound to be made in religious terms. No matter in what terms asserted, though, the deep sense of the oneness of humanity clashed head on with the sense that the lowly members of society must necessarily be possessed of low nature. It was inevitable, then, that the introduction of chattel slavery by Europeans into their American settlements would produce conflict. Perhaps it is a credit to Western culture, however, that there was any tension at all.

CHRISTIAN PRINCIPLES AND THE FAILURE OF CONVERSION

Indications of internal stress bubbled quickly to the surface because the Christian tradition demanded that the souls of men be given spiritual care while still on earth; not just some souls but all, for Christianity was on this point firmly universalist. The obligation of English Christians to convert Indians and Negroes was as obvious and undeniable in the eighteenth century as it had been two hundred years earlier. Yet many of the Englishmen who settled in America proved reluctant or downright unwilling to meet this obligation. In part their failure was owing to practical considerations arising from the necessities of plantation management. Inescapably, however, since conversion was the necessary outward manifestation of the assumption of inner sameness in all men, any opposition to conversion—even when grounded on "necessity"—represented direct denial of inner similarity between the master and his lowly slave. Furthermore, by allowing slaves to remain unconverted, masters were perpetuating the outward differences between the two peoples, and thus in an important sense opposition to conversion fed upon itself.

Not only is it extremely difficult to sort out the practical considerations underlying opposition to conversion of Negroes from more subtle sources of hostility, but it is impossible to determine just how much opposition there actually was. Most of the evidence of opposition derives from indignant assertions by members of the clergy keenly interested in seeing conversion accomplished. Though they were scarcely disinterested observers, it is possible to infer from their reports a good deal about the attitudes of slaveowners: amid the blare of trumpets rallying Christians to the work of God one can easily detect the shuffle of dragging feet.

Many slaveholders felt that no matter how much conversion might benefit the Negroes' souls, it could only make them worse slaves. Occasionally they went so far as to charge that efforts at conversion fostered rebellion rather than piety. Most commonly, though, planters voiced the less specific objection that Christianizing the slaves made them "more perverse and untractable," less amenable to discipline, more discontented with their lot—which may well have been true. Entirely aside from these objections, it seems fair to suppose that one of the major barriers to conversion was unwillingness to put forth the requisite effort. It was a great deal easier simply to forget the slaves on Sunday than to round them up to listen to a sermon.

Perhaps the best assessment of objection to Christian instruction of Negroes came from the astute Swedish visitor to America, Peter Kalm, who wrote that opposition arose "partly by the conceit of its being shameful to have a spiritual brother or sister among so despicable people; partly by thinking that they would not be able to keep their negroes so subjected afterwards; and partly through fear of the negroes growing too proud on seeing themselves upon a level with their masters in religious matters."

What the colonists feared, of course, was the dimly recognized challenge to their distinct status and the mental differentiation upon which it rested. For by Christianizing the Negro, by giving him even the meager crumbs of religious instruction which were prerequiste to baptism, the colonist was making the Negro just so much more like himself. The African's inevitable acquisition of the white settler's language and manners was having precisely this effect. It was virtually inevitable, too, that the colonists should have abhorred the prospect that Negroes might come to resemble them. For if the Negro were like themselves, how could they enslave him? How explain the bid on the block? Slavery could survive *only* if the Negro were a man set apart; he simply had to be different if slavery was to exist at all.

THE QUESTION OF NEGRO CAPACITY

The question of conversion raised an issue concerning the Negro which has become far more important in retrospect than it was at the time. To the relatively lettered English colonists, Africans and Afro-Americans must indeed have seemed ignorant and often downright stupid. As Cotton Mather wrote in *The Negro Chris-*

tianized, "Indeed their *Stupidity* is a *Discouragement.* It may seem, unto as little purpose, to *Teach,* as to *wash an AEthiopian.*" Yet Mather regarded this defect as a challenge rather than a permanent obstacle: "But the greater their *Stupidity,* the greater must be our *Application.*" In fact many proponents of conversion were entirely willing to concede that Negroes were ignorant, stupid, unteachable, barbarous, stubborn, and deficient in understanding. More frequently, many advocates of conversion felt called upon to assert with considerable vehemence that Negroes possessed the same capacities as Europeans and lacked only the opportunity of improvement in order to develop them.

What this argument was groping toward, of course, was the proposition that the Negro's stupidity, far from being inherent, was caused by his condition, and that this condition of slavery had been imposed by white men. By the time of the Revolution, the point at issue had become abundantly clear. In 1770, for instance, a prominent Georgia merchant who was greatly interested in promoting the cause of conversion referred to "the barren, because too generally unimproved Capacities of these poor Creatures," and then hastened to explain himself: "I say unimproved Capacities, as some ignorant people would *foolishly* insinuate, that they are scarcely reasonable Creatures, and not capable of being instructed in the divine Thruths of Christianity; an absurdity too obvious to deserve any refutation."

The ominous implications embedded in these remarks may be readily detected. Proponents of conversion would never have felt compelled to declare the Negro was inherently as intelligent as the European unless they had encountered insinuations to the contrary. To affirm positively that the Negro was the mental equal of the white man was to affirm by indirection that some people thought the Negro was not. In light of later developments in the United States, these affirmations appear to be the first faint rumblings of a long-distant dispute.

It is essential, however, that developments not be read backwards. For one thing, eighteenth-century ideas about human intelligence are almost disconcertingly imprecise when set alongside modern ideas. The bewildering variety of words then used to denote what we call "intelligence" was symptomatic of an underlying vagueness about the abilities in men which, it was half-recognized, were inborn rather than acquired. The concept of intelligence had not yet become disassociated from the idea of capacity for religious experience or even from the idea of wisdom. The attribute(s) which we frequently term "I.Q." did not then appear distinct from attributes which we might call "spirituality," "disposition," and "learnedness."

Paradoxically, the vagueness of the distinction between inherent and acquired attributes in men itself helped pave the way for later assertions of inherent Negro stupidity. To realize this, it is only necessary to consider the way some white men must have been talking in the first half of the eighteenth century. The cultural gulf between the two peoples was enormous, and Negroes fresh from Africa and even their children must have seemed to European settlers very "stupid" indeed. As with any quality in other people which seems extreme, the Negro's stupidity must at times have seemed downright irredeemable, as hopelessly rooted in his essential character; from there it was no step at all to calling him casually a naturally stupid brute. And because there existed no clear distinction between inborn and acquired characteristics, it became easy enough to slip into thinking that the Negro's seemingly natural and intractable stupidity was "innate," without, however, imparting much precision or meaning to the notion.

SPIRITUAL EQUALITY AND TEMPORAL SUBORDINATION

It is no wonder that men interested in the cause of Negro conversion were at pains to strike down such insinuations. These men rightly recognized, however, that the chief obstacle in the path of their program was the slaveholder's fear that conversion might weaken his dominion over his slaves. Accordingly they went out of their way to stress that Christianizing Negroes would make them much better slaves, not worse. These clergymen had been forced by the circumstance of racial slavery in America into propagating the Gospel by presenting it as an attractive device for slave control. The Reverend Thomas Bacon felt no hesitation in telling slaves that they must obey their masters in all things, even when cruelly abused: "your *Masters* and *Mistresses*," he explained glowingly, "are God's Overseers."

After laying down this doctrine of absolute obedience, Thomas Bacon added a highly significant afterthought. Obedience was not required of anyone, Bacon said, if he were commanded to commit a sinful act. This exception, which had long been stressed in Christian and particularly Protestant political thought, was symptomatic of the enormously important fact that the idea of Christian liberty could not be strictly confined to matters of the spirit. Theologians tried manfully to maintain the distinction between spiritual freedom and temporal bondage, but any emphasis on the former was potentially explosive. Because Christianity had always leveled the souls of men before God, it was potentially corrosive of the world's social hierarchies.

It is therefore no surprise that early objection to the Negro's subordination derived not from ideas about earthly equality but from the concept of equality before God. Early antislavery was an application of a religious idea to social practice, an application made possible, however, by the unrecognized gradual weakening of old ideas about natural and inevitable social hierarchy. Certainly it was no accident that early antislavery pronouncements came largely from members of a religious group which had originated at a time of social upheaval. The Society of Friends arose out of the social and religious turmoil of the English Civil War in the mid-seventeenth century and underwent years of persecution partly for doctrinal heresy and partly for their stubborn persistence in pushing the religious principle of equality into areas which nearly everyone else regarded as of purely temporal concern. The twin Quaker doctrines of the Inner Light (which eliminated all intermediaries between men and God) and of the brotherhood of man gave renewed emphasis to the strong streak of equalitarianism which had always run through Christian thought.

There were at least fifteen known written condemnations of slavery in the English colonies before 1750, almost all by Quakers. With deep conviction they struck with almost childlike directness at the moral wrong of slavery, at the *"making Slaves* of them who bear the Image of God, *viz.* their fellow-Creature, Man." The word of God, revealed alike by Scripture and by the Inner Light, declared all men to be one family, brothers in the bosom of the

Christ who died "for all mankind, they being a part, though yet ungathered." Brotherhood demanded love, the brotherly love "which excepts not nor despises any for their Complections." And the demands of love were obvious: "Is there any that would be done or handled at this manner? viz., to be sold or made a slave for all the time of his life? . . . Now, though they are black, we cannot conceive there is more liberty to have them slaves, as it is to have other white ones. There is a saying, that we should do to all men like as we will be done ourselves; making no difference of what generation, descent, or colour they are."

Certainly these antislavery authors were high-minded men, utterly sincere in their pioneering efforts for a noble cause. In virtually every case, however, their opposition to slavery was not based exclusively on moral considerations. Some Quakers pointed to the danger of insurrections (in Pennsylvania in 1688, no less), though of course with pacifist Quakers this danger was moral as well as practical. Ownership of Negro slaves also threatened the Quaker's spiritual purity, or at least a few Quakers thought it did: as one Friend wrote, "If I Should have a bad one of them, that must be Corrected, Or would Run away, Or when I went from home, and Leave him with a women or Maid, and he Should desire or Seek to Comitt wickedness." What then was a loving slaveholder to do?

The early antislavery arguments served to confirm that the Negro's essential nature was equal to the white man's. Compared with the campaign for conversion of Negroes, however, the early antislavery voices were crying in the wilderness. Indeed the two programs diverged rapidly despite their common origin in Christian equalitarianism. Both the Society of Friends and the Church of England started in the seventeenth century urging conversion and better treatment of slaves, yet the Quakers ended in condemning slavery and the Anglican clergy in supporting it. An original identity of purpose was splintered by the rock-hard institution of slavery in America.

INCLUSION AND EXCLUSION IN THE PROTESTANT CHURCHES

The endorsement of slavery by many, though by no means all, proponents of conversion represented the most obvious but clearly not the most important failure of the equalitarian Christian tradition. For the most disastrous failing of the churches in America was embodied in the *kind* of slavery they were at least willing to put up with if not endorse. Especially was this true of the Society for the Propagation of the Gospel in Foreign Parts, the missionary arm of the Church of England, founded in 1701. The slavery which the S.P.G. defended was marked by complete deprivation of rights. Despite the S.P.G.'s somewhat guarded pleas for kind treatment and adequate food and clothing for slaves, neither the S.P.G. nor other proponents of conversion put up much of a fight against the many hideous manifestations of the commercial slavery which deprived blacks of status as human beings.

It has often been said that the very nature of Protestantism was partially responsible for these failures. Of course the various Protestant churches themselves varied appreciably in doctrine and institutional structure. Yet all the Protestant sects, including the Quakers, shared in common a low-church English Protestantism strongly tinged by Calvinism; many of the qualities of mind and temperament which are usually described as Puritan were shared by Anglicans and Baptists and by Quakers as well. The similarities among the Protestant sects were fully as important as the differences.

As far as *the* Puritans were concerned, slavery was simply not a problem. The Puritans who settled in colonies where slavery became a firmly established institution accepted the subordination of the African without protest yet without any special eagerness, and the same was true in Puritan-dominated New England. The Puritans' fondness for the Old Testament and their stress on the depravity of man and the selectivity of salvation might at first sight seem to have led them toward embracing racial slavery with open arms. In the first instance, however, the Old Testament was sufficiently vague on the subject of bond service in ancient Israel that new Israelites could either deny or affirm the legitimacy of Negro slavery by appealing to Scripture. Yet some of the strongest assertions of the Negro's fundamental identity with the white man came from prominent Puritans. Though the Reverend Cotton Mather, for example, exhorted Negroes (and white servants) to remain obedient and content in their bondage, he never minced words on the obligations of their masters: "You deny your *Master in Heaven*," he wrote in *The Negro Christianized*, "if you do nothing to bring your *Servants* unto the Knowledge and Service of that glorious *Master*." The equality of all souls before God was so very real, so axiomatic, and so important to the Puritans that they were virtually precluded from thinking that the Negro was an inherently inferior being.

While there can be no doubt that Puritan theology required that the Negro be regarded as possessing the same nature as the white man, certain ways in which Puritan theology operated in the community may have tended toward exclusion of Negroes from full participation. Embedded in New England Puritanism was a certain tribalism, a sense of being a folk set apart. Their sense of the special character of their religion was matched by a feeling that they were a special people. Migration to an isolated corner of the world certainly did nothing to diminish feelings of specialness and exclusiveness. Yet tribalism was not peculiar to New England, nor to Puritans; in varying measure it pervaded all the Protestant sects in the English colonies. Indeed the sectarian character of Protestantism fostered a spirit of tribalism, since sectarianism meant emphasis on distinctiveness from others and virtual, though inadmissible, abandonment of the ideal of Christian universality. All Protestant history was the history of some people differentiating themselves from others.

While this spirit in Protestantism was probably in some measure responsible for the exclusion of Negroes from the community, the notion that Calvinist belief in predestination led Puritans to think that black men were damned and white men were not is so unbelievably crude as to be utterly incorrect. An African woman was accepted into full membership in a Massachusetts church in 1641, only three years after the first Africans are thought to have arrived in the colony. Protestant doctrine called upon the English settlers to bring strangers into the fold; it was something in the style and spirit of Protestantism as it operated in the community which whispered, "not so fast."

What drastically sapped the energy of Protestant equalitarianism as applied to the Negro was not so much this feeling of exclusiveness as certain glaring institutional weaknesses in the structure of the Protestant churches in America. In New England, of course, the Puritan churches operated from a position of strength. In New England, however, there were not many Negroes. In the southern continental colonies the churches at best were in a weak position to dictate to slaveholders and in some times and places were virtually nonexistent. The burden of sustaining the Christian equalitarian tradition in the face of chattel slavery fell chiefly upon the Anglican Church, which remained predominant, particularly among wealthy slaveholders, in the coastal regions where there was heavy slave concentration. In Virginia and Maryland the Anglican Church's position was relatively firm, but even there it could scarcely be termed a powerful institution; some of the tobacco colonies' parishes lacked ministers and many ministers lacked sanctity and leverage in the community. In the Lower South, the Church of England was even weaker.

All the Protestant sects, including the Church of England, were distinguished from the Catholic Church (which of course prevailed in the Latin American colonies) by a notably different conception of conversion. Protestants felt that true conversion was an arduous and exacting process and required a transformation of the spirit which could not possibly be accomplished by running the heathen through a mill of sacramental rites. As one caustic New Englander put the matter concerning the Indians in 1647, "if wee would force them to baptisme (as the Spaniards do . . . having learnt them a short answer or two to some Popish questions) . . . wee could have gathered many hundreds, yea thousands it may bee by this time, into the name of Churches; but wee have not learnt as yet that art of coyning Christians, or putting Christs name and Image upon copper mettle." For Protestants generally, true converts were nurtured, not minted.

The tedious process of nurturing souls kept great numbers of slaves out of the churches. With all the Protestant sects, converting heathens required instructing them first. Especially during the early years of slavery's rapid growth in the eighteenth century, there were mountainous practical difficulties. An Anglican minister in Virginia replied in 1724 to an official query concerning the "infidels" in his parish (which measured 40 × 8 miles) saying, "A great many Black bond men and women infidels that understand not our Language nor me their's: not any free. The Church is open to them; the word preached, and the Sacraments administered with circumspection." Always, everywhere, there was circumspection.

RELIGIOUS REVIVAL AND THE IMPACT OF CONVERSION

On the other hand, the pronounced strain of individualism in Protestantism which helped make conversion such a hurdle contained implications which operated directly against the tendency toward exclusion. For the most part, these implications remained dormant in the colonies until about 1740, when with remarkable suddenness a wave of religious revivals brought them to life. The spirit of revivalism virtually beckoned Negroes to participate. Schisms ripped through many of the well-established sects, to the benefit particularly of the Baptists and later the Methodists and to the detriment of formalism and orderly procedures of admission. Almost by definition a religious revival was inclusive; itinerant preachers aimed at gathering every lost sheep, black as well as white. The revivals tended to break down the traditional structures of clerical control and emphasize once again the priesthood of all believers. Religious enthusiasm elbowed aside religious sophistication as the criterion of true piety. Nothing could make this tendency more evident than the remarks of one of the foremost critics of the Great Awakening, who lamented the appearance of "so many *Exhorters*," of totally unqualified persons preaching the gospel. As he described them, "They are *chiefly* indeed young *Persons,* sometimes *Lads,* or rather *Boys:* Nay, *Women* and *Girls;* yea, *Negroes,* have taken upon them to do the Business of *Preachers.*"

Nowhere had Negroes previously taken on such a business; indeed in the southern colonies the great masses of slaves stood altogether outside the fold of Christianity. After 1740, Negroes began entering the churches in accelerating numbers. In many localities certain blacks gained considerable reputation as preachers to their own people and in several cases to whites as well. The equalitarian implications in Protestant Christianity were never more apparent; if it was difficult for Negroes to become men of affairs in this world, it became increasingly easy, after the watershed of the Great Awakening, for them to become men of God.

The effects of the Great Awakening on American feelings about the Negro rippled slowly through colonial society. By clearing an avenue down which Negroes could crowd into an important sector of the white man's community, the Awakening gradually forced the colonists to face more squarely the fact that Negroes were going to participate in their American experience. Realization of this fact did not necessarily mean that the Negro would be welcomed; one white Virginian declared that slaves "are grown so much worse" from imbibing New Light ideas. In the long run, indeed, this realization could easily lead to strenuous efforts to find some novel and effective means of barring the Negro from the white community now that heathenism was no longer serving the purpose. Most important of all, however, the Great Awakening re-emphasized the axiomatic spiritual equality of Negroes with white men. It demonstrated once again the staying power and profound influence of the equalitarian strain in Christianity. "Think you," the Reverend George Whitefield asked the planters of the southern colonies in a widely circulated pamphlet, that your children "are any way better by Nature than the poor Negroes? No, in no wise. Blacks are just as much, and no more, conceived and born in Sin, as White Men are. Both, if born and bred up here, I am persuaded, are naturally capable of the same [religious] improvement."

This central theme of religious equalitarianism, that Negroes were "by Nature" the equals of white men because they possessed immortal souls, fenced the thinking of every colonist in America. Despite the Great Awakening and these tendencies, however, many white men were increasingly turning their attention from the spiritual condition of mankind to the place of man in an ordered creation of natural beings. As is true with all aspects of the process of secularization in Western culture, this change was complicated, but however it operated it was bound to make the sheerly physical attributes of Negroes assume a novel importance.

6

The Bodies of Men
The Negro's Physical Nature

The avalanche of geographical discoveries beginning in the fifteenth century had created an increasingly pressing problem for European thought. Old ideas about the natural world were almost buried by a mounting pile of information about distant lands and strange plants, animals, and even men. By the eighteenth century it was obvious that this mass of information had to be squeezed into some logical framework if man were to continue to make sense of the world.

Success in conceptual and technological manipulation of their natural environment led Europeans increasingly to ponder their own place in Nature's scheme. By the eighteenth century, many men no longer fastened their eyes steadfastly upon the drama of salvation. Many intellectuals were ripe for a new center of interest which would bear the weight of their energy and curiosity. And gradually, as they become more interested in themselves as natural creatures, the purely physical differences among men acquired heightened significance and greater relative importance. Viewed in the broadest terms, this growing interest in the physical distinctions among human beings was one aspect of the secularization of Western society.

CONFUSION, ORDER, AND HIERARCHY

Newton had explained the arrangement of the universe with such brilliance as to cast a spell over generations. In contrast, when natural philosophers set about arranging animals and men, they found their materials inherently less easy to manage than the steadily orbiting planets and their findings more liable to unleash disturbing religious and social questions. In the face of these difficulties they nonetheless remained determined to impose order as firmly on the motley variations of men as on all living things. It became apparent in the eighteenth century, however, that there were various ways in which order could be imposed.

In the 1730's Linnaeus took the fateful step of classifying mankind as an integral part of the animal creation, thereby dramatically underlining the fact that man was, after all, a physical being. In his great *Systema Naturae*, which rolled majestically through twelve editions during his lifetime, Linnaeus began his catalogue of all living things with "MAMMALIA: Order 1. Primates" and included in this category the simian apes, the sloth, and "HOMO." Certainly the assumptions underlying this decision were not entirely new, for they had guided the dissecting knife which Edward Tyson had wielded on his "Orang-outang" in 1701. But to throw man into the same "Order" with the "SIMIA" was to make a bald case for regarding man as subject to the same kind of scrutiny as other animals.

Linnaeus's almost governing influence in the eighteenth century did not derive from this classification of men with simians but from his descriptive classification of all living things. Here was a new tool with which order could be hammered into the natural world, and it was as eagerly grasped in America as anywhere. Linnaeus himself gave proof of its power by describing and classifying thousands of plants and the animal kingdom.

Linnaean classification was not, however, the only attractive method of making nature dance to the natural philosopher's tune. An ancient concept with roots deep in classical Greece was reaching full flower in the seventeenth and eighteenth centuries, a concept which had the merit of systematizing all creation and even the Creator himself. The Chain of Being, as usually conceived, commenced with inanimate things and ranged upwards through the lowliest forms of life, through the more intelligent animals until it reached man himself; from man it continued upward through the myriad ranks of heavenly creatures until it reached its pinnacle in God. By definition a chain was without gaps, the more so with the Great Chain forged by the Creator. Man, the middling creature on this scale, was carefully suspended between the heavenly and brute creation. As Edward Tyson had explained in the course of comparing simian and human anatomy, *"Man* is part a *Brute,* part an *Angel;* and is that *Link* in the *Creation,* that joyns them both together."

The "idea" of the Chain functioned at several levels of thought. To summarize baldly for the moment: it served to dramatize the Christian view of man as a creature with a divine soul; it served to formulate men's vague sense of the beast within themselves and their capacity for rising above bestiality; it served to satisfy the eighteenth century's ravenous appetite for hierarchical principles in the face of social upheaval; and it served as a powerful means of organizing the facts of the natural world. No one of these functions was unrelated to any other.

As a means of conceptualizing the differences among natural creatures, the Great Chain of Being differed appreciably from the method forged by Linnaeus. It was one thing to classify all living creation, and altogether another to arrange it in a single great hierarchy. Indeed, to obtain criteria for ranking all creatures on a single scale was virtually impossible. The Great Chain of Being could stand in its traditional form only if the myriad kinds of creation were not viewed in very specific terms. The concept had always been in difficulty the moment men got down to cases. When natural philosophers tried to decide whether the ape, the parrot, or the elephant was next below man, for instance, the grand Chain began to look like an unimpressive heap of ill-assorted links. If anyone ever got down to cases it was Linnaeus.

The Linnaean approach passed into modern anthropology by way of Johann Friedrich Blumenbach, the great physiologist and comparative anatomist who is often called the founder of anthropology. In 1781 Blumenbach described five varieties of men, and in 1795 introduced some badly needed precise terminology, including the inept but remarkably adhesive term *Caucasian.* In each of his editions Blumenbach came down hard on his major point: all men belonged to the same species, and his groupings were merely varieties. The differences among men, he insisted, were not nearly so great as those which separated men from apes.

Far from framing this point in religious terms, Blumenbach approached men and simians physiologically, examining in turn such characteristics as stature, carriage, skull, hair, skin color, and so on. In most or all of these respects, he concluded, the varieties of men differed from each other, yet still more from the apes. Nonetheless, Blumenbach was not without his preferences, for he argued that the original type of man was Caucasian.

While Linnaeus and Blumenbach were able to impose order without hierarchy, many natural philosophers were tempted by the synthesizing power of the Great Chain of Being. Clearly mankind was formed not in one image but in many. If all other created beings were ranked upon a grand scale, why not man? Could it be that the Creator had graded mankind from its noblest specimens to its most brutal savages? The possibilities were there for any European who decided to compare his own society with the "savages" overseas.

Sir William Petty, one of the founders of the Royal Society in mid-seventeenth century, was the first to emphasize the gradation among groups of men on the basis of physical distinctions:

> I say that the Europeans do not onely differ from the . . . Africans in Collour, which is as much as white differs from black, but also in their Haire . . . [and] in the shape of their Noses, Lipps, and cheek bones, as also in the very outline of their faces and the Mould of their skulls. They differ also in their Naturall Manners, and in the internall Qualities of their Minds.

Petty was undecided which animal was next below man on the great scale; on the basis of appearance, the ape nearest resembled man, and on basis of voice, the parrot. But the elephant possessed the greatest intellectual capacities of any animal, and Petty was inclined to award the elephant the rank just below man, though he conceded that most writers preferred the ape. Despite this indirect confession of his inability to arrange even a handful of creatures on the scale, Petty's discussion of the ranks of men was prophetic of developments in the eighteenth century. For Petty had chosen Europeans and Africans as representing the extremities of diversity and had based this decision primarily on physiognomic traits. The work of the Dutch anatomist Peter Camper in the 1770's finally showed where the ideal of hierarchy was leading.

It was Camper who pioneered the idea of the "facial angle" (roughly, a measure of prognathism) and who found in his collection of skulls a regular gradation from apes, through Negroes, to Europeans. "It is amusing to contemplate," he wrote, "an arrangement of these [skulls], placed in a regular succession: apes, orangs, negroes, the skull of an Hottentot, Madagascar, Celebese, Chinese, Moguller, Calmuck, and divers Europeans. It was in this manner that I arranged them upon a shelf in my cabinet." In the long run, this sort of laboratory pastime was scarcely amusing.

In the even longer run, however, this application of the principle of gradation to the facts of anatomy was bound to collapse of its own weight. When examined rigorously the anatomical differences among men (both fossilized and living) simply cannot be forced into a single continuum. It is clear that when Europeans set about to rank the varieties of men, their decision that the Negro was at the bottom and the white man at the top was not dictated solely by the facts of human biology.

While it is easy to see why the European was firmly seated at the top, it is less obvious why Africans, of all the world's peoples, should have been placed at the bottom. Several ways of thinking about the world's "savage" nations were in operation all at once. Color was one means by which people overseas could be categorized, but there were others. Drawing upon a classical tradition, Europeans tended to regard savagery as a function of extreme temperatures. By this logic the cold-ridden natives of Lapland were as radically different from civilized Europeans as were the blacks of tropical Guinea. But Laps were not slaves to Europeans, and Negroes were. Here, surely, was a crucial factor making for the burial of the Negro at the bottom of mankind. Though other peoples, most notably the Indians, were enslaved by Europeans, slavery was typically a Negro-white relationship. This fact in itself inevitably meant that Africans would not be accorded a high place when Europeans set about arranging the varieties of men on a grand scale.

NEGROES, APES, AND BEASTS

One of the most important and enduring influences of the concept of the Chain was its principle of continuity, a principle which operated particularly to emphasize the close affinity of men

with beasts. It was virtually impossible, in fact, to discuss gradations of men without stressing the closeness of the lowest men to
the highest animals. Because the principle of continuity ran counter to the Christian emphasis on the uniqueness of man, moreover, proponents of the Chain were driven to especially strenuous
defense of this affinity. They hammered away to prove that the
Chain's weakest conceptual link was, after all, as strong as any
other. Plainly any elaboration of the Chain of Being was going to
associate some group of human beings with the ape.

By sheer accident, an appalling one in retrospect, Negroes and
apes had already been linked together. European explorers had
stumbled across Africans and the most man-like of the apes simultaneously. The relationship between the travelers' tales and the
concept of the Chain was reciprocal: the "fact" that Negroes and
apes sometimes had "a beastly copulation or conjuncture" served
to demonstrate the affinity of men and beasts; conversely, the
Chain of Being was an admirable way of explaining this "fact."
The chance tales of travelers interlocked with the concept of the
Chain of Being to transform the accidental geographical proximity of Negroes and apes into an association of cosmic significance.

That association was as frequently revealed by denial as by affirmation, for the implications of the association of the Negro
with the ape were profoundly disturbing to faithful Christians
and men of good will. Peter Camper, gazing upon his "amusing"
arrangement of skulls (in which a Negro's stood next to an orang-
outang's), emphatically denied that this proximity implied any
inferiority in the Negro. Just what it did imply, Camper did not
say. To call the Negro a man and the ape a beast was in effect to
shatter the Great Chain, though adherents of that concept could
never admit it. It was impossible for scientists not to sense an
enormous gulf between man, who was rational and immortal, and
an ape, who was neither.

There have been frequent assertions in the twentieth century
that white men in the eighteenth thought Negroes were beasts;
these assertions are incorrect, and they fail to take into account
certain eighteenth-century assumptions about the nature of man.
Everyone knew—then—that man possessed a soul and rationality.
By these twin criteria even the wisest elephant and the most elo-

quent parrot failed admission to humankind. Virtually everyone knew, moreover, that by these criteria Africans were men.

Even during the eighteenth century, however, men interested in converting Negroes and alleviating the brutality of slavery began to charge that the planters thought their slaves were beasts. Usually the accusation was shaped in the simile that the planters regarded and treated their slaves *like* beasts or *as* other men did their cattle. What they *were* saying, in fact, was that the planters were neither treating nor regarding their slaves as human beings ought to be treated and regarded, which was perfectly true. The charge that planters treated Negroes like beasts was particularly effective precisely because the idea that any creatures so obviously human were regarded as animals was profoundly shocking in an age which drew a broad, clear line between men and all other living creatures.

American colonials no more thought Negroes were beasts than did European scientists and missionaries; if they had *really* thought so they would have sternly punished miscegenation for what it would have been—buggery. Yet the charge that white men treated Negroes as beasts was entirely justified if not taken literally. Equalitarian defenders of the Negro were laying bare an inherent tendency of slavery with the only terms they knew how to employ. Chattel slavery in America *did* lead to a mode of thinking about the basest members of society as primarily and merely physical creatures. It was especially the day-to-day business of commercial slavery which placed a premium on the Negro's purely physical qualities. New slaves off the ships were described as "well-fleshed," "strong-limbed," "lusty," "sickly," "robust," "healthy," "scrawny," "unblemished." In South Carolina, Georgia, and the West Indies, slaves were sometimes branded by their owners with a hot iron, usually with the owner's initials. The everyday buying and selling and deeding of slaves underscored the fact that Negroes, just like horses, were walking pieces of property.

Even in the plantations, however, the Negro walked and hoed and talked and propagated like other men. No matter how much slavery degraded the Negro, every daily event in the lives and relationships of blacks and whites indicated undeniably that the

Negro was a human being. White men feared their slaves' desires for freedom, they talked with their Negroes, and they slept with them. These were human relationships, continually driving home the common humanity of all.

RATIONAL SCIENCE AND IRRATIONAL LOGIC

In addition, certain scientific beliefs of the eighteenth century strongly supported the assumption that there was a pronounced dividing line between men and animals. *Species* were generally regarded as fixed in number and in kind—stable, that is, through time. Individual species did not vary beyond distinctly defined limits. It was generally agreed also that the best test of species was interfertility. If union between two creatures could produce fertile offspring, then those two creatures belonged to the same species. Any variations of kind within a species were just that, accidental *varieties* and not species. And there was no doubt that the Negro could mate with other varieties of mankind and that the offspring were themselves fertile: a multitude of reports from the international ethnological laboratory in America provided irrefutable proof.

Yet there was a weak strand in this rope which bound the Negro with the rest of mankind. For it was not completely certain that the Negro was unable to breed with the ape or that the Negro had not sprung from some mixture with that animal. The reports from Africa had done their work. One normally sensible naturalist casually referred to the orang-outang as "equally ardent for women as for its own females," and to Negresses who had forced or voluntary intercourse with apes. Lord Monboddo, an eccentric Scot who made something of a name for himself by contending that apes could speak and were actually a variety of men, airily announced that orang-outangs copulated with human females and almost certainly fathered offspring in this manner. At no time did he suggest that *only* Negroes could have intercourse with apes; but, as it turned out, all his illustrations came from reports about Africa.

The significance of the association of the Negro with the ape was its existence on a variety of levels of mental construction. At one extreme, it appeared in a technical treatise by Linnaeus. At a rather different level of formulation, it cropped up as a crude joke in 1734 when someone inserted an advertisement in the *South-Carolina Gazette* for a runaway "baboon": "He has learn'd to walk very erect on his two Hind-Legs, he grins and chatters much, but will not bite, he plays Tricks impudently well, and is mightily given to clambering, whereby he often shews his A – –. If any one finds him, or will send any news of him to ———— Office, in ———— street, shall be rewarded proportionably to the Merit of the Creature." Still less (self-)conscious was a traveler's much earlier offhand observation that the "genterey" of Barbados "have most of them 100 or 2 or 3 of slaves apes whou they command as they pleas." The sum of these remarks speaks for itself. No one thought that the Negro was an ape, but then there was always the old tale about . . . and so on.

The extraordinarily pervasive and enduring character of this notion was in itself an indication of the diverse functions it served. The notion had scientific value: it forged a crucial link in the Chain of Being and helped explain the Negro's and the ape's prognathism. On a less rational level the notion gave expression to men's half-conscious realization that they were linked to beasts and bestiality. And just as the concept of the Chain ordered every being on a vertical scale, the association of the Negro with the ape ordered men's deep, unconscious drives into a tightly controlled hierarchy. The association was usually conceived in sexual terms, no matter whether remarks about physical resemblance between Negroes and apes were tacked on. The "beastly copulation" and "unnatural mixture" which described the association was vague in one sense and highly specific in another. The specific element is profoundly revealing. The sexual union of apes and Negroes was *always* conceived as involving *female Negroes* and *male apes!* The aggressors were literally beasts; the sexual drive was conceived as thrusting upwards from below. The Negro-ape association was an allegory of the nature of man.

INDIANS, AFRICANS, AND THE COMPLEXION OF MAN

English colonists in America quite naturally fastened their attention particularly upon the two non-European peoples with whom

they had most intimate contact, Indians and Africans. By reason
of their original geographical separation, their dissimilarity in
culture and appearance, and the very different ways they had to
be treated by advancing Europeans, the Indian and the Negro remained what they had been from the first—distinctively different
intellectual problems.

The question which the Indian raised in European minds was
that of his point of origin. The Negro presented an entirely different puzzle. There was no difficulty over how he had arrived at his
homeland in Africa, though there was a great deal of long-
standing difficulty as to the cause of his "peculiar" appearance.
As for the Indian's color, white men both in Europe and America
belittled the importance of his "tawny" complexion or used it
merely as a foil for proving certain points about the Negro's
blackness. Most writers, moreover, saw the Indian as naturally
and innately lighter than he was in fact. As one described them,
"Their skins are naturally white, but altered from their originals
by the several dyings of Roots and Barks, that they prepare and
make useful to metamorphize their hydes into a dark Cinamon
brown." There was little dissent to this commonplace assertion
that the Indians' tawny color resulted wholly or in part from their
custom of daubing themselves with bear grease, oils, or the like
from a well-stocked cabinet of natural cosmetics. White men
seemed to want to sweep the problem of the Indian's color under
the rug.

As for the Negro's "blackness," the reigning mood at the beginning of the eighteenth century was one of puzzlement and
shotgun explanation. As time went on, the theologically oriented
curse on Ham gradually lost its popularity. Most natural philosophers were inclined instead to think that the heat of the sun was
the essential agent, though some talked vaguely of accidental alterations or maternal impressions. With the passage of time, moreover, there was more evidence available concerning the effects of
living in a cold climate on the African's complexion. Buffon, the
great French naturalist, thought that they would become percep-
tibly lighter by the eighth or tenth or twelfth generation, but
Americans generally did not see much improvement.

The source of the confusion over the Negro's color becomes

clearer when the problem is considered in modern terms. Eighteenth-century speculation was based on the assumption that an acquired characteristic (blackness from the heat of the sun) could be transmitted to offspring. Yet this process just did not seem to work in the climatological laboratory: children of white men in the tropics did not inherit the darkened complexion of their parents. The converse situation with Negroes in northern climates did not work for the first generation, nor the children. The problem was insoluble, of course, unless men were willing to distort the facts or until development of the idea of natural selection operating over an unbelievably long period of time.

By far the most common assumption was that the original color of man was white, an assumption which gave special sharpness to the question why the Negro was black. Many commentators treated the Negro's blackness as a degeneration from original color. It was Oliver Goldsmith, the English dramatist, who first pressed this self-comforting conception to its logical conclusion. White, Goldsmith announced, was the natural color of man. "We may consider the European figure and colour as standards," he continued, "to which to refer all other varieties, and with which to compare them. . . . That we have all sprung from one common parent, we are taught, both by reason and religion, to believe; and we have good reason also to think that the Europeans resemble him more than any of the rest of his children." The secret was out: Adam was a white man.

For Europeans in general, the Negro's blackness afforded a certain happiness. No one was lighter than they, a fact that when joined to a feeling of cultural superiority could produce the most extraordinary thoughts in the minds of Europeans. David Hume, the great Scottish philosopher, put the matter more baldly than anyone. Hume was convinced that the peoples near the poles and in the tropics were essentially inferior to those in the temperate zones, a conviction which can be traced historically back through European thought to the Greeks—who also lived in a temperate climate. What Hume did in 1748, though, was to go ancient philosophers one better by hitching superiority to complexion.

> I am apt to suspect the negroes, and in general all the other species of men . . . to be naturally inferior to the whites.

There never was a civilized nation of any other complexion
than white, nor even any individual eminent either in action or
speculation. No ingenious manufactures amongst them, no
arts, no sciences. . . . In JAMAICA indeed they talk of one
negroe as a man of parts and learning; but 'tis likely he is admired for very slender accomplishments, like a parrot, who
speaks a few words plainly.

Here, indeed, was the white man's burden of superiority. Oliver
Goldsmith, in his *History of the Earth* (1774), first decided who
was going to be admitted to his club and then expanded glowingly on the virtues of its members. As he described the various
European peoples, "The inhabitants of these countries differ a
good deal from each other; but they generally agree in the colour
of their bodies, the beauty of their complexions, the largeness of
their limbs, and the vigour of their understandings. Those arts
which might have had their invention among the other races of
mankind, have come to perfection there." By and large, Europeans were a *marvelous* race.

For Americans, the matter of color was more emotionally
charged and of immediate concern. Certainly by the eighteenth
century, blackness was eminently functional in a slave society
where white men were masters. But association of blacks with
slavery will not explain everything. There are other possibilities:
strictly accidental prior cultural valuation of blackness *per se,* in-
stinctual repulsion founded on physiological processes or perhaps
fear of the night which may have had adaptive value in human
evolution, or the association of dirt and darkened complexion
with the lower classes in Europe. The historian, rather like the
modern student of race-awareness in very young children, must
remain tentative and indeed baffled as to why white men re-
sponded adversely to the Negro's color.

Clearly, though, at least by the beginning of the eighteenth century blackness had become so thoroughly entangled with the
basest status in American society that it was almost indecipher-
ably coded into American language and literature. Enslavement
of blacks in a bright land of promise immensely complicated the
meaning of color. It is easy to understand the drama of *Othello;*
it is less easy to comprehend the cryptogram of a great white
whale.

III
Revolutionary Era
1755–1783

7
Self-scrutiny in the Revolutionary Era

The American Revolution has been said to have been primarily a revolution in American consciousness. If this was the case in the realm of politics, it was even more so in the shadowy realm of communal intellect and self-identification. Americans came to realize that they were no longer Englishmen; at the same time they grew conscious of their own "prejudices" concerning Negroes. As they began to question slavery, they began to see that there was a race problem in America and that it was necessary to assert the fundamental equality of Negroes with white men and to combat suggestions to the contrary. In doing so they embraced a mode of thought which for a half-century was to serve the purposes of those who sought to achieve a viable national community: environmentalism became an engine in the hands of republicans asserting their independence from the Old World.

QUAKER CONSCIENCE AND CONSCIOUSNESS

The growth of antislavery remained confined to one religious sect until Americans began protesting, especially after 1763, against certain imperial measures. Although well-known Quaker publicists like Anthony Benezet spread antislavery principles among the world's people from the 1750's onwards, the Quaker antislavery crusade aimed first and foremost at ridding the Society of Friends of the moral taint of slaveholding. Feeling against slavery arose so rapidly after that time that by 1776 Quakers had effectively abolished it—among themselves.

Quaker concentration on the inward sin of degrading Negroes was not, however, unconnected with the increased self-awareness which characterized so much of colonial thought from the Great Awakening onward. Nowhere is this fact so clear as in the writings of John Woolman, the man who as much as any other moved the Quakers to action. Woolman is usually admired as the founding father of Quaker antislavery and as typically, even archetypically, embodying the Quaker spirit of brotherhood and the fellowship of man. Unfortunately, his very saintliness has distracted attention from his perceptive intellect and the astonishingly thorough fashion in which he presaged America's awakening to its racial problem. For it was John Woolman who first clearly exposed the tangle of difficulties which had overgrown the path toward abolition of Negro slavery. By the beginning of the war many Americans who shared his aims but not his religious convictions had discovered the same tangle by means of a similar process of self-evaluation.

In 1743, as if struck by lightning, Woolman suddenly recognized his aversion to human slavery when he was asked to write a bill of sale for a Negro. After returning to New Jersey from a trip through Maryland and Virginia, he jotted down thoughts on the subject which were published as two pamphlets in 1754. His overwhelming sense of empathy led him to explore the feelings of the oppressed: "let us calmly consider their Circumstance; and, the better to do it, make their Case ours."

> Suppose then, that our Ancestors and we had been exposed to constant Servitude, in the more servile and inferior Employments of Life . . . that while others, in Ease, have plentifully heaped up the Fruit of our Labour, we had receiv'd barely enough to relieve Nature, and being wholly at the Command of others, had generally been treated as a contemptible, ignorant Part of Mankind: Should we, in that Case, be less abject than they now are?

In addition to recognizing the crushing effects of slavery upon the enslaved, Woolman's most important insight was recognition of the interactive relationship between the Negro's debased status and the debasement of Negroes in the eyes of white men. The very system of slavery, Woolman insisted, stimulated a pride which was corruption and the reverse of brotherhood: "Placing on Men the ignominious Title, SLAVE, dressing them in uncomely Garments, keeping them to servile Labour, in which they are often dirty, tends gradually to fix a Notion in the Mind, that they are a Sort of People below us in Nature. . . ."

Woolman was acutely conscious of the racial element at the root of this individual and social corruption. "Through the Force of long Custom," he wrote with his customary, almost oblique mildness, "it appears needful to speak in Relation to Colour." White children, "born of Parents of the meanest Sort," were never considered candidates for a lifetime in slavery. "This is owing chiefly to the Idea of Slavery being connected with the Black Colour, and Liberty with the White: and where false Ideas are twisted into our Minds, it is with difficulty we get fairly disentangled." Thus Woolman laid bare the dynamic which made racial slavery different from any other.

In retrospect, the importance of John Woolman's insights lay in the fact that they rapidly became commonplace. His recognition that Americans were "prejudiced" toward Negroes did not remain confined to him or to Quakers. Indeed the concept of "prejudice" toward social groups—*the very term itself!*—came suddenly into wide currency in the years after 1760. Samuel Hopkins, the prominent minister of Newport, asked why white Americans saw blacks as "fit for nothing but slaves." The reason, he explained, was that "we have been used to look on them in a mean, contemptible light; and our education has filled us with strong prejudices against them, and led us to consider them, not as our brethren, or in any degree on a level with us; but as quite another species of animals, made only to serve us and our children; and as happy in bondage, as in any other state. . . ."

What was new about the numerous assertions of the irrelevancy of color to proper social condition was that they achieved wide currency in an atmosphere where slavery seemed not merely wrong but at variance with American professions of attachment to liberty. The logic of color seemed to run counter to the logic of

English liberties. If this wedge of an argument were driven very far home, however, it was bound to split open and expose the fundamental problem: extending liberty to blacks was enormously difficult simply because they did not look like other Americans. As antislavery advocates hammered away, the popular assignment of "the colour as a mark for servitude" was bound to become not only "grossly stupid" but also a major impediment to emancipation. What was at first perceived as a logical absurdity was gradually recognized to be the rock upon which slavery was founded.

ASSERTIONS OF SAMENESS

The eyes of antislavery advocates tended to fall, therefore, upon problems which were sensed to be more easily dealt with than the Negro's complexion. They found that they could—and had to—defend his character. They discovered many discreditable human qualities which were associated with Negroes by the "prejudices" of the popular mind, but if Negroes were "brutish, ignorant, idle, crafty, treacherous, bloody, thievish, mistrustful, and superstitious," perhaps they might be reformed. Better still, these unlovely characteristics in the Negro afforded standing arguments for his emancipation. What better way to reform a man than to free him from the bondage of chattel slavery? Escape from the bondage of sin had always worked wonders. The logic was particularly effective in that it completely inverted a major justification for slavery: the Negro's immorality and ignorance could be completely transformed by saying that these qualities were not a reason for, but the result of, enslavement.

Antislavery advocates had to deal as best they could with the ill-defined, rarely articulated feeling of many Americans, especially in the South, that blacks were inherently stupid and unfeeling. As a young New Englander visiting in the Carolinas complained, rather too strongly, "The Africans are said to be inferior in point of sense and understanding, sentiment and feeling, to the Europeans and other white nations. Hence the one infer a right to enslave the other." Given the not very elevated level of learning among slaves it was not an easy task to transform the Negro into the mental peer of the white man. As early as 1762 Anthony

Benezet explained that he was quoting extensively from the narratives of travelers in Guinea to prove "that the *Negroes* are generally sensible, humane and sociable, and that their Capacity is as good, and as capable of Improvement, as that of the White People." By the 1770's outright denial of Negro mental inferiority had become common. Benjamin Franklin thought Negroes "not deficient in natural Understanding," though Alexander Hamilton seemed less certain when he wrote that "their natural faculties are ~~perhaps~~ probably as good as ours." Equalitarian antislavery advocates were so anxious to find tangible evidence for their contentions concerning mental equality that they almost trampled each other in rushing to acclaim the first exemplar of Negro literary talent. A French official living in America during the war took note of this remarkable prodigy: "Phyllis is a negress," he wrote, "born in Africa, brought to Boston at the age of ten, and sold to a citizen of that city. She learned English with unusual ease, eagerly read and reread the Bible, the only book which had been put in her hands . . . and at the age of seventeen published a number of poems. . . . They are printed, and in the front of the book there are certificates of authenticity which leave no doubt that she is its author." The poems were indeed by Phyllis Wheatley and were first published in London in 1773. The publication of five editions before 1800 and their widespread circulation testified to the importance of the author's race. Their appearance admirably suited the needs of antislavery advocates. Phyllis Wheatley could scarcely have been better for their purposes. She was young, raised in Africa, enslaved, untutored, and a girl to boot. If a Negro laboring under this load of disabilities could write such acceptable poems, how much greater genius might someday be expected to appear among "the sable generation." Phyllis Wheatley, "the negro poetess," became antislavery's most prized exhibit, her name virtually a household term for the Negro's mental equality.

Proponents of Negro equality could scarcely rest their entire case on the poems of one African girl. No matter how successful they were in demonstrating that talent could blossom amidst the weeds of slavery, moreover, equalitarians faced the task of explaining away the embarrassingly "barbarous" condition of unenslaved Negroes in Africa. If, as they contended, the Negro was naturally the equal of the white man, why was he so notoriously barbarous in his natural state? There were several routes around this difficulty. Some writers, notably Anthony Benezet, pooh-poohed the alleged barbarism of the Africans. Eagerly thumbing through reports by European travelers in West Africa, they managed sometimes to portray the life of Africans unmolested by Europeans as one of idyllic simplicity. Others fell back on the time-worn principle of Western anthropology that climate made the man. This argument from natural environment was a highly versatile means of conveying the principle of Negro equality, since it could be steered in any direction. Did the natives of Africa enslave each other? Excessive heat had depraved them. Did the natives live in ease and peaceful indolence? Their tropical surroundings made exertion unnecessary, since nature readily yielded up its fruits without the strenuous human exertions required in colder climates.

More than anyone, Benjamin Rush, a benevolent physician and a firm patriot, rode the crest of this argument toward the goal of fundamental equality. "I shall allow," he wrote disarmingly in 1773, "that many of them are inferior in Virtue, Knowledge, and the love of Liberty to the Inhabitants of other parts of the World: but this may be explained from *Physical* causes." Rush drew himself up for a sweeping summary: "Human Nature is the same in all Ages and Countries; and all the difference we perceive in its Characters in respect to Virtue and Vice, Knowledge and Ignorance, may be accounted for from Climate, Country, Degrees of Civilization, form of Government, or other accidental causes." Writing in 1773 as the eye of the Revolutionary storm passed overhead, Rush epitomized the newly intense concentration of Americans upon their environment.

ENVIRONMENTALISM AND REVOLUTIONARY IDEOLOGY

No line of reasoning—one might almost say no expression of faith —could have better typified the changed pattern of thought in the Revolutionary era. Indeed, the flowering of environmentalism was one of the major historical developments of the second half of the eighteenth century. The environmentalist mode of thought was especially attractive to Americans in the Revolutionary era for a number of reasons. They had always lived in close dependence upon America's natural advantages. In 1760 a people awakening to the benefits of living on a vast and virgin continent (now providentially cleared, to the north and west, of French control) were bound to delight in their surroundings. Then, as the political crisis mounted, they developed a more pressing interest in their habitat. Since they thought of themselves as colonial Englishmen and yet were undergoing an unwelcome estrangement from England, they were compelled to ask what made the child different from the parent, the New World different from the Old, the continent different from the island.

Environmentalist thinking presupposed that differences among men were circumstantial, that they were alterable, and that the core of human nature was everywhere, as Benjamin Rush put it, "the same." This postulating of quintessential human nature was the critical point of contact between environmentalism and the political ideology of the Revolution. The tendency to universalize men into "man" was not new in American political thought when it flowered into the eloquence of 1776. But from the "liberties of Englishmen" it was an easy step to the universalist assertion that all men had a right to be free.

It was inevitable that when mankind was being described as naturally free and equal some men should think of the Negro's condition. Blacks were, as Anthony Benezet put it, "as free as we are by nature." This widely shared presumption led inescapably to realization that Americans were indulging in a monstrous inconsistency. While Americans were claiming liberty for themselves they were denying it to a group of people in their midst. Hundreds of times the appalling gap between word and deed was called to the public's attention. "How suits it with the glorious cause of Liberty," asked a correspondent to a Philadelphia newspaper in 1768, "to keep your fellow men in bondage, men equally the work of your great Creator, men formed for freedom as yourselves." Slavery was inconsistent with the premises of the Revolution. As one antislavery advocate wrote at the end of the war, "We need not now turn over the libraries of Europe for authorities to prove that blacks are born equally free with whites: it is declared and recorded as the sense of America." A group of black men in Massachusetts wrote pointedly in 1777 "that every principle from which America has acted in the course of her unhappy difficulties with Great-Britain, pleads stronger than a thousand arguments in favor of your Petitioners."

THE SECULARIZATION OF EQUALITY

By the time of the Revolution the concept of natural rights was still connected with religious feeling and, in its most common form, with explicitly religious ideas. The right to liberty was spoken of as an endowment by the Creator. More important, all men partook of "natural" rights because, as Thomas Paine wrote in the preamble to Pennsylvania's abolition law of 1780, "all are the work of the Almighty Hand." Within the framework of this orthodox doctrine there was an intellectual shift of major proportions. God had not been removed, but he had been pushed back from the arena of human events. Some men found His will better recorded in the book of Nature than in the Bible. The very term *natural* keynoted this shift in self-conception. For the depersonalization of God into the Author of Nature was also a transformation of man into a natural species originally created by the Deity whom men found increasingly hard to mention without using the definite article. All men, including Negroes, shared in "natural" rights because they were men, not because they were candidates for immortality.

When the storm of rebellion finally broke, the pressure of events acted for the most part to confirm and even implement the logic of secular equalitarianism. Despite the heel-dragging of the two southernmost states, antislavery sentiment had grown sufficiently strong elsewhere to become a factor in political decision-making. The prohibition of slave importations by the Continental Congress of 1774 was aimed primarily at Parliament via the purses of British merchants, but many delegates to the Continental Congress regarded it as a blow for the slave's freedom as well as their own. Before the war was over, Pennsylvania had passed a gradual emancipation act with a high-toned preamble written by Thomas Paine. Even the Negro's right to vote came under discussion during the extended public debate over Massachusetts' proposed new constitution.

In a more direct way, too, the tide of events during the Revolution moved in the Negro's favor. Some slaves won their freedom by fighting for the American cause. Despite the weight of tradition, the fear of slave rebellion, and the uncomfortable feeling that slaves were not suitable recruits for an army engaged in a struggle for liberty, the necessities of war eventually pulled both slave and free blacks into the armed forces, many of them clutching promises of freedom as their eventual reward for fighting for it. An initial refusal to recruit blacks into the Continental Army was reversed because men were desperately needed to fill the ranks. Significantly, South Carolina and Georgia were alone in holding out to the end against slave enlistments. A proposal by John Laurens to authorize formation of a battalion of Negro troops received "contemptuous huzzas" in the South Carolina legislature. John Laurens's more famous father, Henry, was virtually alone among South Carolinians in expressing hope for the eventual disappearance of the institution of slavery. Yet especially in view of the way their grandchildren were talking after 1830, it is important to bear in mind that during the Revolutionary War, despite the virtual absence of antislavery pronouncements in the Lower South and the cautiousness of Virginians on the subject, no one in the South stood up in public to endorse Negro slavery.

From the Revolution on, the increasingly acrimonious debates on slavery and the Negro's nature were grounded in assumptions which, in contrast to those prevailing in pre-Revolutionary America, have a decidedly modern tone. During this third quarter of the eighteenth century, many Americans awoke to the fact that a hitherto unquestioned social institution had spread its roots not only throughout the economic structure of much of the country but into their own minds. As they became conscious of this infiltration they came to recognize that enslavement of the Negro depended upon their assessment of him, that Negro slavery existed within themselves, within their "prejudices," particularly "in Relation to Colour." For equalitarians of whatever stripe, there were two possible ways of effecting a change in the white man's mind. Both necessarily involved an end to slavery, since slavery impaired the feeling of brotherhood within the white man and still more obviously presented an obstacle to the Negro's becoming the white man's equal in actuality. Appeal to environment provided an answer on both counts, and Americans plumped eagerly for a mode of thinking which afforded a prospect of dramatic change both in the Negro and within themselves.

This heightened self-consciousness with which environmentalist thinking was so closely connected was itself closely linked to the crisis known as the American Revolution. Indeed in an important sense the Revolution *was* a great awakening of English colonials in America; it *was* a change in their thinking about themselves. The rise of antislavery sentiment also represented a process of self-evaluation, an integral part of what John Adams recalled as "this radical change in the principles, opinions, sentiments, and affections of the people." The "real American Revolution" involved a newly intense scrutiny of colonial society, including the peculiarly un-English institution of Negro slavery. American thinking about the status of Negroes could never again be characterized by placid and unheeding acceptance.

IV

Society and Thought
1783–1812

8

The Imperatives of Economic Interest and National Identity

For the post-revolutionary generation of white Americans, the most pressing political problem was formation of a viable national union. The existence of the United States of America was not—and it sometimes requires effort of mind to remember this— inevitable. It is easy today to underestimate the disintegrative pressures that bore upon the union of ex-colonies forged by the necessity of uniting against British "tyranny." By examining these pressures, as well as the efforts made to resist them, it is possible to see how closely the primary political problem was interrelated with the presence of Africans in America and with white men's thoughts about black.

The major factor making for sectional division in the United States was the proportion of blacks in the population. By the 1790's it was clear that slavery was going to survive only in the area of high concentration of blacks in the states south of Pennsylvania. Yet in the late eighteenth century sectional division lacked the clarity it was later to take on. Economic differences and the pattern of antislavery sentiment within the South blurred the distinction between northern and southern states, since it was by no means definite that Virginia and Maryland would not become "northern" states by accomplishing general emancipation. Despite the presence in the tobacco colonies of the twin factors which eventually proved determinative, slavery and a high proportion of Negroes, there was every reason to set off the upper

"South" from the lower: proportion of blacks, profitability of slavery, abolition sentiment—the very tone of society. North Carolina served as an anomalous borderland, characterized by a relatively low proportion of Negroes, and a culture which belonged, everyone agreed, almost in a class by itself. There was not one South but two and a half.

While attending to these sectional realities and especially to economic changes which were working to solidify them, it is necessary to bear in mind that sectional discord over slavery depended on the existence of a national union and that existence of a union made the presence of blacks in America a national problem. Discussion of certain issues, especially in the national Congress after 1789, stirred dormant hostilities. Of itself the rise of an independent American nation contained subtle and elusive implications for the Negro which were of far-reaching importance. For the task of building a new nation did not consist simply in laying down the bricks and mortar of national government; a rationale for the new structure was needed. Without some sense of who and why Americans were a people, and therefore a nation, work could not even begin.

THE ECONOMICS OF SLAVERY

Eli Whitney invented the cotton gin in 1793. Its impact may be seen in statistics of cotton production. The nation harvested 6,000 bales in 1792; and 178,000 in 1810. Expansion of cotton production was not, however, the midnight reprieve of a doomed institution, for in 1793 slavery was flourishing in the Lower South.

Thus when South Carolina banned slave importations in 1787 the Assembly was not responding to lack of demand for slaves, nor of course to antislavery sentiment. Many South Carolina planters were in debt; they had purchased more slaves than they could pay for, partly because they had lost slaves to the British occupation. For sixteen years South Carolina stuck by its decision, gingerly extending the ban on imports for two or three years at a time. After 1794 members of the legislature had to face the unpleasant fact that reopening the trade would bring down the outrage of the nation on South Carolina for being the only state to permit slave importation. But the imperatives of expanding agriculture proved irresistible. South Carolina's ports were at last thrown open in 1803. The way west was to be paved with Negroes. Even after the federal prohibition of January 1, 1808, slave importation continued on a much reduced scale as a smuggling operation.

In the Upper South, the dynamics of economic development drove in a different direction. Virginia's principal crop, tobacco, recovered rapidly after the war but underwent no great expansion. Cotton was grown, but not in great quantity. Many tidewater planters, the riches of their soil robbed by tobacco, turned to more diversified farming and especially to grains such as wheat. It was in the tidewater region that blacks were concentrated, an ever-growing proportion of the eastern population. Far from wanting more slaves, many white Virginians wanted to rid themselves of the ones they had. In the 1790's a British traveler reported that Virginia's slave population was increasing rapidly; estates were "overstocked," a "circumstance complained of by every planter," though "humanity" (hopefully) prevented planters selling their slaves or casting them loose. While the unprofitability of slavery in the Upper South pointed toward eventual emancipation, it also suggested a more immediate, rewarding remedy. Superfluous slaves could be sold to the Lower South. And they were. The price differential told the story: in 1797 prices for prime field hands ran about $300 in Virginia and $400 in Charleston.

UNION AND SECTIONALISM

Even prior to these developments there had of course been sectional disagreements. The first rumblings of sectional discord appeared with the first tenuous "continental" union in 1774. Members of the Continental Congress argued over inclusion of blacks in the army and whether slaves should be counted when taxes were apportioned among the states. After the war the slavery issue reappeared in novel form when Congress debated the future of the Northwest Territory. In 1784 a vote in the Congress to exclude slavery north of the Ohio River was lost for the inelegant reason that a New Jersey delegate was home sick in bed. The sectional pattern of voting was clear. Northern delegates were unanimous for exclusion, while only two southerners voted for it. On the third try, in 1787, proponents of excluding slavery were successful.

That same year, when the Constitutional Convention met in Philadelphia, delegates found that forging a new national government necessitated dealing with the hard facts of slavery. One major issue concerned slave representation and taxation: the several states' very different proportions of blacks raised the question whether slaves were persons or property. If slaves were to be included when apportioning representation, northerners asked, why not cattle as well? Despite the implications of this question, the dispute involved political definition and practice, not ethical evaluation of Negroes. No one claimed that slaves were not human beings. In the end, of course, the Convention decided to count three-fifths of a state's slaves for apportionment of representation and taxes. This famous compromise was a practical resolution of political interests, but it embodied more logic than has commonly been supposed. For the slave was, by social definition, both property and man, simultaneously partaking of the qualities of both; the three-fifths rule treated him accordingly, adding only a ludicrous fractional precision. Framing a national constitution forced men to say it outright: the Negro as a slave was only three-fifths a person.

Manifestly the Convention could not consider even the eventual abolition of domestic slavery; proposals for this would have sent half the delegates packing. The overseas slave trade, so widely deplored, was another matter. An overwhelming majority of delegates wanted to ban the traffic immediately or after a few years. But South Carolina and Georgia were, as James Madison put it, "inflexible on the point of the slaves." C. C. Pinckney of South Carolina warned that, while he did not favor the traffic personally, the two southernmost states would most certainly reject the Constitution if denied slave imports. The founders wanted—and the point requires emphasis—union more than an end to the slave trade. With the aid of New England votes obtained by concessions on navigation laws, the twenty-year prohibition on federal action was inserted in the Constitution, a monument to pragmatic politics and to the ideal of national union.

Far from soothing sectional disagreements, creation of a new national government fostered sectional tension over slavery. A powerful federal Congress looked like a magnificent fulcrum to antislavery organizations, and in 1790 petitions against the slave trade were presented to the House of Representatives. Several southern Representatives wanted the House to refuse consideration of the petitions, and the debate which followed laid bare sectional interests before the nation. Representative Thomas Scott of Pennsylvania set forth the antislavery case in language which would have been almost inconceivable a generation earlier: "I look upon the slave trade to be one of the most abominable things on earth; and . . . I . . . oppose it upon the principles of humanity, and the law of nature." William Loughton Smith of South Carolina, whose bitter speech on the same issue lasted two hours, dwelt insistently on the horrors of racial intermixture, to which every man in the House, he hoped, had the utmost aversion. Like so many southerners after him, Smith lectured the nation on the peculiar sociology of the South: "The truth is," Smith declared, "that the best informed . . . citizens of the Northern States know that slavery is so ingrafted into the policy of the Southern States, that it cannot be eradicated without tearing up by the roots their happiness, tranquillity, and prosperity." Smith's angry speech revealed the near impossibility of defending slavery without derogating the Negro: "It is well known that they are an indolent people, improvident, averse to labor: when emancipated, they will either starve or plunder." Pennsylvania's Scott, appalled beyond eloquence, could only gulp in reply that advocacy of slavery was *a Phenomenon in Politics.*

As time went on, sectional anger over slavery seemed to subside. For several sessions after 1800 Congress was undisturbed by the slavery issue. Antislavery groups no longer petitioned the House—a reflection of growing timidity and declining zeal in the antislavery movement. Relative quiet might have prevailed until the end of the slave trade's twenty-year immunity from congressional prohibition had not South Carolina reopened old wounds in 1803. Legal resumption of the traffic in South Carolina aroused proposals in Congress for a $10 duty on imported slaves, the maximum permitted by the Constitution. Debate was warm but not unrestrained. Samuel Latham Mitchell of New York, though strongly antislavery, stressed joint sectional responsibility: "the citizens of the navigating States bring negroes from Africa, and sell them to the inhabitants of those States which are more distinguished for their plantations." Such careful phraseology was characteristic of the debate. More striking still was the pathetic need for reassurance that the slave trade received no public support: speaker after speaker arose to declare that he and everyone present abhorred the noxious traffic, and South Carolina's Representatives, while vigorously opposing the tax, were at pains to point out that they personally would have opposed their state's action.

It became clear, though, that the international trade would be ended. When the Constitution finally permitted action, in the session of 1806–7, congressional debates on the bill prohibiting the trade were hard-fought and bitter, but significantly they bore on enforcement and on disposal of contraband slaves, not on whether a bill should be passed. And with enactment of the law banning the international slave trade which took effect January 1, 1808, slavery was no longer a really divisive issue in the Union. The chief aggravation was relieved: the albatross of the slave trade was no longer strung around the national conscience. The prevailing sense of victory and elation was heightened by Britain's prohibition of the trade that same year. Congress and the nation turned their energies to quarreling with Great Britain about other matters, and, when the Second War for Independence came in 1812, it brought, in striking contrast to the first, no benefit to black Americans. Not until westward expansion reintroduced sectional bitterness in the Missouri Compromise debates of 1819–20 did Congress find itself troubled again by Negro slavery. Americans had learned to fear its divisive power, particularly after the first and bitterest clash in 1790. Jefferson's "firebell in the night," in 1820, was actually a second alarm. The first fire had been brought under control, many thought, in 1807.

NATIONHOOD AND IDENTITY

To many of Jefferson's contemporaries the Revolution was not the end but the beginning of a glorious chapter in the history of man, the opening act of a glorious drama to be played out on the open stage of a virgin continent, with sympathetic vibrations confidently expected in the Old World. It was not the past which required elucidation so much as the present and future—including the future of America's Negroes.

Americans inherited from their Revolution instruction as to the future in only one area—government. Thus the Revolution gave a peculiarly *political* bias to American nationalism; it provided instructions to establish governments suitable for the "republican genius" of the American people. But it failed to give guidance concerning the peculiar nature of the American people other than that they were "republican," which was principally a political concept. Important questions were left unanswered: Who were these people to be governed? What were they like? Why was there any reason to place them under one national government?

To some extent the assumption of republicanism answered these questions. As it bore upon Afro-Americans the republican self-image was logically negated or blurred by chattel slavery, and as the national destiny continued to unfold, the antislavery people seized upon what was in a very real sense a violation of self. As Theodore Dwight proclaimed in 1794, "If any thing can sound like a solecism in the ears of mankind, it will be this story—That in the United States of America, societies are formed for the promotion of freedom." While Americans knew themselves to be a republican, virtuous, and politically independent people, however, their character—as they saw it—nonetheless remained unclear. Their struggle for cultural independence involved fighting on two fronts, proving both difference from the Old World and unity among Americans. With non-political institutions, perceptible progress was possible. Americans could point, for example, to more than a dozen new colleges, scores of academies, and hopes for a national university. Genuine cultural independence from England could not, however, be adequately assured by a proliferation of extra-political organizations. How could Americans be *sure* that they had acquired their own truly independent culture?

For a century and a half the white people of the American continent had thought of themselves primarily as colonial Englishmen. The Revolution undercut this self-conception with disconcerting suddenness. Political independence discredited the old self-image by strongly implying that Americans were not in fact Englishmen of any sort. To proclaim convincingly non-Englishness as an accomplished fact was at once essential and impossible; the clash between political independence and the inertia of cultural heredity made for uncertainty and ambivalence. Americans still spoke English. Institutions such as family, churches, learned societies, and representative government had arisen on English models, no matter how markedly transformed by New World conditions. White Americans could scarcely toss these aside as mere excess baggage.

For additional confirmation of their own distinctive character, Americans might perhaps have seized upon the indisputable fact that their continent had not been settled by Englishmen exclusively but by peoples from all the western regions of the Old World. In defining themselves, Americans might have pointed to a new amalgam of nationalities as confirmation of American distinctiveness. Physically, by blood, the American could accurately have been described as a new man. On this matter it has been customary to quote St. Jean de Crèvecœur's *Letter from an American Farmer* (1782):

> . . . whence came all these people? they are a mixture of English, Scotch, Irish, French, Dutch, Germans, and Swedes. . . . What then is the American, this new man? He is either an European, or the descendant of an European, hence that strange mixture of blood, which you will find in no other country. Here individuals of all nations are melted into a new race of men. . . .

These are striking words; few observations on the American people have been quoted more frequently, with approval, as demonstrating both the fact of amalgamation and America's warm welcoming of the process. But in fact Crèvecœur (a naturalized American who was born, and died, in France) was not expressing a common view, and historians have since relied heavily on his words because at the time virtually no one else was saying the same thing. Certainly no one else put such emphasis on the fusion of bloods. In the late eighteenth century the idea that the "American" was a "new man" by reason of physical amalgamation was the exceptional opinion of a romantic French immigrant.

Of course physical amalgamation had in fact occurred. Non-English people had flocked to America in large numbers and in many cases had lost their genetic distinctiveness. But they had lost as well their *cultural* distinctiveness to the voracious dominance of English customs, institutions, and language. Especially, one of the most powerful forces making for cultural homogenization in the colonies was the overwhelming preponderance of the English tongue, which was native to many "non-English" settlers, such as the Scots, Irish, and Scotch-Irish. This is to say that Americans had good reason for thinking of themselves as modified Englishmen rather than as products of a European amalgam.

The postwar need for strong unified government tempted Americans to emphasize the nation's unity even to the point of utterly ignoring existing diversities. As John Jay wrote in the first Federalist paper, "Providence has been pleased to give this one connected country, to one united people, a people descended from the same ancestors, speaking the same language, professing the same religion, attached to the same principles of government, very similar in their manners and customs." This thinking left Afro-Americans in an obvious place—out.

To assess the nature of the American people was to assess the Negro by implication, simply because blacks lived in America. Because they viewed the architecture of their culture as modified-English rather than fused-European, most white Americans were not led to ponder the dynamics of cultural amalgamation in America, much less the pronounced African element involved. In fact there was little consideration given to the possibility that African language and manners had contributed to American uniqueness. Even more so with physical intermixture. Even St. Jean Crèvecœur could praise physical amalgamation in America only by ignoring utterly the single most important element in the process as it was actually occurring: "What then is the American, this new man? He is either an European, or the descendant of an European. . . ." Presumably the Negro was not an American.

9

The Limitations of Antislavery

The Revolution ended with all the states having prohibited the slave trade but with only two having moved against slavery itself. Yet it was perfectly clear that the principles for which Americans had fought required the complete abolition of slavery; the question was not *if*, but *when* and *how*. Although the majority of Americans failed to face this question, thus effectively answering the *when* with *later*, some men felt that abolition must come soon if not at once. No one, of course, pondered the possibility of direct revolutionary action—except, as will become evident in the next chapter, by Negroes themselves.

THE PATTERN OF ANTISLAVERY

Most antislavery societies formed after the Revolution were ostensibly state-wide, but in fact their memberships and activities centered in the larger cities, where organization was most feasible. The first secular antislavery organization was founded in Philadelphia in 1775. Inactive during the war, the Pennsylvania Society reorganized in 1784 and bent its efforts especially toward "the relief of free negroes unlawfully held in bondage." Kidnapping of free Negroes centered in Pennsylvania, though the problem existed in all states. In New York, where slavery remained on secure legal footing, a Manumission Society was founded in 1785. Then, as the country pulled out of the economic depression of the mid-1780's and debated the question of a national government, there was a spasm of organizational effort. By 1792 state and local antislavery societies were scattered from Massachusetts to Virginia. While antislavery writing was dominated by obscure and often anonymous men, the societies enlisted the names though not always the efforts of eminent and respectable gentlemen.

The new concentration of political power in a federal government provided both an example and a point of attack for antislavery organizations, and early in 1794 some twenty-five delegates from nine societies gathered in Philadelphia and proceeded to memorialize everyone, including their own membership and the federal Congress. Thus refreshed, the Convention published its proceedings and resolved to meet on an annual basis. But this original energy dissipated rapidly. An apparently promising organizational movement came apart at the seams within a dozen years. In 1798 the somewhat bewildered Convention sadly recorded its pessimism: "In many of the United States a peculiar degree of caution in the management of this business becomes necessary." From about 1806 until after the War of 1812, the national organ of antislavery was virtually dead, and the most healthy of its component organizations, the New York and Pennsylvania societies, were less active than ever before.

While many factors contributed to this process, organized antislavery contributed to its own decline by achieving one of its major goals. A measure of success had come rather rapidly. Vermont banned slavery in its 1777 constitution. Pennsylvania, appropriately, was first to pass an abolition law (1780). In the next few years judicial decisions in Massachusetts found slavery to be a violation of the state's new constitution. Elsewhere, emancipationists pushed through gradual abolition laws in Rhode Island (1784), Connecticut (1784), New York (1799), and New Jersey (1804). Northern slavery seemed almost to be withering gradually away.

In all these states except Vermont and Massachusetts, cautious legislators were at pains to provide that emancipation not be abrupt. Generally, the acts declared that all Negroes born after the date of passage, or soon (often July 4) thereafter, were to be free; these young blacks were to serve their mother's owner until some such age as twenty-one or twenty-eight. Freedom was thus conferred upon a future generation, and the living were given merely the consolation of a free posterity. Yet this apparent reluctance should not obscure the dimensions of the achievement: slavery had been put on the road to extinction in the eight states from Pennsylvania northwards.

In Georgia and South Carolina, of course, the antislavery movement ended by never beginning, and the same was largely true of North Carolina except among the Quakers. In Virginia, Maryland, and Delaware, however, criticism of slavery was at least acceptable. Antislavery societies represented a visible but very small portion of this sentiment. After the Revolution, particularly in Virginia, men of various backgrounds denounced slavery in private conversation and in print and in the legislature. During the 1790's, however, there was a pronounced change in mood. Indeed during the very early years of the new century the antislavery movement of the Upper South faded away like some wispy vision. In 1805 Thomas Jefferson confided gloomily, "I have long since given up the expectation of any early provision for the extinguishment of slavery among us."

Yet southern antislavery was neither utopian nor a total failure. Its principal success lay in the passage of laws facilitating private manumission. In this way the states from Delaware to North Carolina conceded a certain legitimacy to individual antislavery sentiment while balking at the sweeping action which the state alone could effect. Frequently memorialized by the antislavery societies and by Friends' Meetings, the legislatures of the five states which constituted what may be called the antislavery South one by one opened the door to private action, first in Virginia in 1782.

As with the antislavery organizations, however, the tide turned. In 1791 the Maryland House of Delegates roundly denounced the Maryland Abolition Society. In 1795 Virginia reinforced the master's position in freedom suits and in 1798 barred members of emancipation societies from sitting on juries considering such cases. Finally, an increasingly vigorous campaign to stem the flood of private manumissions succeeded in the Virginia General Assembly in 1806; by law, slaves freed thereafter were required to leave the commonwealth within twelve months. This was, of course, a key decision in a key state. Virginia's neighboring states to the north and west, faced with an influx of freshly manumitted slaves, hastily prohibited immigration of free Negroes.

Even a brief review of efforts at abolition in the American states makes possible detection of certain important patterns of development. Divided according to final results, the states fell into the two groups made so very familiar by events later in the nineteenth century. Divided according to their willingness to entertain the hope of abolition rather than by hindsight, however, four distinct groups of states emerge. Between 1777 and 1804, all states from Pennsylvania northwards provided for the eventual abolition of slavery. In the same period, in the antislavery South the tide of public sentiment and action moved tentatively in the direction of abolition until the 1790's, but then in that decade turned and, after 1800, flowed so swiftly that by 1807 it was clear that the region was committed to slavery for many years to come. South Carolina and Georgia never took steps toward abolition and even tightened up long-standing restrictions on manumission after 1800. North Carolina followed a middle course.

In themselves these patterns do little to explain the fact that antislavery, as a national mood and program, lost its vigor after the 1790's. Initially, abolitionists had hoped for eventual total victory. The first Philadelphia Convention had proudly said of its own member societies in 1794, they "hope, their labours will never cease, while there exists a single slave in the United States." Yet ten years later the national organ of antislavery had gone a fair way toward disintegration. Plainly something had gone wrong.

THE FAILINGS OF REVOLUTIONARY IDEOLOGY

Much of the energy of antislavery had derived from the Revolutionary struggle against Great Britain. The triumphant achievement of independence at Yorktown and Paris gave added stature to the ideology of the Revolution, of which antislavery was a part, by sealing it with success. But in the postwar years the natural rights philosophy, no longer needed as a handbook for action, easily became a diploma of republican achievement. During the postwar years of governmental drift and economic depression, moreover, the rhetoric of natural rights became increasingly irrelevant to the nation's problems. Americans found that the philosophy of rights, bedrock of the Revolution, could not be made to serve as the cornerstone of effective government.

Even in full force the Revolutionary philosophy was of limited benefit to black Americans. For one thing, the ideas of freedom and equal rights were intimately linked with the concept of private material property. As Locke had said, men possessed a "property" in both themselves and their possessions; they had a natural right to their life, liberty, and "estates." American revolutionaries saw no reason to readjust this view of private property as a basic natural right; more important, they rarely thought of the right of private property as distinct from, much less antagonistic to, other natural liberties. Arbitrarily deprive a man of his possessions, and you had a slave. The issue of private property was central to Revolutionary agitation, and for the colonists this issue was not financial or economic. It was characteristic of the Revolution that some of its earliest martyrs were delinquent taxpayers.

The absence of any clear distinction between what are now called "human" as opposed to "property" rights formed a massive roadblock across the route to abolition of slavery. It was obvious —much more obvious at the time than we find easy to comprehend—that compulsory manumission would violate the right of masters to their own property. Insofar as slaves were property, their masters possessed an inherent right to do with them as they wished. A revolution carried forward in the name of this right was in this sense a serious and enduring impediment to compulsory abolition. In Massachusetts the preamble to the state's constitution had been taken literally by the courts, all slaves had been freed, and some men evidently felt that such interpretation violated an even more basic principle. As Judge James Winthrop complained, "By a misconstruction of our State Constitution, which declares all men by nature free and equal, a number of citizens have been deprived of property formerly acquired under the protection of law." Almost a century afterwards Abraham Lincoln seriously considered the possibility of paying slaveowners for their human property.

Despite this limitation, the concept of natural rights was ideal as a weapon against personal or national slavery. Yet it was permeated by a strong tone of negativity. The only duty it enjoined on government and men was negative—that they *not* violate the rights of other men. It afforded few hints about protecting life against the four horsemen, about preserving liberty in the face of more subtle threats than outright enslavement, or about providing necessary property to those who somehow had acquired none. John Locke had laid down a trinity of rights—life, liberty, and property—which Revolutionary Americans generally found sufficient and self-explanatory. There were virtually no elements in the character of the Revolutionary struggle which might have served to broaden this definition. Accordingly white Americans were led to seek an end to the Negro's slavery and to feel that they had fulfilled their obligation once they had ceased to violate his "rights." The natural rights philosophy was virtually silent on how black people were to be treated when they became "free." Accordingly, it was characteristic of the situation that little was done to meet the most obvious needs of newly freed Negroes (except in Quaker Philadelphia), for preparing slaves to deal with the burdens of freedom, and, more surprisingly, little proposed.

THE QUAKER VIEW BEYOND EMANCIPATION

On this matter Quakers were the exception. Quakers were especially concerned with the Negro's plight because they felt that enslavement was morally wrong, not merely a denial of rights. It was characteristic of this feeling that many Friends, once they discovered a concern to free their slaves, actually compensated them for back wages. Indeed, Quaker attitudes toward Negroes seemed to operate in an atmosphere of moral bookkeeping. Quaker religious principles made the Negro their brother, whom they had wronged. More than for other white Americans, slavery for them was a particularly crying defect in moral social relations.

In fact, Quakers far more than other Americans interested themselves in the Negro's condition *after* emancipation. They concentrated especially on education of blacks. Anthony Benezet, a virtual one-man abolition society, established a Negro school in

1759 and exercised his concern for Negro education until his death in 1784. After the war, many other Friends took a hand in the work. In 1789 one group organized the Philadelphia Society for Free Instruction of Colored People, which carried on a correspondence with Quakers of similar mind elsewhere. A Newport, Rhode Island, group hoped its work would help demonstrate to the world that blacks "are of the Same species as Ourselves; possessing the same Capacities, and that Education only, forms the Apparent Contrast between us." In this view, instruction of blacks would be instructive to whites. Fully as important and revealing as these Friendly attempts at education of blacks was the pervasive Quaker influence in the abolition societies and in the national Convention begun in 1794. Though the societies carried famous names on their membership rolls, much of the real work was done by Quakers.

As far as the national Convention was concerned, the Negro's status as a slave did not constitute the entire problem nor abolition the complete answer. In 1795, for example, the Convention in Philadelphia was vigorously explicit in outlining the broader duties of the Negro's friends: "even should that great end [entire abolition] be happily attained," the Convention wrote, ". . . when we have broken his chains, and restored the African to the enjoyment of his rights, the great work of justice and benevolence is not accomplished." Instruction of blacks would serve three good purposes: it would render the Negro "capable and desirous of fulfilling the various duties he owes to himself and to his country"; it would "do away the reproach and calumny so unjustly lavished upon us"; and it would demonstrate that Negro slaves were "in no wise inferior to the more fortunate inhabitants of Europe and America."

The pervasive Quaker influence in organized antislavery points up the continuing vitality of religious equalitarianism. Certainly it was the specifically religious impulse in antislavery, in contrast to the natural rights philosophy, which provided the energy and vision necessary to think and act beyond abolition of slavery. In one sense, education, jobs, and protection for Negroes was taken up as the half-loaf imposed by the seeming impossibility of complete abolition, but this very refusal to demand all-or-nothing, as the philosophy of rights did, contained the critical affirmation that outward legal status was not all that mattered.

Yet the religious view of the problem of racial debasement contained a special ambivalence. Sermons addressed to black slaves were invariably freighted with assertions of inherent equality before God and the utter rightness of inequality on earth. When the Reverend Cary Allen urged upon a group of Virginia blacks the central fact that Christ had died for them, as well as for whites, he was no more a "Christian" than the Reverend Jedidiah Morse (who hated slavery) when he cautioned Negroes, "Many eyes are upon you. . . . Be contented in the humble station in which providence has placed you." The tenor of this admonition was, of course, new neither to America nor to Christianity. From St. Paul through Martin Luther to Cotton Mather and Bishop Asbury, Christianity had to grapple with the profoundly revolutionary implications of its own doctrine. Social stability had always depended upon maintenance of rigid distinction between two spheres, earth and heaven. For some, but by no means all Anglo-Americans, the mode of thought and beliefs which informed the American Revolution had considerably blurred the traditional distinction; indeed some white Americans became caught up in a round of thought which imbued mankind with the spark of divinity by a circular process of naturalizing God, deifying Nature, and naturalizing man, a process which brought heavenly equality to earth, literally.

HUMANITARIANISM AND SENTIMENTALITY

The religious demand for *"amelioration"* found a new ally during and after the Revolutionary era. The growth of humanitarianism, one of the most profound, widespread, and least explicable developments of the eighteenth century, resulted in increasingly humane treatment of slaves. More than that, humanitarian feeling was quietly but effectively equalitarian. Insofar as humanitarianism limited brutality it tended to undercut the notion that the Negro was a brute. It tended to legitimize the Negro's claim to humanness and to compel explicit recognition that Negroes, in such matters as family affection and physical pain, were similar to other men.

A number of circumstances combined to nurture an especially strong humanitarian movement in America. Perhaps most important was the pervasiveness of environmentalist thought: human misery had come to seem less inherent in the human condition and more a function of the surroundings in which man was placed. The decay of social hierarchy helped level the mental wall which separated the wealthy and powerful from the suffering of the less fortunate. And while some religious sects contributed conspicuously to the humanitarian movement, so did the decline of religiosity. It had become less possible to shrug off suffering as inherent in the God-ordained social order. Growing rationalism meant witches hustled off to hospitals and debtors sprung from jails. And driving all these and other factors was a snowball dynamic: the less suffering there was, the less reason why there should be any.

If ever there was a deserving claimant to humanitarian ministration, it was American slavery and the slave trade. Abuse of Negroes was a compelling invitation to reform, and widespread awareness of this abuse vigorously stimulated the humanitarian impulse. The humanitarian mood was always deeply earnest and serious minded, and the hideousness of slavery at its worst reinforced this bent. Humor is never possible when hyperbole fails to dwarf reality, as one writer unwittingly demonstrated by suggesting that the bodies of dead Negroes be used as currency, with fractional currency to be obtained by chopping them up and salting the extremities. The less lovely aspects of slavery kept popping into the open in an embarrassing way, as in Charleston where in 1805 there was much indignation about "dead bodies" thrown from slave ships into the harbor.

Slavery did in fact become somewhat less cruel physically. The new laws which prohibited gross maltreatment of slaves and made murder of a slave an offense equal to murder of a white man, no matter how well or badly observed in practice, were expressions of an important change in standards. The supreme irony in this happy development, however, was that with slavery humanitarian victories over brutality left the real enemy more firmly entrenched than ever. As slavery became less brutal there was less reason why it should be abolished. Humanitarianism was less a program of reform than a quality of human need; as such it was satisfied by piecemeal accomplishments. The dangers inherent in such an approach to human slavery have perhaps never been more obvious. By concentrating on elimination of inhumane treatment, the humanitarian impulse helped make slavery more benevolent and paternal and hence more tolerable for the slaveowner and even for the abolitionist. In revealing contrast to this situation in the American South, slavery in the British West Indies helped doom itself by its notorious cruelty. To the extent that cruelty was inherent in slavery, humanitarian amelioration helped perpetuate cruelty.

Closely intertwining with the growth of humanitarianism in late eighteenth-century America was a growing mood of sentimentality. As a cast of mind, a mode of approach, sentimentality brought to good-hearted benevolence a half-intended emotionalism, a partially deliberate titillation of human sympathies. No matter how fluttery, sentimentality heightened empathy; as a mode of approach to Negro slavery, it implied that Negroes had feelings as deep and legitimate as white men.

With its penchant for pretty feeling, sentimentality found its natural outlet in literature. While humanitarianism played somber fugues on the theme of human suffering, sentimentality pulled all the stops. Antislavery writers increasingly put themselves in the Negro's place by employing a simple literary device: "We were dancing on the green in the evening, and we dreaded not the hour of danger. But the tall ship anchored in the stream, and treachery lurked for our captivity. In vain we wept." Africa was thus transformed into the despoiled sylvan idyl of aggrieved and tear-stained humanity.

In becoming more sentimental and more a specifically literary genre, antislavery writing seemed merely to reflect a change in American mood and taste. At a deeper level of development, however, this shift toward a romantic sentimentalism was a symptom of, and perhaps a subtle yet readily intelligible social signal for, a retreat from rational engagement with the ethical problem posed by Negro slavery. Even if the more extravagantly sentimental antislavery tales are disregarded, it remains true that the rhetoric of antislavery as a whole was changing in the direction of *extrava-*

gance, a term whose derivation suggests very neatly what was happening.

> Why shrinks yon slave, with horrors from his meat?
> Heavens! 'tis his flesh, the wretch is whipp'd to eat.
> Why streams the life-blood from that female's throat?
> She sprinkled gravy on a guest's new coat!

The hyperbole inherent in the new approach represented, on the surface, a willingness to face the grim realities of slavery; but excessive exaggeration, as it so often does, exposed an inner inability to face reality, an *un*willingness to admit the true dimensions of the problem. In an important sense, atrocity-mongering attested less to a decline in rationalism than to a failure of nerve. In the long run, too, this shift toward extravagant sentimentality tended to weaken antislavery as a program of action. Removal from the political arena and failure to attend to practical goals made for a weaker grasp on future problems and for blindness to the economic and social mechanics of slavery. As for the Negro's future, the contribution of sentimental antislavery literature was to cloud it with tears.

THE SUCCESS AND FAILURE OF ANTISLAVERY

The slave trade was notoriously the most brutal facet of the Afro-American labor system, and it became a principal target for humanitarian indignation. Blame for its brutalities might readily be foisted onto the British, even though everyone knew that some New England traders were (illegally) very active, Rhode Island being "the most exuberant in iniquity." Most important, the slave trade invited attack after the war because it was on its last economic legs. Slave importation was stopped as much by lack of demand for slaves as by antislavery attack. Yet many states prohibited residents from participating in the trade, and the federal government reinforced these laws in 1794 by barring all United States citizens from participation. On no matter of policy concerning the Negro was there anything like such national consensus. From Virginia northwards the traffic was almost universally condemned.

In moving against the slave traffic, Americans attacked the most vulnerable aspect of the "Negro problem." The political, religious, humanitarian, and sentimental approaches toward Negro slavery—it sometimes seems useful to separate the inseparable—all converged upon this one point. The result was fairly effective suppression of the slave trade, yet success on this front proved damaging to the campaigns on others. A series of local triumphs against the trade and the long-awaited national victory of January 1, 1808, caused men to forget that much remained undone; it was partly for this reason that the antislavery drive began to sputter after about 1790 and finally stalled around 1810. The successful movement against the slave trade engrossed much reformist energy and, more important, salved the nation's conscience that *something* was being done about slavery. While the program against the trade rested upon the equalitarian assumption of human sameness, it said nothing definite about Negroes already in America and afforded a comfortable alternative to thinking about that problem.

10

The Cancer of Revolution

Although the Revolution did not result in the abolition of slavery in the eighteenth century, it is well known that the Revolution helped spark successful attempts at freedom elsewhere. Ironically, the first triumphant imitators were Negro slaves.

The reaction of Americans to the shocks of revolution which swept through France and, in a different way through the West Indies, was mixed. They hoped for the triumph of liberty in the world but not for a complete one. They delighted to talk of freedom but wished their slaves would not. They assumed that their Negroes yearned for liberty but were determined not to let them have it. To trace the spread of African rebellion in the New World and to examine American responses to what they saw as a mounting tide of danger is to watch the drastic erosion of the ideology of the American Revolution. It is also to glimpse a chronological pattern, beginning in 1791, which virtually matched the courses of nation building, agricultural change, and the fortunes of antislavery.

ST. DOMINGO

On New Year's Day 1804 the Republic of Haiti became the second independent nation in the hemisphere, ruled by triumphant revolutionaries who were, of all things, black. France had lost the pearl of her empire (St. Domingo, as Americans called it), hundreds of thousands of people on the island had lost their lives, and millions of white men in other lands wondered what had happened. Standing before a crowd of shouting blacks, Jean-Jacques Dessalines, the new black ruler, seized the tricolor in furious hatred and tore from it the band of white.

As much as they were repelled by events in the island, Americans remained fascinated. The popular press regaled its readers with tales of horrible atrocities ("Who can read this and not drop a tear?"). St. Domingo assumed the character of a terrifying volcano of violence, liable to new eruption at any moment. A single black rebellion was bad enough, but this was never-ending, a nightmare dragging on for years. Worst of all, the blacks were successful, and for the first time Americans could see what a community really looked like upside down.

In 1793 white refugees from Haiti came streaming into American ports, many bringing their slaves with them. That year saw growth of a peculiar uneasiness, especially in Virginia, where many refugees had congregated. In Richmond one Virginian reported that he had overheard two blacks discussing a plot against the whites and referring to what the slaves had accomplished in the "French Island." Another citizen wrote the governor that "since the melancholy affair at Hispaniola" the inhabitants of the lower counties "have been repeatedly alarmed by some of their Slaves having attempted to raise an Insurrection, which was timely suppressed in this county by executing one of the principal advisors of the Insurrection." Similar alarms were raised in Charleston, where there were also many refugees. As one newspaper described the situation, ". . . the NEGROES have become very insolent, in so much that the citizens are alarmed, and the militia keep a constant guard. It is said that the St. Domingo negroes have sown those seeds of revolt, and that a magazine has been attempted to be broken open." Few prospects could have been so alarming. In 1794 South Carolina barred entry of free Negroes from the West Indies or any part of the Americas except the United States.

Had Americans successfully shut out every dangerous West Indian Negro, they would still have felt themselves in jeopardy.

Complete quarantine was impossible, for while news traveled slowly in the eighteenth century, some governments were unwilling and none were efficient enough to erect an effective iron curtain. Most slaves were screened off to some degree by illiteracy, but many slaves lived so close to whites that they could hardly miss picking up topics of general conversation. Some blacks, moreover, could read; it was advantageous if one's trusted slave could do so—if one could trust him. And it certainly was no comfort that literacy among so-called free Negroes was more common than among slaves.

It was therefore an important result of the reverberating disaster of St. Domingo that many Americans came increasingly to feel that slavery was a closed subject, entirely unsuitable for frank discussion. Southern delegates in Congress began to claim that public airing of matters bearing on slavery was downright dangerous. In the midst of heated debate on a free Negro petition in 1800 an angry John Rutledge of South Carolina threw off the customary cloak of caution to bare the alarming facts: "There have been emissaries amongst us in the Southern States"; Rutledge cried, "they have begun their war upon us; and actual organization has commenced; we have had them meeting in their club rooms, and debating on that subject. . . . It might be wrong in me to mention these things, because many of those people can read and write, and will be informed of what I am now saying. . . ." The ostentatiousness of all this caution is suggestive: beyond a reasoned fear of domestic insurrection seems to have lain a desire to banish the reality of St. Domingo.

But of course no one could forget. The height of feeling came with complete black independence in the island in 1804, for now the worst had happened; even the finest Napoleonic armies had proved incapable of preventing it. St. Domingo suggested an awful progression in racial slavery: white rule, insurrection, black usurpation. Southerners were unwilling to concede inevitability to the process, for obvious reasons, but the possibility of such progression could scarcely be denied. John W. Eppes of Virginia rattled the windows of Congress with a fanfare of indignation: "Some gentlemen will declare St. Domingo free; if any gentleman harbors such sentiments let him come forward boldly and declare it. In such case, he will cover himself with detestation. A system that will bring immediate and horrible destruction on the fairest portion of America." Eppes's concluding phrase revealed how rapidly Negro slavery was pushing Americans into a stance so familiar in the nineteenth century and, indeed, in the twentieth.

THE CONTAGION OF LIBERTY

Especially striking in all this bluster was the total lack of surprise that rebellion had occurred. For one thing, many Americans living in 1800 were old rebels; if rebellion had taken place in America, why not France and St. Domingo? Americans proudly regarded their revolutionary doctrine of natural rights as highly contagious. By 1797 a deeply disturbed Thomas Jefferson fretted that "if something is not done, and soon done, we shall be the murderers of our own children . . . the revolutionary storm, now sweeping the globe, will be upon us. . . . From the present state of things in Europe and America, the day which begins our combustion must be near at hand; and only a single spark is wanting to make that day to-morrow." From the very first, St. Domingo seemed a threat to American security.

Americans were fully aware where the "epidemical contagion" of "the rights of man" had originated. By definition these rights belonged to all men, despite the lurking temptation to regard them as essentially Anglo-American in origin and character. For Americans particularly, denial of the universal applicability of natural rights would have deprived their own Revolution of its broader meaning and of its claim upon the attention of the world. Denial would have shrunk the new nation from a grand experiment to an episodic instance. If men throughout the globe possessed a right to liberty, there was no good reason why they should not fight for it. Americans had shown the way. Who was to say where all this would stop?

Not that Americans were eager to spell out the dynamics of rebelliousness. Though consciously the heirs of revolution, as custodians of a new government they were perforce no longer revolutionary, at least not at home. Daniel Shays and the Pennsylvania Whisky Boys had shown once again that every revolution must suppress its successors. There is no need to label the new mood a reaction; a doctrine of revolution simply no longer served American interests and was, indeed, counter to them.

The Negro as potential rebel was of course presumed to crave liberty. Indeed if there was one thing about which Americans of the eighteenth century were certain (in fact there were a great many) it was that men everywhere yearned for freedom. Nothing would have surprised them more than to learn that later generations spoke knowingly of the contented slave. Surely God would not have conferred the natural right of liberty on all men and then failed to provide them with the desire to realize it! This appetite was *inherent* in *slaves,* nonetheless real for being unwelcome. What could be more obvious than that a natural right was bound to be naturally and rightly sought after? When the American Negro grasped desperately at freedom too, he confirmed America's great expectations, as well as America's greatest fears.

SLAVE DISOBEDIENCE IN AMERICA

Nor were the fears of white Americans unfounded. There was, in fact, a period of pronounced unrest among American slaves just after word arrived of racial turmoil in St. Domingo. There had been no revolts involving large numbers of slaves for many years after the 1740's. During the Revolution, British armies provided many opportunities for escape to freedom, but no important slave rebellions took place. A period of continued quiet after the war abruptly terminated in the spring and summer of 1792. Virginia was most seriously affected. The governor received numerous requests for arms, and white men reported hearing muffled Negro conversations about the "French Island." This was the first summer following news of the slave uprising in St. Domingo. The source of the effect seems clear, but it is impossible to tell whether white men or black men, or both, had been affected.

Certainly white Americans knew from grim experience that slaves could be dangerous as individuals, and in the South, at least, they were understandably apprehensive of slaves in combination. Toward the end of a hot summer in 1800 the long-dreaded disaster finally struck: Virginia was confronted with genuine rebellion. Led by a tall slave named "General" Gabriel, slaves in the Richmond neighborhood collected what arms they could lay hands on and gathered themselves for a march on the capital. Apparently they hoped that capture of key points in the city would trigger a general revolt throughout the state and beyond. Their plans were frustrated by two blacks who warned authorities and by a torrential downpour which rendered a vital bridge impassable. The time was long past when such heavenly intervention was clearly purposeful, and Virginians knew themselves lucky to have escaped so easily. No whites or blacks had been killed, but future safety called for executions. Within six weeks the affair was officially closed by thirty to forty hangings, Gabriel, "the main spring and chief mover," on October 7.

Virginians could not possibly permit themselves to doubt their ability to suppress any black revolt, but they were thoroughly shaken by the magnitude of the Gabriel plot. While it confirmed their fears about the Negro, it jarred their picture of slavery and themselves. They had taken pride in the gradual amelioration of slavery. The revolt, some Virginians felt, should logically have come much earlier and, indeed, elsewhere than Virginia. Young Governor James Monroe thought it somewhat "strange" that "this novel and unexampled enterprise" had occurred in an enlightened day when slaves were better treated and there were relatively fewer of them. Sustaining these thoughts was a feeling of unrequited rectitude, and one can detect here the seeds of an important change in attitude toward slave revolt. Yet Monroe went on to say, in words which were not yet a sterile formula, "Unhappily while this class of people exists among us we can never count with certainty on its tranquil submission."

It was not long before Virginians realized that they were far from rid of danger. In 1802 several genuine conspiracies were unearthed; hangings that year ran to thirty-two—three times the annual norm. Violence and rumors of violence subsided somewhat after 1802, but not so far as to ease the public mind entirely. Violence was built into the system of racial slavery which rested, in the final analysis, on coercion. Violence perpetuated itself, permitting brutalities which contrasted anomalously with humanitarian amelioration. In 1805, for instance, a slave plot was discovered in North Carolina with the following swift results: one woman was burned alive for poisoning her master, mistress, and two other white persons; three slaves were hanged, one transported, one "pilloried, whipped, nailed, and his ears cut off"; others were whipped or discharged. Fear seems to have been so great that there was no public protest.

If white men rightly feared for their lives, they also feared for their women, but whether rightly is open to question. During the Virginia disturbances in 1802 one slave was reported as testifying that two blacks intended to kill certain white men and "take" their wives. On the other hand another black's note of warning said all whites were to be killed, including "wemin and children," and a white man reported that all white men between eight and eighty were supposed to die at the hands of blacks "and not a white woman on earth to live." A straightforward "J.R." of Martin County, however, reported conspiratorial Negroes as saying they aimed at killing all white males over six or seven together with white and Negro women over a "certain age" but that "the young and handsome of the white women" they would "keep for themselves" and the young Negro women to be spared as "waiters." Perhaps such reports were well founded. Hatred of the white man might easily have generated an urge to take his woman, to take the one liberty most emphatically denied. Perhaps the bewildered black conspirator under pressing examination got the idea from his anxious questioner. Perhaps white reporters invented these assertions to satisfy their itch to discover Negroes libidinously yearning for white women. In fact, during this entire period of slave unrest there is *no* evidence of Negroes sexually assaulting white women. Though this lack is hardly final proof of anything, at very least it suggests that the danger of sexual violence by Negroes was exaggerated by white men. Certainly white men had compelling reasons to exaggerate. They had been doing so for a long time.

THE IMPACT OF BLACK REVOLT

Certainly, too, there can be no doubt concerning the great impact of the plots on white Americans. Gabriel, the terrible figure with the devastatingly ironic name, was set against a backdrop of black rebellion which included not only the "scenes of St. Domingo" but flashes of individual violence and revelations of conspiracies at home. The outburst of violence at the opening of the century had the immediate effect of hardening the determination of white Americans that slaves should have no opportunity for success. Virginia's black conspirators did not kill any whites, but they did a remarkably effective job on Virginia antislavery. The Virginia Abolition Society reported pessimistically that the plot had rendered its work much more difficult, an understatement at best. In 1805 a member of the by-then defunct Alexandria Society named the revolt as one cause of the Society's collapse, explaining gloomily, "We are in fact dead; and I may say, I have no hope of reanimation."

Of all reactions to slave insurrection by far the most complex occurred in Virginia. South Carolina, by comparison, reacted directly and with confident dispatch, enacting laws which directly dealt with the "problem." Virginia displayed a hesitancy which betrayed inner conflict. Since the roots of Virginia's distress lay tangled in a multitude of factors other than revolt, further discussion needs to be withheld, except for the bald suggestion that Virginia reacted to a revolt of slaves by turning on freemen. That the freemen were black affords striking demonstration that American slavery lay deeply enmeshed in problems of race which immeasurably complicated the dynamics of exploitation. No free blacks were implicated in the Gabriel plot. During this period of slave agitation beginning in 1792 there seems to be no clear record of "free Negroes" actually involved in conspiracy of any kind.

This was not, for white Virginians or for white Americans generally, the point. In the quarter-century after the Revolution they had, many of them, come to regard the prospect of Negro freedom with considerably less enthusiasm as Negroes began to take a hand in the work. The Revolution had entailed upon the institution of slavery a gigantic question mark and upon white Americans the necessity of facing up to the prospect of what it would be like actually to have blacks free. As they were forced to face this prospect they backed off from its inherent implications. In this period of economic and political reorganization, of successful and unsuccessful antislavery, of reverberating revolts, whites and blacks in America became separated from each other in ways which fitted the pace and direction of social change in post-Revolutionary America.

11

The Resulting Pattern of Separation

Shortly after the Revolution, Americans began to legislate Negroes into an ever-shrinking corner of the American community. Blacks became more than ever walled off from whites in a chronological pattern which coincided with the patterns of change in the economics of southern agriculture, national and sectional feeling, antislavery, and fear of slave revolt. For ten years after the war there were some signs of relaxation, but then came a trend which included tighter restrictions upon slaves and especially on free Negroes, separation of the races at places of social gathering, and the founding of all black churches.

THE HARDENING OF SLAVERY

There was a period of uncertain eddying before the tide clearly turned. Before the mid-1790's many states extended to Negro slaves the right of trial by jury in capital cases. In harmony with the spread of humanitarian feeling, some states made their slave codes more humane and occasionally less restrictive. To prevent circumvention of their gradual emancipation laws, many northern states prohibited selling slaves out of state, thereby demonstrating that they valued liberation of blacks over riddance of them. Northern states and Maryland, Virginia, and North Carolina, as late as 1800, attached severe penalties to kidnapping of free Negroes, a not uncommon crime few people were willing to condone.

Feeling on this matter was strong: a North Carolina man was executed for this offense in 1806.

After 1800, however, slave codes in the South were tightened up, though the brutal punishments of an earlier day remained discarded, at least from the statute books. The principal occasion, of course, was Gabriel's plot, but, while this was an important turning point, the pattern of restrictions on Negroes makes clear that Gabriel was not "the main spring and chief mover" behind the new mood among white men. Two years earlier, for example, Virginia clamped down hard on harboring of fugitive slaves. As late as 1804 Virginia restricted night-time religious meetings of slaves but the next year revised the law to permit whites to take their slaves with them to public worship.

In somewhat random fashion, the structure of slavery was hardened and polished. Between 1796 and 1806, mounting irritation with antislavery agitation and free Negroes resulted in more stringent requirements for private manumission. Particularly where slavery was economically most viable it began to assume the qualities of the familiar ante-bellum institution; it was becoming a "way of life." One senses, especially in South Carolina, not only the effects of time and handsome profits but a settling-in which could have come only from a feeling of permanence or at least a feeling that it was going to be a long siege. It was scarcely possible to doubt the perpetual existence of the social system when so much was at stake. Who could see the absurdities involved? Probably only a foreign critic could have dissected Charleston with one brief slice of description, as a British traveler did so neatly about 1807:

> I expected to find the Charleston stage well supplied with *sooty negroes,* who would have performed the *African* and *Savage* characters, in the dramatic pieces, to the life; instead of which the delusion was even worse than on our own stage; for so far from employing *real negroes,* the performers would not even condescend to *blacken* their faces, or dress in any manner resembling an African. This I afterwards learnt was occasioned by motives of *policy,* lest the negroes in Charleston should conceive, from being represented on the stage, and having their colour, dress, manners, and customs imitated by the white

people, that they were very important personages; and might take improper liberties in consequence of it. For this reason, also, Othello and other plays where a black man is the hero of the piece are not allowed to be performed; nor are any of the negroes or people of colour permitted to visit the theatre.

What had been drama two hundred years before was now life.

RESTRAINT OF FREE NEGROES

After 1790 it became increasingly apparent that southerners were less worried and irritated by black slaves than by blacks who were not slaves. Mounting hostility to free Negroes was chiefly responsible for the retraints on private manumissions, for in the Upper South, at least, men did not mind freeing Negroes so much as having them around once freed. There seemed to be more of them every day. From 1790 to 1810 the proportion of free Negroes in the total black population in the United States went from almost 8 per cent to more than 13 per cent. The increase was greatest in the Upper South. Almost one-quarter of Maryland's Negroes were free by 1810.

Attempts to deal with the "problem" of free Negroes during the thirty years after the Revolution afford the clearest index to important changes in attitudes toward the Negro in that period. Most traditional restrictions on the freedom of free Negroes were continued or strengthened. In addition to this clarifying of a third legal status of persons in the South, many laws aimed at specific abuses and dangers arising from the presence of free Negroes. Maryland particularly, with the largest free Negro population, claimed to be plagued by free Negroes operating as receivers for goods stolen by slaves. Everywhere they were regarded as thievish: a French traveler explained that in Maryland "the judges attribute the multiplicity of robbers to the free negroes" and that he had "heard the same accusation preferred against them in all the states where slavery is permitted." Worse still, free Negroes seemed a threat to effective police control of slaves, more than ever now that slaves seemed to have been inoculated with the doctrine of liberty. Everywhere in the South the free Negro was pelted with restrictions, miscellaneous in character, growing in severity, and similar in underlying intent.

How much this legislative tinkering represented a response to actual thievery, harboring of fugitives, and so forth must remain open to question, though surely free Negroes were not paragons of planter morality. Whatever their behavior, free Negroes constituted a threat to white society, which was not owing so much as generally supposed to the fact that Negro freedom threatened to undermine the structure of slavery, for in many quarters men hoped genuinely for the institution's eventual extinction. It arose within the white men as a less than conscious feeling that a people who had always been absolutely subjected were now in many instances outside the range of the white man's unfettered power. The dislike, apprehension, and fear of free Negroes, which clearly had swelled out of proportion to any possible overt threat they might have posed, was thus in part an almost predictable response to loss of a once firm sense of control. Long accustomed to absolute dominion, white men could not readily or calmly surrender it, yet they could find compensation in despising what could no longer be absolutely controlled. It was a tragic paradox that the growth of manumissions after the Revolution tended to heighten the white man's distaste for Negroes as such.

NEGRO CHURCHES

Separation of Negroes from white persons—"segregation" now—assumed a new rigidity and meaning wherever slavery was abolished, though the pace of this change was slowed by the gradualness of abolition. Slavery was a genuine, if crude and perverse common bond, which abolition snapped. Manumission of slaves resulted in fewer blacks actually living in white families, a long step toward residential separation made firmer by Negro poverty. Slavery had formalized and ritualized relations between blacks and whites and accordingly had served to clarify the status of both. After abolition, only by separating the Negro, by law or by some less formal means, could clarity be retrieved. Clarity as to status was essential, since uncertainty about the Negro's position was proportionately as unwelcome as the Negro himself. In the period before about 1810, one can just begin to detect the origins of segregated institutions.

That Negroes were generally not welcomed as equal partici-
pants among American churches helps account for the development in the years after the Revolution of a dramatic and novel
variety of separation of Negroes from the white community.
Throughout the nation but most obviously in Philadelphia and
other northern cities, the "Black sheep" of Christ's flock began to
gather "by themselves." At least two independent Negro congregations had been founded in the South before the end of the war,
but the rush of blacks into "African" churches began in the same
year and in the same city as the Constitutional Convention.

The critical break was led by two prominent Philadelphia
blacks, Richard Allen and Absalom Jones, but they received
ample encouragement from influential white men. Jones and
Allen were leaders of a group of blacks who worshipped at St.
George's Methodist Church. There in 1787 they were told to take
seats around the wall and then, one day, in the gallery. Though
they complied, one of the church's "trustees" attempted to haul
Absalom Jones to his feet during prayer. The indignant blacks,
who had recently subscribed to refurbishment of the church,
walked out "in a body" when the prayer was over. Apparently
on their own initiative, but with assistance from some Quakers,
they formed a Free African Society which for a time showed promise of becoming a very Quaker-like organization. Although the
Free African Society lasted for more than a decade, it was rendered a rump in 1791 by the exodus of Jones and Allen, both of
whom had been pupils at Anthony Benezet's school, and a number of their followers. Out of their efforts soon grew the first
black Episcopal church in America, led by Jones, and the African
Methodist Episcopal Church, of which Allen became the first
bishop.

The erection of the "African Episcopal Church of St. Thomas"
in 1793 occasioned a moving display of interracial harmony.
After the roof-raising, there was a festive dinner under some
spreading trees at the edge of town where about one hundred
white persons, many of them carpenters, were waited upon by the
Negroes. Afterwards about fifty "black people sat down at the
same table" and were waited upon by "Six of the most respectable
of the white company."

The building was finally readied for public worship in July 1794. On a slab of marble on the outside wall of the church was inscribed, with the best intention, an appalling irony: "The People That Walked in Darkness Have Seen a Great Light." The Reverend Samuel Magaw, delivering the opening discourse in the church, dwelt tediously—and with no greater perceptiveness than the piece of marble—upon the "darkness" from which Negroes were so fortunately emerging. Turning from freemen to slaves, Magaw rang the changes on an age-old theme. "Your present situation," he counseled them, "gives you some advantages above what others have: yes, and very possibly, above what your Masters have,—in that your humbleness of mind, your patience, faithfulness, and trust only in God, will add to the greatness of your future happiness." He went on to remind the free blacks of the debt of gratitude they owed their earthly benefactors, especially to Lay, Woolman, Benezet, Franklin, the Pennsylvania Abolition Society, and not least, the citizens of Philadelphia. He cautioned them to guard against pride, which was said to be increasing among them, and explained (with perfect accuracy) that "less allowance will be made for your failings, than for those of other people." Among the virtues they should cultivate, he suggested, was "an obliging, friendly, meek conversation."

In the ensuing years, the generally amicable pattern of separation in Philadelphia was repeated, with variations, in New York, Boston, and other northern cities. The circumstances varied, and some of the new churches had white ministers at first, but the trend toward racially separate churches was well under way in the 1790's. The same process operated in the slave states as well. Not that the now-familiar arrangement of mutual exclusion had yet been approximated: in many churches, blacks and whites attended together. But unquestionably there were an increasing number of racially exclusive congregations.

Few developments could have been so symptomatic of the changes which white attitudes underwent after the Revolution. The splintering of the churches along racial lines was not simply a matter of blacks recognizing that they would be more welcome elsewhere. It symbolized an increasingly clear-cut and pervasive separation. It meant that the one institution which was at all prepared to accept the Negro as an equal was shattered—completely, as it turned out. The new Negro churches were equal but separate, prototypes of "separate but equal." When Christian equalitarianism ran head on into racial mores the result was, institutionally and in the public mind, gradual separation along racial lines.

Many Americans seemed unable to tolerate equality without separation. This inability proved critical in the years after the Revolution, for it raised the question of what would happen to the commitment to equality if separation seemed impossible. If Negroes were going to remain in America and in increasing numbers become free, white men would have every reason to ask more intensely than before the Revolution what manner of men these Negroes were. Thus while social relationships between whites and blacks were undergoing change and examination the very nature of the Negro was coming under close scrutiny.

V

Thought and Society
1783–1812

12

Thomas Jefferson: Self and Society

Against the backdrop of changing attitudes and actions concerning Negroes and Negro slavery, the writings of one man become a central point both of reference and influence. In the years after the Revolution the speculations of Thomas Jefferson were of great importance because so many people read and reacted to them. His remarks about Negroes in the only book he ever wrote were more widely read, in all probability, than any others until the midnineteenth century. In addition to his demonstrable impact upon other men, Jefferson is important—or perhaps more accurately, valuable to historical analysis—because he permits (without intending to) a depth and range of insight into the workings of ideas about Negroes within one man as he stood in relationship to his culture. Jefferson's energetic facility with the pen makes it possible, uniquely so in this period of history, to glimpse some of the inward springs of feeling which supported certain attitudes toward Negroes. It then becomes possible to see the intricate interlacing of one man's personality with his social surroundings, the values of his culture, and the ideas with which he had contact. Thomas Jefferson was scarcely a typical man, but his enormous breadth of interest and his lack of originality make him an effective sounding board for his culture. On some important matters, therefore, he may be taken as accurately reflecting common presuppositions and sensitivities, even though many Americans disagreed with some of his conclusions.

To contemplate any man-in-culture is to savor complexity. It will be easiest to start with Jefferson's central dilemma: he hated slavery but thought blacks inferior to whites. His remarks on the Negro's mental inferiority helped kindle a revealing public controversy on the subject which deserves examination. But it will also be necessary to return again to Thomas Jefferson, to his inward world where Negro inferiority was rooted. There it is possible to discern the interrelationship between his feelings about the races and his feelings about the sexes and thence to move once again to the problem of interracial sex in American culture. Finally, by tacking back to Jefferson and to the way he patterned his perceptions of his surroundings, it becomes easy to see how he assimilated the Indian to his anthropology and to America. His solution with the Negro was very different.

JEFFERSON: THE TYRANNY OF SLAVERY

Jefferson was personally involved in Negro slavery. On his own plantations he stood confronted by the practical necessity of making slave labor pay and by the usual frustrating combination of slave recalcitrance and inefficiency. Keeping the Negro men and especially the women and children clad, bedded, and fed was expensive, and keeping them busy was a task in itself. Nor was his load lightened by daily supervision of a system which he genuinely hated, nor by realization that his livelihood depended on its continuation. This dependence almost inevitably meant that, for Jefferson the planter, Negroes sometimes became mere objects of financial calculation. "I have observed," he once wrote, "that our families of negroes double in about 25 years, which is an increase of the capital, invested in them, of 4. per cent over and above keeping up the original number." For a man of Jefferson's convictions, entanglement in Negro slavery was genuinely tragic. His hopes for transforming his slaves into tenants evidenced a desire to seek a way out, but financial considerations perpetually precluded action. In the end he freed a very few of them, but more than a hundred remained in slavery.

Jefferson's heartfelt hatred of slavery did not derive so much from this harassing personal entanglement in the practicalities of

"farming" .s from the system of politics in which he was enmeshed mentally. "Enmeshed" seems the appropriate term because the natural rights philosophy was the governing aspect of
his theology and his science; it formed a part of his being, and
his most original contribution was the graceful lucidity with
which he continually restated the doctrine. Yet in Jefferson's
hands natural rights took on a peculiar cast, for he thought of
rights as being natural in a very literal sense. Rights belonged to
men as biological beings, inhering in them, as he said in his draft
of the Declaration of Independence, because "all men are created
equal and independent" and because "from that equal creation
they derive rights inherent and inalienable." The central fact
was creation: the Creator, whose primary attribute was tidiness,
would scarcely have been so careless as to create a single species
equipped with more than one set of rights. The natural world
dominated Jefferson's thinking. Creation was the central "fact"
because it explained nature. And Jefferson was awed by nature,
if "awe" may be used in connection with a man so immensely
capable of placid receptivity. While apparently working from a
"Supreme Being" to an orderly nature, in fact Jefferson derived
his Creator from what He had created—a nature which was by
axiom orderly. In the same way, he derived God-given rights from
the existence of the class of natural beings known as men. To
know whether certain men possessed natural rights one had only
to inquire whether they were human beings.

Without question Negroes were members of that class. Hence
Jefferson never for a moment considered the possibility that they
might rightfully be enslaved. He felt the personal guilt of slaveholding deeply, for he was daily depriving other men of their
rightful liberty. With "my debts once cleared off," he wrote with
a highly revealing slip of the pen, "I shall try some plan of making their situation happier, determined to content myself with
a small portion of their ~~liberty~~ labour." His vigorous antislavery
pronouncements, however, were always redolent more of the
library than the field. Slavery was an injustice not so much for the
specific Africans held in bondage as for any member of the human
species. It was not simply that Jefferson was a benevolent master
and had little contact with the cruelty of slavery, but that his

approach to human society was always phylogenic. His most heart-felt denunciation of the notorious horrors of the slave trade, for example, consisted of a reference to "the unhappy human beings . . . forcibly brought away from their native country." Wherever he encountered human cruelty, as he assuredly did in France, he saw not cruelty but injustice; as in so many other matters he was inclined to universalize particulars. Yet he was always the observer of particulars and too much interested in the welfare of Virginia to let his vision of slavery remain entirely academic. Slavery was an evil as well as an injustice, and from this standpoint Jefferson wrote one of the classic denunciations of the institution. In his *Notes on the State of Virginia,* written in 1781–82 in reply to queries from the secretary of the French legation in Philadelphia, François Barbé-Marbois, Jefferson answered a question on the "particular customs and manners that may happen to be received in that state" by discussing one matter only—the damaging effects of slavery.

> There must doubtless be an unhappy influence on the manners of our people produced by the existence of slavery among us. The whole commerce between master and slave is a perpetual exercise of the most boisterous passions, the most unremitting despotism on the one part, and degrading submissions on the other. Our children see this, and learn to imitate it; for man is an imitative animal. . . . The parent storms, the child looks on, catches the lineaments of wrath, puts on the same airs in the circle of smaller slaves, gives a loose to his worst of passions, and thus nursed, educated, and daily exercised in tyranny, cannot but be stamped by it with odious peculiarities. The man must be a prodigy who can retain his manners and morals undepraved by such circumstances. . . . With the morals of the people, their industry is also destroyed. For in a warm climate, no man will labour for himself who can make another labour for him. This is so true, that of the proprietors of slaves a very small proportion indeed are ever seen to labour. And can the liberties of a nation be thought secure when we have removed their only firm basis, a conviction in the minds of people that these liberties are of the gift of God? That they are not to be violated but with his wrath?

While he recognized the condition of slaves as "miserable," the weight of Jefferson's concern was reserved for the evil effects of slavery upon masters. With slavery's effect on black men he simply was not overly concerned.

Indicative of Jefferson's approach toward the institution was his horror of slave rebellion. His apprehension was of course shared by most Americans, but he gave it expression at an unusually early date, some years before the disaster in St. Domingo. When denouncing slavery in the *Notes on Virginia* he gave vent to forebodings of a possible upheaval in America in a passage clouded with dark indirection. "Indeed I tremble for my country," he wrote passionately, "when I reflect that God is just: that his justice cannot sleep forever: that considering numbers, nature and natural means only, a revolution of the wheel of fortune, an exchange of situation, is among possible events: that it may become probable by supernatural interference! The Almighty has no attribute which can take side with us in such a contest." The depth of his feeling was apparent, for he rarely resorted to exclamation marks and still less often to miracles without skepticism. Later, African rebellion in St. Domingo confirmed his fears, the more so because he was utterly unable to condemn it. Always blandly receptive to revolution as a mechanism of change, he foresaw a strange future for the Caribbean islands. "I become daily more and more convinced," he wrote in 1793, "that all the West India Islands will remain in the hands of the people of colour, and a total expulsion of the whites sooner or later take place." From the islands he gloomily turned to his own country. "It is high time we should foresee the bloody scenes which our children certainly, and possibly ourselves (south of the Potomac,) have to wade through, and try to avert them." St. Domingo, he became convinced, was merely "the first chapter"; and his mind dwelt on the possible second chapter almost morbidly: "if something is not done," he wrote melodramatically in 1797, "and done soon, we shall be the murderers of our own children." Then in the summer of 1800 the second chapter appeared to open, and Jefferson wrote self-consolingly from Monticello: "We are truly to be pitied." Twenty years later at the time of the Missouri Compromise he was still murmuring of his fears. Still adamant that blacks must be free, he characteristically fused obligation with future fact: "Nothing is more certainly written in the book of fate than that these people are to be free." Only the means were at question: white men must liberate black men in justice, or black men would liberate themselves in blood.

While Jefferson thus hitched fear of rebellion to the antislavery cause, he refused to allow strong feelings on both matters to override his judgment as to the appropriate course of practical action. As a youth, in the first blush of Revolutionary enthusiasm, he had urged upon his native Virginia a program of gradual emancipation. "But it was found," he wrote years later in 1821, "that the public mind would not yet bear the proposition, nor will it bear it even at this day." As early as the 1780's, Jefferson fully recognized the difficulties involved in any practical program for freedom and shrank from publishing his *Notes on Virginia* because it contained strong antislavery expressions. He was acutely conscious of "the passions, the prejudices, and the real difficulties" compounded in American Negro slavery.

JEFFERSON: THE ASSERTION OF NEGRO INFERIORITY

His sensitive reaction to social "passions" and "prejudices" was heightened by dim recognition that they operated powerfully within himself, though of course he never realized how deepseated his anti-black feelings were. On the surface of these thoughts lay genuine doubts concerning the Negro's inherent fitness for freedom and recognition of the tensions inherent in racial slavery. He was firmly convinced, as he demonstrated in the *Notes on Virginia,* that blacks could never be incorporated into white society on equal terms.

> Deep rooted prejudices entertained by the whites; ten thousand recollections, by the blacks, of the injuries they have sustained; new provocations; the real distinction which nature has made; and many other circumstances, will divide us into parties, and produce convulsions which will probably never end but in the extermination of the one or the other race.—To these objections, which are political, may be added others, which are physical and moral.

The "real distinction which nature has made" was for Jefferson not only physical but temperamental and mental. Blacks seemed to "require less sleep," for "after hard labour through the day," they were "induced by the slightest amusements to sit up till midnight, or later" though aware that they must rise at "first dawn." They were "at least as brave" as whites, and "more adventuresome." "But," he wrote, withdrawing even this mild encomium, "this may perhaps proceed from a want of forethought, which prevents their seeing a danger till it be present. When present, they do not go through it with more coolness or steadiness than the whites." Negroes were "more ardent," their griefs "transient." "In general," he concluded, "their existence appears to participate more of sensation than reflection. To this must be ascribed their disposition to sleep when abstracted from their diversions, and unemployed in labour." Within the confines of this logic there was no room for even a hint that daily toil for another's benefit might have disposed slaves to frolic and to sleep.

Of far more serious import for the Negro's future were Jefferson's remarks on mental capacity. More than any other single person he framed the terms of the debate still carried on today.

Comparing them by their faculties of memory, reason, and imagination, it appears to me, that in memory they are equal to the whites; in reason much inferior, as I think one could scarcely be found capable of tracing and comprehending the investigations of Euclid; and that in imagination they are dull, tasteless, and anomalous. It would be unfair to follow them to Africa for this investigation. We will consider them here, on the same stage with the whites. . . . It will be right to make great allowances for the difference of conditions, of education, of conversation, of the sphere in which they move. Many millions of them have been brought to, and born in America. Most of them indeed have been confined to tillage, to their own homes, and their own society; yet many have been so situated, they might have availed themselves of the conversation of their masters; many have been brought up to the handicraft arts, and from that circumstance have always been associated with the whites. Some have been liberally educated, and all have lived in countries where the arts and sciences are culti-

vated to a considerable degree, and have had before their eyes
samples of the best works from abroad. . . . But never yet
could I find that a black had uttered a thought above the level
of plain narration; never see even an elementary trait of
painting or sculpture.

Despite his stress on the necessity for "great allowances," Jefferson seemed unable to push the logic of environmentalism very far;
in fact he stopped at just the point where that logic made a case
for Negro inferiority. He seemed incapable of complimenting
Negroes without immediately adding qualifications. "In music,"
he continued, picking up a widespread popular belief, "they are
more generally gifted than the whites with accurate ears for tune
and time, and they have been found capable of imagining a small
catch." Further ability was "yet to be proved."

Not content with a general assessment, Jefferson went on to disparage the widely known Negroes who had been puffed by the
antislavery people as examples of the Negro's equal capacities.
Those known to him were poets, and by speculating on the effects
of slavery upon poetry he twisted the environmentalist logic into
anti-Negro shape. "Misery is often the parent of the most affect-
ing touches in poetry.—Among the blacks is misery enough, God
knows, but no poetry. Love is the peculiar oestrum of the poet.
Their love is ardent, but it kindles the sense only, not the imagination." He dismissed Phyllis Wheatley with the airy remark that
she was "not . . . a poet. The compositions published under her
name are below the dignity of criticism." Ignatius Sancho he
treated with more respect but decided that Sancho's works did
"more honour to the heart than the head" and substituted "sentiment for demonstration." Sancho was the best of his race, but
among literary figures in England "we are compelled to enroll
him at the bottom of the column," if, Jefferson added pointedly,
he was in fact the real author of the material "published under
his name."

Jefferson was thoroughly aware that the environmentalist argument could serve (and actually had) to make a case for Negro
equality, and hence he went to great lengths to prove that the
Negroes' lack of talent did not stem from their condition. He
turned to the slavery of classical times and wandered happily and

discursively among the Romans and the Greeks, arguing that ancient slavery was more harsh than America's yet produced slaves of talent and demonstrable achievement. Unaware that he might be inverting cause and effect he noted that some ancient slaves excelled "in science, insomuch as to be usually employed as tutors to their master's children." There had been slaves, then, who had demonstrated significant attainments; and those who had "were of the race of whites." As for Negroes, he concluded, "It is not their condition, then, but nature, which has produced the distinction."

Having baldly stated his belief in innate inferiority, Jefferson immediately introduced his next subject by reopening the question he had just closed: "Whether further observation will or will not verify the conjecture, that nature has been less bountiful to them in the endowments of the head. . . ." What he now asked was suspension of decision, for he became increasingly aware of how far he had allowed himself to go. Genuine alarm underlay his admonition, toward the *end* of his passage on Negroes, that caution must be exercised "where our conclusion would degrade a whole race of men from the rank in the scale of beings which their Creator may perhaps have given them." But he extricated himself in highly satisfying fashion by dumping the whole problem in the broad lap of American science, thus permitting qualification of his previously stated position to the point of inconsistency. "The opinion, that they are inferior in the faculties of reason and imagination, must be hazarded with great diffidence. To justify a general conclusion, requires many observations, even where the subject may be submitted to the Anatomical knife, to Optical glasses, to analysis by fire, or by solvents. How much more then where it is a faculty, not a substance, we are examining; where it eludes the research of all the senses. . . ."

Growing happier with his solution he thus labored the obvious fact that assessing mental ability was an immensely difficult task. With nearly audible relief he remodeled an anti-Negro diatribe into a scientific hypothesis, thus effectively depersonalizing a matter which was for him obviously of some personal importance. "To our reproach it must be said, that though for a century and a half we have had under our eyes the races of black and of red men, they have never yet been viewed by us as subjects of natural history. I advance it therefore as a suspicion only, that the blacks, whether originally a distinct race, or made distinct by time and circumstances, are inferior to the whites in the endowments both of body and mind. It is not against experience to suppose, that . . . [they] may possess different qualifications." A "suspicion only" of "different qualifications" represented a rather different proposition from "It is not their condition then, but nature, which has produced the distinction."

In assessing one important quality in Negroes, however, Jefferson always remained firmly consistent. The "moral sense" was as fully developed in blacks as in whites. On this subject Jefferson suddenly pressed environmentalist logic as far as it would go. "That disposition to theft with which they have been branded," he declared categorically, "must be ascribed to their situation." With dry detachment he explained the justice of Negro thievery: "The man, in whose favour no laws of property exist, probably feels himself less bound to respect those made in favour of others." Might not the slave "justifiably take a little from one, who has taken all from him?"

Jefferson's strikingly divergent conclusions on the Negro's moral sense and on his intellect were reached without a particle of inconsistency, for the two qualities were, as far as he and many of his post-Revolutionary contemporaries were concerned, very much distinct. The "moral Sense, or conscience," as Jefferson explained, was "as much a part of man as his leg or arm" and was "made a part of his physical constitution, as necessary for a social being." To say that the Negro possessed it was the Jeffersonian analogue of the Christian axiom that the Negro possessed a soul. Just as the traditional Christian God had provided the soul, the Jeffersonian Creator had endowed men with the properties necessary for their existence, and no kinds of men could be assumed to lack what they could not live together without. Had the Creator not provided men with a moral sense He would have been "a pitiful bungler." The moral sense might be temporarily impaired by slavery, but Negroes must be said to possess it, else Negroes could never be free. Indeed they could not even be men without it. No such requirement, on the other hand, pertained to the Negro's intellectual endowment.

In the years before the Revolution antislavery men had increasingly recognized the importance, even the necessity, of asserting Negro mental equality, but Jefferson's suspicions as advanced in the *Notes on Virginia* greatly heightened the urgency of the question and stimulated much more widespread debate. Publication of the *Notes* in the 1780's was followed almost immediately by public criticism of Jefferson's views as well as by a marked increase in the frequency of speculation on the matter in general terms. In 1792 Gilbert Imlay, a man of strange fortunes who had lived for a time in Kentucky, set out to refute Jefferson at some length, saying flatly that "it is certain" that blacks and whites "are essentially the same in shape and intellect." Jefferson's whole case for mental inferiority, Imlay declared, was absurd because it rested on comparison between slaves and free men. Equally specific attacks on Jefferson became more frequent after his involvement in national politics. Clutching the lamp of environmentalism, the antislavery people set out to discover an equality of mental capacity in the Negro, a discovery necessary both to the logic of their cause and to vindication of the Negro's ability to lead life in freedom. An "Address to the Public" by the Pennsylvania Abolition Society, signed by its president, Benjamin Franklin, in 1789, declared that the chains which bound the slave's body "do also fetter his intellectual faculties; and impair the social affections of his heart." William Pinkney of Maryland, later to attain fame as an orator, raised his huge bulk in the state legislature to attack slavery on two occasions in 1789. Negroes and whites, Pinkney rumbled, were "endued with equal faculties of mind and body." Warming to his work, Pinkney summed up the antislavery case in twenty-two words: "Thus the ignorance and the vices of these wretches are solely the result of the situation, and therefore no evidence of their inferiority."

One reason for the outbreak of interest in mental equality

around 1790 was the sudden, and far from fortuitous, appearance of several Negroes to whose fresh example men might readily appeal. Benjamin Rush, first engaged in antislavery controversy in 1773, was responsible for bringing to light the strange case of Thomas Fuller, a Maryland Negro who perfectly embodied the hopeful proposition that a slave might demonstrate great natural talent despite his slavery. "Negro Tom" was a *"self-taught Arithmetician"* born in Africa and brought to America at age fourteen. This "famous African Calculator" humbly commenced his mathematical career by counting hairs on the tails of cows and horses he had been set to tend, and, though illiterate, became able to perform complicated arithmetical calculations in his head. When called upon to calculate the number of seconds a man has lived when age 70 years, 17 days, and 12 hours, he popped out the answer after only a few minutes' thought and, upon being charged with error, correctly suggested to his examiners that they had failed to account for leap years. What better possible evidence of native ability than this? Overnight he became an antislavery hero, often referred to simply as "the Negro mathematician."

The most widely known exemplar of the interracial brotherhood of science was Benjamin Banneker, also something of a mathematician. Born free in Maryland, he interested himself in mathematical puzzles, supposedly constructed a clock, and when loaned some books by a neighboring Quaker, became fascinated by astronomy. He was appointed member of the commission to survey the new national district; the Georgetown *Weekly Ledger* reported in March 1791 the arrival of Major Pierre Charles L'Enfant, a second member, and "Benjamin Banneker, an Ethiopian whose abilities as surveyor and astronomer already prove that Mr. Jefferson's concluding that that race of men were void of mental endowment was without foundation." Banneker's fame rested particularly, however, on his almanac. The Baltimore printers of the first issue left no doubt as to the purposes for which the *Almanac* was to be used. It "must be considered an extraordinary Effort of Genius" by a Negro "who, by this Specimen of Ingenuity, evinces, to Demonstration, that mental Powers and Endowments are not the exclusive Excellence of white People, but that the Rays of Science may alike illumine the Minds of Men of every

Clime . . . particularly those whom Tyrant-Custom hath too long taught us to depreciate as a Race inferior in intellectual Capacity."

When Banneker sent a manuscript copy of his almanac to Jefferson he gave no hint that he knew of Jefferson's views on the Negro's nature but confined his long letter to a brief suggestion that the almanac was evidence of Negro ability and to lengthy remarks on the injustice of slavery. Jefferson replied to the old man briefly and courteously. Both letters were almost immediately published as a pamphlet.

> No body [Jefferson wrote] wishes more than I do to see such proofs as you exhibit, that nature has given to our black brethren, talents equal to those of the other colors of men, and that the appearance of a want of them is owing merely to the degraded condition of their existence, both in Africa and America. I can add with truth, that no body wishes more ardently to see a good system commenced for raising the condition both of their body and mind to what it ought to be, as fast as the imbecility of their present existence, and other circumstances which cannot be neglected, will admit.

It was a careful, courteous, and resoundingly ambiguous letter; the condition of the mind and body of the Negro was to be raised "to what it ought to be." Jefferson was still unconvinced, still awaiting the dictates of science.

Jefferson promptly shipped off the manuscript almanac to the Marquis de Condorcet. He was "happy," he wrote Condorcet, to proffer this evidence that a Negro had become "a very respectable mathematician." "I have seen," Jefferson continued, "very elegant solutions of Geometrical problems by him. Add to this that he is a very worthy and respectable member of society. He is a free man. I shall be delighted to see these instances of moral eminence so multiplied as to prove that the want of talents observed in them is merely the effect of their degraded condition, and not proceeding from any difference in the structure of the parts on which intellect depends." As these remarks so clearly indicate, Jefferson had been thrown into confusion by his unsettling confrontation with Banneker. Having attempted to transform Banneker's achievement into an instance of "moral eminence," thereby dodging the problem of intellectual ability, he forced himself back to the issue at hand and suggested that "moral eminence" might offer proof that Negroes were not deficient "in the structure of the parts on which intellect depends." In light of his firm conviction that the "moral sense" and the intellect constituted completely separate entities, this simply made no sense.

Jefferson's confusion at times became monumental. On the one hand he had intellectually derived his belief in human equality from the existence of an orderly creation which had shaped every natural species each to its own mold; and on the other he possessed a larger unquestioning faith, strengthened by his political experience, which predisposed him toward equality. The problem of the Negro's intellect stripped these approaches of their apparent congruity. For he could not rid himself of the suspicion that the Negro was naturally inferior. If this were in fact the case, then it was axiomatic that the Creator had so created the Negro and no amount of education or freedom or any other tinkering could undo the facts of nature. Thus Jefferson suspected that the Creator might have in fact created men unequal; and he could not say this without giving his assertion exactly the same logical force as his famous statement to the contrary. His science-theology rammed squarely into his larger faith, and the result was intellectual wreckage. In the *Notes,* for example, he explained the Indian's apparent deficiencies as resulting wholly from environmental influences. Yet in 1785 he wrote to the Marquis de Chastellux, "I believe the Indian then to be in body and mind equal to the whiteman. I have supposed the blackman, in his present state, might not be so. But it would be hazardous to affirm that, equally cultivated for a few generations, he would not become so." This was all very well as a declaration of faith, but intellectually it made no sense at all. Logically the Indian could retrieve an original equality. But if the Negro was not originally equal he could never "become" so, not if equality really stemmed from "that equal creation" from which Jefferson had derived it in the Declaration.

For Jefferson's contemporaries, it was the scientific aspect of Banneker's achievement which confirmed his celebrity, and that also of Fuller. If evidence of intellect was sought, what more likely field than science? Banneker was better proof even than Phyllis Wheatley. Nothing could point more clearly to the late eighteenth-century separation of intellect from morals than the arresting fact that no abolitionist seized upon Negroes like Richard Allen, Absalom Jones, and Prince Hall as exemplars of Negro capacity. Allen and Jones, both well-known ministers in Philadelphia, and Hall, leader of the active black community in Boston, were in all probability more able men than Banneker. Benjamin Rush was well acquainted with Allen and Jones, yet he never attempted to parade them as examples of Negro equality, nor did any other antislavery writer. White Americans simply assumed that Negroes possessed religious and even quasi-political abilities; doubts on this point would have been doubts about the Negro's status as a human being. The Negro was to be judged on a thoroughly distinct matter—his intellectual capacity.

Until well into the nineteenth century Jefferson's judgment on that matter, with all its confused tentativeness, stood as the strongest suggestion of inferiority expressed by any native American. This fact in itself suggests, at very least, strong feeling on his part, an uncommon need to discourse upon the subject. And the structure of his relevant passage in the *Notes*, where his appeal to science followed lengthy and very definite pronouncements on Negro inferiority, indicated clearly that his appeal to that highest court was not the starting point for his thoughts about Negroes but a safe refuge from them.

JEFFERSON: PASSIONATE REALITIES

Jefferson started, in fact, with a brief assertion of the necessity for colonizing Negroes elsewhere once they had been freed. "Why not retain and incorporate the blacks into the state?" Only later did his answer find wide acceptance in Virginia, especially after September 1800. "Deep rooted prejudices entertained by the whites; ten thousand recollections, by the blacks, of the injuries they have sustained; new provocations; the real distinctions which nature has made; and many other circumstances, will . . . produce convulsions which will probably never end but in the extermination of the one or the other race." His ensuing remarks made evident which factor carried greatest weight with him, for he immediately entered into a long discussion of other "objections" which were "physical and moral." "The first difference which strikes us" he wrote in accurate summary of his countrymen's perceptions, "is that of colour." And he continued, "Whether the black of the negro resides in the reticular membrane between the skin and scarf-skin, or in the scarf-skin itself; whether it proceeds from the colour of the blood, the colour of the bile, or from that of some other secretion, the difference is fixed in nature, and is as real as if its seat and cause were better known to us." For Jefferson, the overwhelming aspect of the Negro's color was its *reality;* he simply shelved the important scientific question of its cause. Even when he considered the question in a more neutral context, in his discussion of albino blacks in the section on "Productions Mineral, Vegetable and Animal," he refused (or perhaps was unable) to offer a word of speculation about a matter on which other scientists speculated freely. Instead he rushed on, spilling forth words which revealed what the "reality" of the "difference" was for Thomas Jefferson. The passionate underpinnings of his feelings were laid bare.

> And is this difference of no importance? Is it not the foundation of a greater or less share of beauty in the two races? Are not the fine mixtures of red and white, the expressions of every passion by greater or less suffusions of colour in the one, preferable to that eternal monotony, which reigns in the countenances, that immoveable veil of black which covers all the emotions of the other race? Add to these, flowing hair, a more elegant symmetry of form, and their own judgment in favor of the whites, declared by their preference of them, as uniformly as is the preference of the Oran-ootan for the black women over those of his own species. The circumstances of superior beauty, is thought worthy attention in the propagation of our horses, dogs, and other domestic animals; why not in that of man?

With this geyser of libidinal energy Jefferson recapitulated major tenets of the American racial complex. Merely on a factual level he passed along several notions which had long been floating about, some since the first years of confrontation in Africa. Red and white were the ingredients of beauty, and blacks were pronouncedly less beautiful than whites; Negroes desired sexual relations especially with whites; black women had relations with orang-outans. On a deeper level the pattern of his remarks was more revealing of Jefferson himself. Embedded in his thoughts on beauty was the feeling that whites were subtler and more delicate in their passions and that blacks, conversely, were more crude. He felt Negroes to be sexually more animal—hence the gratuitous intrusion of the manlike ape. His libidinal desires, unacceptable and inadmissible to his society and to his higher self, were effectively transferred to others and thereby drained of their intolerable immediacy. Having allowed these dynamic emotions perilously close to the surface in the form of the orang-outan, he had immediately shifted to the safe neutral ground of horse-breeding, thus denying his exposure by caricaturing it. Without fully recognizing the adversary within, he continued to flee, taking refuge on higher and higher ground. "They have less hair on the face and body." Not quite safe enough, but he was reaching the safe temple of science. "They secrete less by the kidnies, and more by the glands of the skin," he wrote, carefully placing the rationale before the important fact, "which gives them a very strong and disagreeable odour." Having taken as given the facts of Negro secretion, about which many contemporaries were uncertain, he applied them as proof to a less emotion-laden folk belief. "This greater degree of transpiration renders them more tolerant of heat, and less so of cold, than the whites." He came to rest finally in convoluted speculation. "Perhaps too a difference of structure in the pulmonary apparatus . . . may have disabled them from extricating, in the act of inspiration, so much of that fluid from the outer air, or obliged them in expiration, to part with more of it."

Yet Jefferson was never completely at rest. His picture of blacks as crudely sensual beings, which was at once an offprint of popular belief and a functional displacement of his own emotional drives, kept popping up whenever blacks came to mind. That it did not appear on other, irrelevant occasions indicated that there were limits to its personal importance, yet most of Jefferson's widely-read remarks on the Negro were tinged by it. When discussing the Negro's over-all temperament he wrote, "They are more ardent after their female: but love seems with them to be more an eager desire, than a tender delicate mixture of sentiment and sensation." Elsewhere in the *Notes* he commented in defense of the masculinity of Indian men despite the sparsity of their hair: "Negroes have notoriously less hair than the whites; yet they are more ardent."

While the depth of emotional intensity underlying his thinking about the Negro seems sufficiently evident, the sources of his feeling remain obscured by his unsurprising failure to articulate emotional patterns and processes of which he was unaware. As has often been remarked about him, few men have written so much yet revealed so little of themselves. This fact is in itself enormously suggestive, though it has been a disappointment to historians that he did not include in his papers some remarks on parents and childhood, some few letters to his beloved wife. Yet if one draws back the velvet curtain of his graceful style to regard the *pattern* of his life and thought, it is possible to detect certain of the currents running beneath the structure of his intellect.

JEFFERSON: WHITE WOMEN AND BLACK

Two interrelated currents seem especially relevant to his thoughts on the Negro, the more deep-seated one having to do with his relationships with members of the opposite sex. Jefferson grew up in a world of women. His father, a man of more imposing physique even than Jefferson, died when his son was fourteen. At that critical age he was left with a mother about whom we know almost nothing, four sisters, and one brother. He was never really congenial with his brother, and he never said much concerning his mother and sisters. As a young man, he filled his letters with talk about girls, but his gay chitchat ended abruptly after a keenly disappointing one-sided romance with Rebecca Burwell, an attractive sixteen-year-old orphan. Consoling himself with outbursts of misogyny, Jefferson turned to the companionship of men. Nearly ten years later he made a level-headed match with Martha Skelton Wayles, a twenty-three-year-old widow. The marriage lasted from 1772 until her death in 1782, but again Jefferson left no picture of the woman sharing his life. She bore him six children: three girls died in infancy, as did their only son (whom Jefferson referred to as such before the birth!), and two daughters survived. His wife's failing health worried him terribly—it was in this period that he wrote the *Notes*—and her death left him shattered with grief, not untinged, as so often happens, with self-pity.

Throughout his life after the Burwell affair, Jefferson seemed capable of attachment only to married women. Several years before his marriage he had made, on his own much later admission, improper advances to the wife of a neighboring friend. In Paris, as a widower, he carried on a superficially frantic flirtation with Mrs. Maria Cosway, a "love affair" in which the "love" was partly play and the "affair" non-existent. The only other woman outside his family for whom he formed some attachment was John Adams's remarkable wife, Abigail; with good reason he admired her intellect. With women in general he was uneasy and unsure; he held them at arm's length, wary, especially after his wife's death, of the dangers of overcommitment. Intimate emotional engagement with women seemed to represent for him a gateway into a dangerous, potentially explosive world which threatened revolution against the discipline of his higher self. His famous "Dialogue of the Head and the Heart," written to Maria Cosway, revealed his dim awareness of the struggle within, for beneath its stiltedness one senses a man not naturally cool but thoroughly air-conditioned. Of necessity, the Head emerged victorious in the dialogue, just as it did in real life, declaring pontifically to the Heart, "This is not a world to live at random in as you do." The sentence might have served as a motto for his life.

As Jefferson matured, he seems to have dealt with this inner tension by imputing potential explosiveness to the opposite sex and by assuming that female passion must and could only be controlled by marriage. Certainly Jefferson lived in a culture which assumed dutiful wifely submission, but there was a particular urgency in his stress upon the necessity of female decorum. In any age, his strictures on toilet and dress to his unmarried daughter would seem egregiously detailed. "Nothing is so disgusting to our sex," he warned her, "as a want of cleanliness and delicacy in yours." It is scarcely surprising, therefore, that when living in

Paris, Jefferson dashed off frequent warnings of the sexual cor-
ruptions awaiting American youths in Europe. If unrestrained sex
seemed a dangerous trap to Jefferson, he was deeply certain which
sex had set it. On one occasion, in his rough "Notes on a Tour of
English Gardens," he jotted down an arresting mental picture, in
an otherwise matter-of-fact account, of "a small, dark, deep hol-
low, with recesses of stone in the banks on every side. In one of
these is a Venus pudique, turned half round as if inviting you
with her into the recess." It was a revealing description, as much
of Jefferson as of the statue. Most revealing of all was a letter to
James Madison in 1786. The recent revisal of Virginia laws had
included mitigation of criminal punishments, but harsh punishments had been preserved in two cases, death for treason or murder and castration for rape and buggery, etc. Jefferson wrote from
Paris an interesting commentary. "The principle of retaliation is
much criticised here, particularly in the case of Rape. They think
the punishment indecent and unjustifiable. I should be for alter-
ing it, but for a different reason: that is on account of the temptation women would be under to make it the instrument of venge-
ance against an inconstant lover, and of disappointment to a
rival." Evidently women loomed as threats to masculinity, as
dangerously powerful sexual aggressors.

Jefferson's transferal of sexual aggressiveness to women helps
explain certain otherwise puzzling aspects of his expressions on
the Negro. He was greatly concerned with the Negro's lack of
beauty—in his culture a highly feminine attribute. Moreover,
Jefferson failed to offer even a hint concerning the Negro male's
supposedly large organ, and though this failure may have stemmed
from an understandable reluctance to broach the matter publicly,
he gave no suggestion even indirectly of the sexual aggressiveness
of Negro men; nor did he ever do so privately. In fact—and it is
an arresting one upon re-reading the passage—his previously
quoted remarks concerning beauty and breeding had reference
not to Negro men, nor to Negroes in general, but, in implicit yet
highly specific fashion, to Negro women!

It is in the light of this emotional pattern that Jefferson's
widely discussed relationship with the Hemings family should
be considered. The subject is an unpalatable one for many Amer-

icans: the assertion that a great national figure was involved in miscegenation—this is the central supposed "fact" of the Hemings matter—is one that white Americans find difficult to treat as anything but a malicious accusation. Malice *was,* indeed, the animating force behind the original claim, but we need to brace ourselves into an intellectual posture from which we can see that the importance of the stories about black Sally Hemings and Thomas Jefferson lies in the fact that they seemed—and to some people still seem—of any importance. The facts of the matter require attention not because Jefferson's behavior needs to be questioned but because they are of some (but not very much) help in understanding Jefferson's views about miscegenation and, far more, because they shed light on the cultural context in which he moved and of which we are heirs. Viewed in the context of his feelings about white women, the problem of Jefferson's actual overt behavior becomes essentially irrelevant to the subject of this book; it is to the inner world of his thought and feeling that we must look for significant patterns and, even more, to his culture for the larger significance of the matter.

In 1802 James T. Callender charged in the Richmond *Recorder* that it was "well known" that Jefferson kept Sally, one of his slaves, as concubine and had fathered children by her. Callender was a notorious professional scandalmonger who had turned upon Jefferson when the President had disappointed his hope for federal office. Despite the utter disreputability of the source, the charge has been dragged after Jefferson through the pages of formal and informal history, tied to him by its attractiveness to a wide variety of interested persons and by the apparent impossibility of utterly refuting it. Jefferson's conduct has been attacked from several angles, for in fact the charge of concubinage with Sally Hemings constitutes not one accusation but three, simultaneously accusing Jefferson of fathering bastards, of miscegenation, and of crassly taking advantage of a helpless young slave (for Sally was probably twenty-two when she first conceived). The last of these, insofar as it implies forced attentions on an unwilling girl, may be summarily dismissed. For one thing, indirect evidence indicates that Sally was happy throughout her long period of motherhood, and, more important, Jefferson was simply not capable of violating every rule of honor and kindness, to say nothing of his convictions concerning the master-slave relationship.

As for bastardy and miscegenation, the known circumstances of the situation at Monticello which might support the charges were, very briefly, as follows. The entire Hemings family seems to have received favored treatment. Sally's mother was mulatto and had come to Jefferson with her still lighter children from the estate of his father-in-law, John Wayles, in 1774. Most of Sally's siblings were personal servants; Sally herself and her mother were house servants. All the slaves freed by Jefferson were Hemingses, and none of Sally's children were retained in slavery as adults. She bore five, from 1795 to 1808; and though he was away from Monticello a total of roughly two-thirds of this period, Jefferson was at home nine months prior to each birth. Her first child was conceived following Jefferson's retirement as Secretary of State with nerves raw from political battling with Hamilton. Three others were conceived during Jefferson's summer vacations and the remaining child was born nine months after his very brief return to Monticello for the funeral of his daughter. In short, Jefferson's paternity can be neither refuted nor proved from the known circumstances or from the extant testimony of his overseer, his white descendants, or the descendants of Sally, each of them having fallible memories and personal interests at stake.

If we turn to Jefferson's character we are confronted by evidence which for many people today (and then) furnished an immediate and satisfactory refutation. Yet the assumption that this high-minded man *could not* have carried on such an affair is at variance with what is known today concerning the relationship between human personality and behavior. If the previous suggestions concerning his personality have any validity, Jefferson's relations with women were ambivalent, and in the Hemings situation either tendency could have prevailed.

Assuming this ambivalence in Jefferson, one can construct two reasonable (though not equally probable) and absolutely irreconciable cases. It is possible to argue on the one hand, briefly, that Jefferson was a truly admirable man if there ever was one and that by the time he had married and matured politically, in the

1770's, his "head" was permanently in control of his "heart." Hence a liaison with a slave girl would have been a lapse from character unique in his mature life. It would have represented, on a deeper level, abandonment of the only grounds on which he was able to maintain satisfactory relations with women, their safe incarceration in the married state. It would have meant complete reversal of his feelings of repulsion toward Negroes and a towering sense of guilt for having connected with such sensual creatures and having given free rein to his own libidinous desires, guilt for which there is no evidence. On the other hand, however, it is possible to argue that attachment with Sally represented a final happy resolution of his inner conflict. This would account for the absence after his return from Paris in 1789 of evidence pointing to continuing high tension concerning women and Negroes, an absence hardly to be explained by senility. Sally Hemings would have become Becky Burwell and the bitter outcome of his marriage erased. Unsurprisingly, his repulsion toward Negroes would have been, all along, merely the obverse of powerful attraction, and external pressures in the 1790's would easily have provided adequate energy for turning the coin of psychic choice from one side to the other. One is left fully persuaded only of the known fact that any given pattern of basic personality can result in widely differing patterns of external behavior.

The question of Jefferson's miscegenation, it should be stressed again, is of limited interest and usefulness even if it could be satisfactorily answered. The *Notes* had been written years before, and Jefferson never deviated from his "aversion," as he wrote just before he died, "to the mixture of colour" in America. One aspect of the history of the Hemings family, however, offers possible clarification on several points. It appears quite probable that Sally and some of her siblings were the children of his father-in-law, John Wayles. It must have been a burden indeed for Jefferson, who probably knew this, to have the Hemingses in the same house with their half-sister and aunt, his beloved wife, who almost certainly was ignorant of the situation. This burden might well have embittered his thoughts on miscegenation in general and have helped convince him to his dying day that it was a social evil. It would also have heightened his conviction that slavery was degrading to white men. And while it does not settle anything concerning his relations with Sally, it would explain the favored treatment the Hemings family received at Monticello.

The larger significance of the Hemings matter lay not in Jefferson's conduct but in the charges themselves. The charge of bastardy was virtually lost in the clamor about miscegenation. Hamilton's admission of sexual transgressions with a white woman had done little to damage *his* reputation. Jefferson's offense was held to be mixture of the races, and Callender and his fellow scandalmongers strummed the theme until it was dead tired.

> In glaring red, and chalky white,
>   Let others beauty see;
> Me no such tawdry tints delight—
>   No! black's the hue for me!

> Thick pouting lips! how sweet their grace!
>   When passion fires to kiss them!
> Wide spreading over half the face,
>   Impossible to miss them.

INTERRACIAL SEX: THE INDIVIDUAL AND HIS SOCIETY

Callender's grossness played upon very real sensitivities. Beneath everyone's pronouncements on the undesirability of racial mixture lay a substructure of feeling about interracial sex. Jefferson's feelings were of course partially molded by specific beliefs about Negroes which constituted readily visible manifestations of feelings prevailing in his culture not merely about Negroes but about life in general. It seems legitimate and profitable to speak of an entire culture as having feelings, partly because every society demands—and gets—a large measure of the behavior it "wants" (i.e. needs) from individuals and partly because in a literate culture expressions of individual feeling accumulate through time, thus forming a common pool of expressed feelings. Usually, but by no means always, these expressions are highly intellectualized, that is, detached from direct functional connection with powerful emotional drives. Sometimes they are not, as they sometimes were not when Thomas Jefferson wrote about Negroes. It seems evident that his feelings, his affective life, his emotions—whatever term one prefers—were being expressed in some of his beliefs or opinions about blacks. His opinions were thus sometimes quite directly the product of his repressions. And it seems axiomatic, given the assumptions about the nature of culture prevailing in the twentieth century, that variants of his repressions operated in so many individuals that one can speak of deep-seated feelings about the Negro as being social in character, that is, as characterizing an entire society. The explicit *content* of social attitudes stemmed not directly from the emotions being repressed but from the mechanisms of repression. The resultant attitudes, moreover, through constant communication within society, acquired an autonomous energy and a viability independent of emotional underpinnings. Hence many individuals subscribed to beliefs about Negroes which performed no very vital function in their personality, and these beliefs may be considered as being part of the cultural environment.

The relationship between miscegenation and society was intricately reciprocal. While miscegenation altered the tone of society, the social institution of slavery helped reshape the definition of miscegenation from fusion of that which was different to fusion of higher and lower; hence slavery was of course responsible for much of the normative judgment implied in the concept of miscegenation. Yet both slavery and miscegenation rested, in the final analysis, upon a *perception of difference* between the races, a perception founded on physiognomic fact. When Jefferson, for example, set out to prove that emancipated blacks must be removed from white society he predicated "the real distinctions nature has made," moved immediately into a discussion of appearance, and only then went on to less tangible differences in temperament and intellect. Underlying his discussion of the Negro, and everyone else's, was an axiomatic separation of blacks from whites based on appearance.

JEFFERSON: A DICHOTOMOUS VIEW OF TRIRACIAL AMERICA

Yet Jefferson laid *uncommonly* great stress on the physical distinction between blacks and whites. This emphasis derived partly from his emotional responses to women but also from a pervasive temperamental characteristic, a habit of mind not unconnected with his views of the opposite sex. He always regarded the world of men as utterly distinct from the strange world of women in which he could never feel at ease; his division was even sharper than that of the culture in which he lived, which was sharp enough, to be sure. (The English word *sex* itself derived from Latin terms indicating cutting, separation, division.) On a different level, in terms of his "thought," Jefferson gave every evidence of a predilection for bifurcating men and issues and even his perceptual environment, for thinking of the world in terms of—it is significant that we cannot avoid a play on words here—black or white. His approach to the external world became most obvious perhaps during his involvement in the stormy partisan politics which elicited in so many Americans a tendency to regard the political world as composed of two conflicting opposites, Republican and Federalist, France and England, honest men and knaves. Jefferson pressed this tendency as far as anyone. He always insisted that hard-core Federalists were "monocrats," i.e. utterly antirepublican, and that, on the other hand, the great body of Federalists were really Republicans at heart. This inability to admit a possible middle ground assumed only slightly different shape in his famous statement in the First Inaugural—"We are all republicans: we are all federalists"; here he resolved wide differences by a doubly incorrect denial of their existence. This was partly a matter of shorthand phrasing, but no terminology is innocent of meaning; earlier Jefferson had frequently described European social and political conflicts with such pairs as "hammer and anvil" and "sheep and wolves." He never shared in the contemporary enthusiasm for a balance of powers in government; indeed his picture of society as composed of the people and their enemies precluded any necessity for balancing various interests. Jefferson was at his best on occasions calling for the vigor of simple dichotomy, as in 1776 when he contrasted the virtues of a free people to the crimes of a tyrannical king.

A similar penchant for orderly division became apparent in his relations with individual persons. With a mind too intelligent to classify all men as good or bad, Jefferson nonetheless was temperamentally incapable of subtle analysis of other men's character. Gouverneur Morris sensed this quality when he wrote in his diary after a call upon Jefferson in Paris, "I think he does not form very just estimates of character, but rather assigns too many to the humble rank of fools, whereas in life the gradations are infinite and each individual has his peculiarities of fort and feeble." For his most famous love letter Jefferson seized upon the one literary form which could most adequately convey his conception of his own personality, a "dialogue" between "the head and the heart."

Jefferson's pervasive temperamental bent for order, symmetry, and normative dichotomy was nowhere more obvious than in his anthropology. It helped Jefferson to find a highly satisfying resolution of the problem posed by the American Indian. Here his individual temperament came into contact with his society's perception of Indians as being utterly distinct from Negroes. Indians did not in fact look like white persons, yet Americans showed either indifference or downright unwillingness to admit the fact. With Jefferson the unwillingness was monumental. Confronted by three races in America he determinedly turned three into two by transforming the Indian into a degraded yet basically noble brand of white man. Some of the most heartfelt passages in the *Notes on Virginia* were devoted to a defense of the Indian against the famous French naturalist, Buffon, whose aspersions Jefferson declared to be "just as true as the fable of Aesop." Indians, he asserted, were actually brave and manly and by no means deficient in attachment to family and friends. They were notably eloquent. In contrast with Negroes "they astonish you with strokes of the most sublime oratory; such as prove their reason and sentiment strong, their imagination glowing and elevated." Physically, too, Jefferson argued, the Indian was by no means inferior to the white man.

With both Indians and Negroes Jefferson appealed decisions on mental powers to the court of facts, but he clearly expected radically differing verdicts. In contrast to his "suspicion" concerning Negroes, he announced that with the Indians "we shall probably find that they are formed in mind as well as in body, on the same module with the 'Homo sapiens Europaeus.'" Nothing could demonstrate more clearly Jefferson's prejudgment of the verdict than the different slants with which he made his appeal to environmental influences. While comparing Negroes unfavorably with Roman slaves, he declared that a comparison of Indians "in their present state with the Europeans North of the Alps" during the Roman Empire "would be unequal" because of the greater density of European population. Consistency of argument was no barrier when the final judgment had already been made.

In defending the Indian Jefferson was vindicating the American environment, for his remarks on the Indian in the *Notes* formed only part of his refutation of Buffon's claim that animals in the New World were smaller and weaker than in the Old, and of the Abbé Raynal's extension of that claim to white Americans. These charges stung Jefferson not only as nationalist but also as scientist, since they imputed inferiority to his natural laboratory equipment. In employing an environmentalist defense of the Indian he had to work carefully, however, since the Indian was both a part of the American environment and the product of it. In order not to disparage his own natural environment he was careful to avoid any suggestion that the backwardness of the Indians was the effect of their surroundings.

Nowhere was Jefferson's effort to Americanize the Indian more apparent than in his reiterated hope for cultural and physical amalgamation of Indians with white Americans. Together they formed one nation: "We, like you," he once addressed an Indian chief, "are Americans, born in the same land, and having the same interests." His purchase of Louisiana raised the possibility of encouraging the Indians to remove beyond the Mississippi, but he preferred that they be encouraged to give up hunting for farming and cede the resultant surplus of land to the United States. "In truth," he wrote, "the ultimate point of rest and happiness for them is to let our settlements and theirs meet and blend together, to intermix, and become one people." This would "best promote the interests of the Indians and ourselves, and finally consolidate our whole country to one nation only." Ten years later in 1813 he wrote regretfully that war had now intervened: "They would have mixed their blood with ours, and been amalgamated and identified with us within no distant period of time."

Amalgamation and identification, welcomed with the Indian, were precisely what Jefferson most abhorred with the Negro. The Indian was a brother, the Negro a leper. While Americans had always regarded the two peoples as very different, Jefferson underlined the dichotomy with a determined emphasis not matched by other men. His derogation of the Negro revealed the latent possibilities inherent in an accumulated popular tradition of Negro inferiority; it constituted, for all its qualifications, the most intense, extensive, and extreme formulation of anti-Negro "thought" offered by any American in the thirty years after the Revolution. Yet Thomas Jefferson left to white Americans something else which may in the long run have been of greater importance—his prejudice for freedom and his larger equalitarian faith. It was this faith which must have caused him to fall gradually more silent on a subject which many of his fellow intellectuals were taking up with interest. For Jefferson more than for any of his known contemporaries, the subject was not an easy or a happy one.

13

The Chain of Being
and the Stamp of Color

Natural philosophers in the young republic were less willing than previously to act as humble collectors for the learned naturalists of Europe, less willing, that is, to accept colonial status in the empire of science. In the face of this change, however, the structure of their conceptual world remained fundamentally the same: they remained committed to a world view which was remarkable for its cohesiveness, energy, and passion for system.

By the final quarter of the eighteenth century the ordering concept of the Great Chain of Being had become highly popular and widely popularized. Yet the Linnaean tradition of classification remained as a separate, viable means of imposing order on the Creation. The eminent naturalist's terminology and reputation still dominated the study of natural categories in America. While the supply of systematizing concepts thus remained much the same as earlier in the century, political and social developments after the Revolution worked to heighten the temptation to draw upon them. The Negro had become an issue for many Americans and they began to discuss what they thought was his essential nature far more than they ever had before.

TWO MODES OF EQUALITY

In 1787, an aspiring college president undertook the first major American study of the races of mankind. Samuel Stanhope Smith was the son of a Presbyterian minister, became professor of moral philosophy at Princeton, married the college president's daughter, and succeeded to his father-in-law's post in 1795. He stood in the front rank of American academicians, partly owing to his *An Essay on the Causes of the Variety of Complexion and Figure in the Human Species.*

Smith's point of departure in the *Essay* revealed his basic purpose. At the outset, he took notice of the theories which held mankind to be different stocks and summarily dismissed them: "we are not at liberty to make this supposition." The impossibility of determining the exact number and types of originally separate human species, Smith argued, was clear indication that they had never existed. Having thus cleared the stage in a few short pages Smith turned to constructive work, and it took him the rest of the book to demonstrate his basic proposition—that mankind constituted a single species and that human varieties had come to differ in appearance through the operation of natural causes, which were, as he described them, "climate," "state of society," and "habits of living." The energy of his argument plainly derived from Smith's abhorrence of the contrary possibility that men varied in appearance because they had originally been cast in different molds.

In effect, Samuel Stanhope Smith marshaled Linnaean classification and the power of environmental influences in support of the Book of Genesis. Yet his book was not the work of a reactionary minister; rather it represented an age of special faith that inquiry into the natural world could do nothing but support the tenets of revealed religion because true inquiry could only reveal the handiwork of God. It was in this sense that the Reverend Mr. Smith shared the same cosmology with the other principal author on race in 1787, Thomas Jefferson.

Smith's *Essay* and Jefferson's *Notes on Virginia* did not, however, offer similar conclusions concerning the Negro. It was not that the two men began with radically different views about man, but rather that they elaborated their assumptions with different basal modes of logic. Both started with human equality. After grounding equality in the *brotherhood* of man as embedded in the story of Genesis, Smith could scarcely permit merely physical distinctions among men to override the fundamental kinship of all human beings within one family. But Jefferson, by grounding human equality in men's common taxonomic participation in a natural species, was forced to suppose that physical distinctions among men were of the utmost importance.

Not merely the dangerousness of Jefferson's biologic conception of equality but also the ambiguousness of the *Notes on Virginia* and the profundity of his disparagement of the Negro stand out all the more sharply when viewed in the light of Linnaean terminology and the Great Chain of Being. His remarks in the *Notes* bore all the earmarks of an attempt to dodge the implications arising from his deep-seated sentiments. At a conscious level Jefferson's evasiveness involved gingerly referring to Negroes as a "race," a term then characterized by total absence of any precise meaning. (At best the term *race* was used, as one writer explained, "merely to express the fact, that differences do exist.") Thus Jefferson hedged himself doubly when he hesitated to declare the Negro inferior in mental capacities because such a conclusion "would degrade a whole race of men from the rank in the scale of beings which their Creator may perhaps have given them."

At a less conscious level, the Great Chain enabled Jefferson to express the charged sexuality with which he had vested relations between the two races. Here he was able to draw upon a centuries-old tradition, probably without even knowing it. He revealed to his readers his picture of an ordered hierarchy of sexual aggressiveness by referring to the Negroes' "own judgment in favour of the whites, declared by their preference of them, as uniformly as is the preference of the Oran-ootan for the black women over those of his own species." Here at last, proclaimed in language at once passionate and clinical, was what Jefferson saw as the Negro's true rank in nature's scale—exactly midway between ("as uniformly as") the white man and the most manlike ape.

This enduring merger of sexual myth and intellectual construct was one of the most bizarre in Western history; it may serve as a striking reminder that the "mind" of any age arises from widely disparate levels of psychic activity and that "ideas" persist according to the measure of their deep-rootedness in psycho-social necessities. Ever since the days of confrontation in Africa the sexual connection between Negro and ape had served to express the deep-seated feeling that the Negro was more animal— and accordingly more sexual—than the white man; or put another way, the Negro-ape connection served as a sufficiently indirect means by which the white man could express his dim awareness of the sexual animal within himself.

THE HIERARCHIES OF MEN

The union of sexuality and the Chain was most glaringly apparent in the abrasive remarks of the Jamaican historian Edward Long. In the opening months of 1788 the *Columbian Magazine* dredged up Long's *History of Jamaica* (1774) and reprinted certain passages under the title "Observations on the Gradation in the Scale of Being between the Human and Brute Creation. Including Some Curious Particulars Respecting Negroes." Long's "particulars" were indeed "curious," for his description of Negroes proved to be a romp through the garden of infantile sexuality. With the greatest sobriety he enumerated the Negro's "covering of wool, like the bestial fleece," round eyes, thick lips, large nipples on the females (to fit the lips, Long suggested), black lice, and "bestial or faetid smell." Long's formulations on the Negro's less tangible qualities were not much further removed from the lost pleasures of the nursery: Negroes were "void of genius" and had "no moral sensations; no taste but for women; gormandizing, and drinking to excess; no wish but to be idle."

Long turned to reinforcement of what he rightly sensed might be considered the weakest portion of his Chain. He hammered away industriously at proving that the "orang-outan" (the chimpanzee) was nearly human: Apes ate at dinner tables; the mechanic arts of the Negroes were no more than an orang might be brought to do; orang-outans might be taught to speak. Orangs did not "seem at all inferior in the intellectual faculties to many of the negroe race; with some of whom it is credible that they have the most intimate connexion and consanguinity. The amorous intercourse between them may be frequent; the Negroes themselves bear testimony, that such intercourses actually happen; and it is certain, that both races agree perfectly well in lasciviousness of disposition." Long found this sexual theme irresistible, and he was eminently successful at weaving it into the Great Chain. "Ludicrous as the opinion may seem, I do not think that an oran-outang husband would be any dishonour to an Hottentot female."

In transforming the most manlike ape nearly into a man and by emphasizing his affinity to the Negro, Long did *not* imply that the Negro was actually a beast, even though he was tempted, he said, to think that blacks and whites were not of the same species and did not have common parents. It is of the utmost significance that the most virulent defamers of the Negro were forced to wildly strenuous and preposterous attempts at proving that the orang-outan was nearly human. Essentially what Long's attempt involved was eradication of the clear distinction between men and beasts, and such an attempt (even with powerful assistance from the concept of the Chain) was clearly going to have considerable difficulty wiping out a basic presupposition thousands of years old. The Judaic-Christian tradition had always been inflexible on the distinct nature of man created "in his own image" as contrasted to "the fish of the sea," "the fowl of the air," "the cattle," and "every creeping thing that creepeth upon the earth."

ANATOMICAL INVESTIGATIONS

Edward Long had no standing in the scientific community, but a number of reputable scientists were reaching conclusions similar to his. The study of human anatomy and physiology advanced rapidly during the final quarter of the century. It was the blossoming interest in the nature of the human body, indeed, which revealed how thoroughgoing a shift had taken place toward a primarily naturalistic view of man. The alteration was centuries in the making, to be sure, but the introduction of anatomical investigation into the longstanding problem of differences among human groups came with relative suddenness. When, after 1775, large numbers of human corpses were brought under the same scrutiny which Edward Tyson had applied to his "orang-outang" in 1700, there were bound to be repercussions upon ideas about the Negro.

The appeal to the hard facts of anatomical structure was carried furthest by an English surgeon whose book was largely responsible for the subsequent re-entry of Samuel Stanhope Smith into the field of controversy. Dr. Charles White was a reputable member of the Royal Society and author of a treatise on midwifery which was well known in America. He eventually took an interest in the subject of comparative anatomy when he one day saw a friend's collection of skulls lined up in order of declining facial angles. The downward progression of European, Asiatic, American Indian, Negro, orang-outan, and monkey impressed White enormously, and it occurred to him "that Nature would not employ gradation in one instance only, but would adopt it as a general principle." Even the parrot and elephant, he suddenly realized, possessed high facial angles! When White turned in 1799 to apply his "general principle" to man, he discovered that of all the sorts of men, Europeans were highest and Africans lowest on the scale.

Thus charged, Charles White went on to compose a lengthy catalogue of the particular ways in which the Negro more closely resembled the ape than did the European. He carefully examined skeletons of Europeans, Africans, Tyson's orang-outan, and a monkey, as well as the bodies of living whites and blacks. The Negro's skull, he announced, had a smaller capacity than the European's. The Negro possessed longer arms, thicker skin, ranker smell, shorter life span and earlier maturation, larger breasts, and "gibbous" legs. Negroes excelled Europeans, on the other hand, in certain areas where apes excelled man—seeing, hearing, smelling, and memory. For support of his contention that Negroes were inferior mentally, White relied not only upon his own "evidence" of lesser cranial capacity but on the authority of an eminent American scientist, Thomas Jefferson.

Dr. Charles White's book was of considerable importance not only because it was read (not widely but in important quarters) in America but because it established a striking precedent for grounding opinions about the Negro in the ostensibly irrefutable facts of comparative anatomy. His case for Negro inferiority rested upon an unprecedented (if unreliable) array of physiological detail. To discover whether the Negro was in fact a highly sensual creature, for example, one had only to turn to White's scientific evidence. "That the PENIS of an African is larger than that of an European," he announced airily, "has, I believe, been shewn in every anatomical school in London. Preparations of them are preserved in most anatomical museums; and I have one in mine." His own investigations of living Negroes had confirmed this: "*Haller,* in his *primae Liniae,* speaking of the Africans, says, '*In hominibus etiam penis est longior et multo laxior*'; but I say *Multo firmior et durior.*" Furthermore, lest the facts of human anatomy be allowed to repose slag-like in meaningless disorder, White had assembled them in a fashion guaranteed to provide white men with gratifying satisfaction:

> Ascending the line of gradation, we come at last to the white European; who being most removed from the brute creation, may, on that account, be considered as the most beautiful of the human race. No one will doubt his superiority in intellectual powers. . . . Where shall we find, unless in the European, that nobly arched head, containing such a quantity of brain . . . ? Where the perpendicular face, the prominent nose, and round projecting chin? Where that variety of features, and fulness of expression . . . ? In what other quarter of the globe shall we find the blush that overspreads the soft features of the beautiful women of Europe, that emblem of modesty, of delicate feelings, and of sense? Where that nice expression of the amiable and softer passions in the countenance; and that general elegance of features and complexion? Where, except on the bosom of the European woman, two such plump and snowy white hemispheres, tipt with vermillion?

Where indeed?

Such contentions were bound to alarm the defenders of human unity, and President Samuel Stanhope Smith of Princeton emerged once again in 1810 to defend the "outworks" of true fidelity and to carry his attack "into the enemy's camp." As his combative language suggested, Smith sensed how much the situation had changed since his initial attempt in 1787 to explain the causes of human physical variations. During the quarter-century between the two editions of his *Essay,* important transformations had occurred in his immediate social world, in the American nation, in world politics, and in the international realm of ideas.

With complete assurance that sound study of natural philosophy could only confirm the revealed Word, Smith manfully attempted to battle Charles White and others on their own ground. Indeed he could scarcely dodge a challenge which had arisen from the inductive principles of science, and he scurried about the kitchens of Princeton bravely brandishing a foot rule and thermometer. Smith concluded that his opponents had failed to take into account the changes which the American environment was producing especially in domestic slaves and free Negroes. Was the formation of the jaw, the teeth, or the nose of the Negro of inferior quality? This portrait was "sufficiently accurate" for the Negro in Africa but "in the United States, the physiognomy, and the whole figure and personal appearance of the African race is undergoing a favorable change." Were the legs of the Negro more gibbous? So they were in Africa and almost as much so among the neglected field slaves of America, but among the domestics of the South and even more among the free Negroes of Princeton are limbs "as handsomely formed as those of the inferior and laboring classes, either of Europeans, or Anglo-Americans."

All this was written in defense of the Negro, but in effect Smith was denying *inherent* inferiority while conceding *present* inferiority. His whole book shouted that the Negro was going to be the *equal* of the white man only when the Negro came to look like one.

ERASING THE STAMP OF COLOR

But how could black men ever come to look like white? For Smith, the answer was that American Negroes were becoming lighter as the result of a more favorable "climate," "manner of living," and "state of society." For Dr. Benjamin Rush, distinguished antislavery advocate, active leader in the conventions of abolition societies in the 1790's, publicizer of talented Negroes, the answer was more specific. He published his explanation in 1799: "Observations Intended to Favour a Supposition That the Black Color (As It Is Called) of the Negroes Is Derived from the

Leprosy." Why Africans particularly should have contracted leprosy was no mystery, Rush announced, since it was well known that an unwholesome diet often led to the disease and that Africa was characterized by "greater heat, more savage manners, and bilious fevers." Leprosy sometimes resulted in a blackening of the skin and a "smell" which "continues with a small modification in the native African to this day." It was no objection that many Negroes lived on into old age, for a disease of local character would not impair longevity. Further evidence of a leprous quality in Negroes lay in their notorious sexuality: "Lepers are remarkable for having strong venereal desires. This is universal among the negroes, hence their uncommon fruitfulness when they are not depressed by slavery; but even slavery in its worst state does not always subdue the venereal appetite, for after whole days, spent in hard labor in a hot sun in the West Indies, the black men often walk five or six miles to comply with a venereal assignation."

Rush's central contention possessed no reputable contemporary scientific validity, nor, indeed, any basis in fact. No matter. Benjamin Rush was not a man to permit such puny obstacles to impede the swath of his convictions. Nor was he willing to let the reader escape the "reflections" to be drawn from his "facts and principles." "If the color of the Negroes be the effect of a disease, instead of inviting us to tyrannize over them, it should entitle them to a double portion of our humanity, for disease all over the world has always been the signal for immediate and universal compassion." Rush seemed totally unaware of the irony involved in transforming Negroes into lepers: of all diseases leprosy had for ages been treated with something less than "compassion" and "humanity."

Yet Rush knew the reputation of the disease and seized upon it for a second revealing "reflection." "The facts and principles which have been delivered, should teach white people the necessity of keeping up that prejudice against such connections with them, as would tend to infect posterity with any portion of their disorder." With supreme ease Dr. Rush had transformed what he called "the existing prejudices against matrimonial connections with them" into an obviously necessary measure of human hygiene.

Rush reserved his most far-reaching "reflection" to the last, in what was surely one of the most optimistic pleas of Baconian science. "Is the color of the negroes a disease? Then let science and humanity combine their efforts, and endeavour to discover a remedy for it." This was no utopian hope. "Nature has lately unfurled a banner upon this subject. She has begun spontaneous cures of this disease in several black people."

No matter how sandy the foundations, Rush's edifice had a certain magnificence. If only blackness were leprosy, blackness could be cured by science, and slavery and intermixture would stand condemned and Scripture and humanitarian benevolence confirmed. It was a big *if*, though; nobody even bothered to refute his suggestion. In retrospect, it seems remarkable how absurd Rush could be, but it is also worth noting that his central contention was, as far as white men were concerned, correct and impressively predictive: Negroes have been regarded in America as outcast and diseased. At an important level of human logic, Dr. Rush's diagnosis of blackness was entirely accurate.

More representative of American environmentalists was Hugh Williamson, a Pennsylvanian who lived in the South. In his "Remarks on the Different Complexions of the Human Race" (1811), he proved eager to see his findings agree with Revelation, which they easily did since he was convinced that mankind had been varied by natural causes. The number of human races, he pointed out, could as well be considered fifty as five since the colors of man formed a spectrum without demarcations. Were cows of differing colors to be considered separate species? The features and color of all human beings could be altered by changes in "climate, food, and education or habits." It was no surprise, therefore, that the Negro's color and features were being altered in America, although it was far harder for black men to become white than vice versa. Climate (which like all things in the material world was governed by "the constant, universal agency of the God of nature, who is every where present always") invariably but eventually altered men to suit them to itself. Later generations of white Americans were less sure, but as late as 1811 an American intellectual was elaborating the case for the power of environment in general and the American environment in particular. In that, essentially eighteenth-century view, black Africans were to be changed, though not in the twinkling of an eye. It would *not* be through their efforts: whiteness was to be *bestowed* upon them by America. The new land was not for black men; even the Indians, Williamson pointed out, had not been rendered black despite their savagery because the climate was not hot enough. Here, in the language of natural philosophy, was the absolutely literal claim: America was a white man's country.

14

Toward a White Man's Country

If there was one thread of development which showed how deeply white Americans felt about Negroes, it was a campaign which developed in the 1790's especially in Virginia for ridding the state (and the entire nation) of black people. Perhaps "campaign" is too strong a term for the wishful proposals which were so obviously doomed to failure, but it was the enormousness of the obstacles rather than any weakness in the wish which kept the early colonization movement from accomplishment. The proposals are worth examining precisely because they could not have been implemented and because they therefore suggest the existence of extraordinary pressures making for pathetic hopes.

One of the most revealing aspects of American attitudes was the nearly universal belief that emancipation of blacks from slavery would inevitably lead to increased racial intermixture. What is arresting about this opinion is that no one attempted to give reasons *why* such a development was inevitable and that there *were* in fact no good reasons. (So far, a century and a half later, emancipation has actually lessened the rate of intermixture.) The problem becomes, then, one of inquiring why Americans adhered (and in many quarters still adhere) to this belief.

Perhaps the real reasons for this expectation (those other kinds of human "reasons") lay in the hopes that white men had invested in America. A darkened nation would present irrefutable evidence that sheer animal sex was governing the American destiny and that the great experiment in the wilderness had failed to maintain the social and personal restraints which were the hall-marks and the very stuff of civilization. A blackened posterity would mean that the basest of energies had guided the direction of the American experiment and that civilized man had turned beast in the forest. Retention of whiteness would be evidence of purity and of diligent nurture of the original body of the folk. Could a blackened people look back to Europe and say that they had faithfully performed their errand?

THE BEGINNINGS OF COLONIZATION

Just as publication of the *Notes on Virginia* in 1787 helped spark discussion of the Negro's nature, it seems to have helped generate sentiment for colonization of Negroes. Some men thought Negro removal indispensable to the accomplishment of emancipation. An anonymous New Hampshire author, who summarized his indictment of American slavery, in his title *Tyrannical Liberty-men,* declared that emancipated slaves must be put in "a state of dependence and discipline" because they were unused to free-dom. Perhaps some should be returned to Africa, he suggested, but preferably they should be sent to lands in the West and supplied wih provisions and magistrates. He conceded that "diffi-culties would attend the achievement" but pointed out "what a flattering project would it open to the wellwisher of mankind."

> We might reasonably expect soon to see a large province of black freemen, industrious and well regulated, improving in arts and learning, happy at home and at peace with us. . . . Might not the establishment of such a colony be of extensive influence in bringing about the universal spread of light, lib-erty, and benevolence. Ye republican Pharaohs, how long will ye harden your hearts, and not let the people go!

The sons of Ham were to be repatriated to a new, separate land of Canaan.

Certainly a majority of antislavery advocates in the North were not especially attracted by such proposals. The Convention of Abolition Societies in Philadelphia was virtually silent on the matter, which suggests hesitancy to endorse colonization but also that they saw no great evil or danger in Negro removal. No one denounced colonization as a proslavery instrument, as the next generation was to do, for the very good reason that the project was supported only by men of genuine antislavery feeling.

THE VIRGINIA PROGRAM

Only in Virginia did wholesale emancipation look at once extremely difficult yet seemingly within the realm of possibility. The statute of 1782, facilitating private manumissions, seemed a good beginning. Eventually, of course, statesmen like Jefferson came to realize that emancipation was not to be the work of their generation, but in fact there was some basis for the assumption by contemporaries that Virginia would be the first southern state to act against slavery. In the last quarter of the century Virginia's leaders, who had been foremost in expounding the doctrines of the Revolution, provided capable aristocratic leadership. More important, there was in Virginia little economic justification for continuing slavery and, by comparison with South Carolina at least, a manageable proportion of Negroes. A unique combination of favorable circumstances meant that of all the states where slavery's deep entrenchment precluded easy solution, Virginia was the one where the question of emancipation seemed furthest open. And in Virginia there lived 40 per cent of the nation's black population.

After Jefferson opened the discussion in 1787 the possibility of Negro removal had to be considered by anyone interested in emancipating Virginia's blacks. In 1788 James Madison cautiously endorsed a plan for an African settlement as a means of encouraging manumission. As the situation now stood, Madison explained, general emancipation would benefit neither society nor freedmen. For the well-being of society "a compleat incorporation" of freedmen would be required, but this development was "rendered impossible by the prejudice of the whites, prejudices which proceeding principally from the difference in colour must be considered as permanent and insuperable." A settlement on the African coast was preferable to the American interior because in the West Negroes would be destroyed by the "Savages" if too distant and would soon be at war with the whites if too near.

The idea of Negro removal spread rapidly in Virginia during the 1790's. An observant Frenchman touring the United States in the 1790's described the idea of removal almost as if it were the subject of daily conversation in Virginia: "They talk here of transporting all the negroes out of the country at once, either to Africa or to the southern parts of America, in order to found a colony." The Duc de La Rochefoucauld-Liancourt went on to complain that the measure was "so full of difficulties in its execution" and "attended with so many unpleasant consequences, that it cannot possibly be carried into effect." But he had no doubts why Virginians favored the measure: "The plan is supported by the fear which manifests itself in those who espouse it, that a mixture in the blood would take place if the Negroes were emancipated, or suffered to remain in the country: 'in future generations,' say they, 'there would not be a countenance to be seen without more or less of the black colour.' "

It was all very well for a foreign visitor to call this problem an "inconvenience," but white Virginians thought it was something rather more serious. Their fears cried out in every proposal for colonization. Ferdinando Fairfax, whose plan in 1790 was the first put forward in detail, declared that it was "agreed" that manumitted Negroes could never be allowed *all* the privileges of citizens." "There is something very repugnant to the general feelings," Fairfax continued, "even in the thought of their being allowed that free intercourse, and the privilege of intermarriage with the white inhabitants, which the other freemen of our country enjoy. . . . The remembrance of their former situation, and a variety of other considerations, forbid this privilege—and as a proof, where is the man of all those who have liberated their slaves, who would marry a son or a daughter to one of them? and if *he* would not, who would?" These "prejudices, sentiments, or whatever they may be called," Fairfax concluded, "would be found to operate so powerfully as to be insurmountable."

Certain assumptions underlying Fairfax's remarks were revealing and important because almost certainly they were shared by a great many other white Virginians. The desirability of emancipation, presumably a "radical" measure, was as much taken for granted as the "conservative" right of protection for private property. Still more obvious was Fairfax's presumption that the white man's claim to purity was of higher order than the Negro's claim on his future condition. Finally, prejudices ("or whatever they may be called") did not suggest alterability or remedial action; they were to be accepted for what they appeared—"insurmountable"—and action taken accordingly.

Another major proposal for abolishing slavery in Virginia came from St. George Tucker, distinguished law professor and judge. A general simultaneous emancipation, Tucker felt, would be impossible. The habits of slavery had rendered blacks unfit for freedom, and whites incapable of treating freedmen as equals. Tucker proposed a "middle course" between slavery and freedom which was bold, ingenious, and complicated. It amounted to freeing as yet unborn *female* slaves and eventually their children. At the same time most civil "privileges," what we would call "civil rights," would be denied to all blacks for the foreseeable future. Tucker conceded that his plan "may appear to savour strongly of prejudice," but he protested that he was merely trying to level as many obstacles to abolition of slavery as possible. He protested, too, that his proposal denied no one his lawful property since no man could rightly claim ownership of persons yet unborn. Significantly, Tucker was unable to thrust from his mind the hope that someday America would be rid of Negroes. "Though I am opposed to the banishment of the Negroes," he wrote pregnantly, "I wish not to encourage their future residence among us. By denying them the most valuable privileges which civil government affords, I wished to render it their inclination and their interest to seek those privileges in some other climate." With the exception of this pitiful lingering hope that Negroes would solve the fundamental problem by simply going away, Tucker's plan was not in fact ridiculous. As things turned out, a century later the Negro *was* "free" but, in a condition which, in an informal way, materially resembled the one he proposed!

INSURRECTION AND EXPATRIATION IN VIRGINIA

Tucker forwarded copies of his *Plan* to the Virginia General Assembly when it met that autumn of 1796. Reaction was mixed though scarcely heartening, and Tucker gloomily wrote that he had abandoned hope: "Actual suffering will one day, perhaps, open the oppressors' eyes. Till that happens, they will shut their ears against argument."

The first "suffering" descended upon Virginians all too soon, and their eyes and ears were indeed opened by the alarming events of the summer of 1800. Proposals for Negro removal suddenly assumed a somewhat changed character. After 1800 the colonizationist movement became in much larger measure an effort to free Virginia from the danger of slave insurrection.

That conviction settled especially on George Tucker, a young cousin of St. George. Shortly after the Gabriel plot he published anonymously a pamphlet which announced dramatically that "the late extraordinary conspiracy has set the public mind in motion: it has waked those who were asleep, and wiped the film from the eyes of the blind." The situation in Virginia was "an eating sore" and fast becoming worse: blacks were increasing more rapidly than whites despite the heavy sale of slaves to the southern states; the "progress of humanity" precluded more rigorous discipline; and "the advancement of knowledge among the Negroes of this country" was turning them into just so many incendiaries. George Tucker knew the spirit of revolution when he saw it.

> Every year adds to the number of those who can read and write. . . . This increase of knowledge is the principal agent in evolving the spirit we have to fear. The love of freedom, sir, is an inborn sentiment, which the God of nature has planted deep in the heart. . . . This celestial spark, which fires the breast of the savage, which glows in that of the philosopher, is not extinguished in the bosom of the slave. . . . Thus we find, sir, there never have been slaves in any country, who have not seized the first favorable opportunity to revolt.

Especially was this so in America: "The very nature of our government, which leads us to recur perpetually to the discussion of natural rights, favors speculation and enquiry."

In one sense, Tucker had offered a prosaic reason for suggesting that blacks be removed from Virginia: no matter what one's political philosophy, one throws a menacing tiger out of the house. But he had also effectively demonstrated the appalling fact that "the very nature of our government" was "the spirit we have to fear." Like virtually every commentator on the Gabriel plot, he detected the spark of liberty burning in the slave, a spark which made the specter of Negro rebellion the more abhorrent because it confirmed that the rebellious Negro was merely responding to the claims of his nature and asking what was rightly his. Slave revolt was a deadly reminder that slaveholding violated the purpose for which the nation existed. Yet emancipation as such, Tucker felt, was no remedy: blacks "would never rest satisfied with any thing short of perfect equality"—and he was not prepared to extend this privilege. "The most zealous advocates for a general emancipation, seeing the impossibility of amalgamating such discordant materials, confess the necessity of qualifying the gift of freedom, by denying the negroes some of the most important privileges of a citizen." Having thus predicated that equality would result in amalgamation, Tucker proceeded to toss the Negroes out. Africa was too expensive and the West Indies too cruel, but western lands would be entirely suitable and might be obtained from the federal government. It would be an exclusively black community under United States protection.

George Tucker's proposals found a far more receptive audience than his cousin's had five years earlier. The General Assembly was now very much in a mood for Negro removal. When it met several months after the insurrection the Assembly's first thought was safety; behind "closed doors" and without recording the customary public minutes, both houses passed a resolution asking the Governor to correspond with the President of the United States concerning some area outside the state to which blacks might be removed. Governor James Monroe dutifully wrote to his friend President Jefferson, who proved no more able to provide a practical solution than anyone else.

The Louisiana Purchase aroused a spasm of interest within Virginia's legislature. Still cloaking discussion in secrecy, both houses adopted resolutions favoring Negro removal in 1804 and 1805; everyone agreed with the Governor that it was a "delicate business." The resolution of 1805 instructed Virginia's congress-

men to press for a portion of the Louisiana Territory for settlement of Negroes already free, freed in the future, and those who
became dangerous to society. It was the last such resolution until
1816.

THE MEANING OF NEGRO REMOVAL

A variety of factors contributed to the sudden disappearance of
clamor for colonization after 1806. The nation was sucked into a
whirlpool of international conflict, and removal of Negroes overseas seemed more out of the question than ever. The official abolition of the slave trade lessened the apparent need for immediate
action, and at the same time the energy of the antislavery drive
was flagging rapidly, thereby weakening a major impulse behind
colonization proposals. Furthermore, the early movement for Negro removal was riddled with inconsistencies and confronted by
insurmountable obstacles. There was no general agreement on
the key question whether blacks were to be allowed, enticed, or
forced to leave, and no thoughtful consideration of the problem.
There was no realistic appraisal of what a Negro colony would
be like if one ever got started. In order even to approach success,
a program for Negro removal would have had to have been
backed by massive popular support, by prodigious wealth, and by
long-standing familiarity with both the necessity and the tech-
niques of organized large-scale social engineering. None of these
existed. Division of power in a federal system of government was
also a hurdle; the national government had no authority to fi-
nance a program of black removal, and Virginia had no authority to acquire an external colony. So Virginia appealed (in vain)
to the national government for assistance with her racial problems. Sixty years later there would be an end to *that* spectacle.

The early movement for Negro removal needs to be recognized
for what it was and not for what African colonization later became. The ten-year period before the founding of the American
Colonization Society in 1816–17 marked an alteration in purpose.
During those years, warhawk expansionism claimed the West for
the American white man; thenceforward colonizationists thought
in terms of Africa or sometimes the Caribbean. And by the 1820's

and 1830's some, perhaps most, of the support for colonization came from men interested in perpetuating slavery; here was a complete reversal of intention. On the other hand, the same thread of abhorrence for the presence of emancipated blacks was woven into the fabric of colonization in both periods. An underlying hostility to blacks as equals in freedom was fundamental to any program of colonization, whether pro- or anti-slavery.

That the notion of colonizing America's Negro population in some remote region was so persistent while so preposterously utopian suggests that it was less a quirk of fancy than a compelling fantasy. That Virginians among the founding fathers, men noted by posterity as political realists above all, should have stressed the utter necessity of accomplishing what was clearly an impossibility suggests that in this instance they were driven men. Caught, as they thought, between the undeniable necessity of liberating their black slaves and the inevitability (as they thought) of disaster if they did, they clutched desperately at the hope that the problem, Negroes, would simply go away.

There was, however, in the apparently preposterous proposition to colonize Negroes an important element of realism. During this period, in Virginia at least, some men were facing up to the necessity of doing something about slavery before it was too late, and at the same time they were also facing squarely the existence of "prejudices" and attempting to do the only thing they thought possible—to accommodate themselves to the reality that white men would not accept blacks as equals. By acceding to this reality, of course, they hardened it and rendered it still more intractable. On the other hand, to think that "prejudices" would simply go away would have been as utopian as hoping Negroes would. The measure of the tragedy was that white Virginians were so paralyzed by the rigid and forbidding character of "prejudices" that they were unable to nourish any hope that time and effort might change them. As time went on in the nineteenth century, white Virginians, realizing that colonization was utterly impractical, turned more and more to the self-solacing thought that "prejudices" were inevitable, innate, and right. Indeed they came to think that their opinions about blacks were not prejudices at all but merely objective assessments of the realities of Negro inferiority. Eventually the defense of Negro slavery necessitated forthright vindication of the rationale upon which slavery rested, but as yet few people were *happy* that white Americans regarded black Americans as inferior human beings.

Epilogue

15

Exodus

I shall need, too, the favor of that Being in whose hands we are, who led our forefathers, as Israel of old, from their native land, and planted them in a country flowing with all the necessaries and comforts of life; who has covered our infancy with his providence, and our riper years with his wisdom and power; and to whose goodness I ask you to join with me in supplications, that he will so enlighten the minds of your servants, guide their councils, and prosper their measures, that whatsoever they do, shall result in your good, and shall secure to you the peace, friendship, and approbation of all nations.

These words concluded the second inaugural address of President Thomas Jefferson in 1805. Coming from him, from the Enlightenment, from rationalism and natural philosophy, from Virginia, they provide special illumination. It was two and a half centuries since Englishmen had first confronted Africans face to face. Now, what had once been the private plantations of the English nation were transformed into an independent state seeking not only the "peace" but the "approbation" of all nations. The transformation had been accompanied by similarly impressive alterations in the character of society and thought. The people had become what so many sixteenth-century Englishmen feared they might become—the governors. As Jefferson said, magistrates were "servants" of the people. God no longer governed—much less judged— his people immediately; indeed "that Being" was now to be given "supplications" so that his "goodness" might endorse a people's continuance in peace and prosperity.

It would seriously mistake the meaning of Jefferson's words to see them as entirely a bland acclamation of the new society in America or as merely another stanza to God-on-our-side. They were these and more. His explicit identification of Americans with the covenanted people of Israel suggests that all Americans were very much in touch with what has been called too narrowly the old New England firm of Moses and Aaron. The American people had been led out "from their native land," though here there was a crucial difference, for Americans had once been truly "native" to England in a way that Israel had never been in Egypt. They had been planted in a land "flowing" with "comforts," a land of plenty, a land surely of milk and honey. In their earliest years, as the process of maturation was so persuasively described, they had "providence"; later they had "wisdom and power." As they grew they dispossessed the tribes of the land and allotted it in various portions to themselves. They killed and enslaved those people not of their own house, both the dispossessed tribes and the black sons of the cursed Canaanites whom their very ancient intellectual forefathers had driven out and killed when they achieved *their* deliverance from bondage.

All of which suggests that the most profound continuities ran through the centuries of change. Particularly, there were the tightly harnessed energies of a restless, trafficking, migrating people emerging from dearth and darkness into plenty and enlightenment. These were a people of the Word, adventuring into a New World; they sought to retain their integrity—their identity— as a peculiar people; they clamped hard prohibitions on themselves as they scented the dangers of freedom.

Which in turn rings of the twin themes which coursed through Elizabethan England—freedom and control. The same themes were changed upon in America; they may be summarized and at the same time most clearly illuminated by looking at a single, undramatic development in the heart of Jeffersonian America.

In 1806 Virginia restricted the right of masters to manumit their slaves. On its face not a remarkable measure, in fact it was the key step in the key state and more than any event marked the reversal of the tide which had set in strongly at the Revolution. It was the step onto the slippery slope which led to the South's surrender to the North at Appomattox and beyond.

There had been some sentiment in Virginia favoring restriction of manumission ever since passage of the law permitting private manumissions by will or deed in 1782. However, the appearance of widespread and insistent demand for restriction may be dated precisely at September 1800. Public pressure mounted during the next few years, especially as it became apparent that the Assembly's resolutions on colonization were not going to bring results. In 1806 the Assembly passed a bill providing that any slave freed in Virginia had to depart the state within one year or face reenslavement. This was in fact a drastic restriction on manumission and was intended as such. At the time of passage, Ohio already prohibited the entry of Negroes, and within a year the other three key states, Kentucky, Maryland, and Delaware, predictably forbade Negroes from entering to take up permanent residence.

No record of debate on the provision has survived, if in fact there was any. Fortunately, however, the spirited debates on two directly restrictionist bills of 1805 and 1806 were partially reported in the Richmond newspapers. Brief as they are, these reports reveal with unusual clarity the attitudes which led the Virginia legislature to repudiate Virginia's most tangible expression of dedication to the principle of liberty for all men.

Easily the most significant element in these debates was the deep sub-stratum of *agreement* which underlay the opposing arguments. Every speaker echoed the general consciousness that restriction of private manumission would constitute a betrayal of the faith of the Revolution. John Minor, the most vigorous friend of manumission, passionately reminded the House that "In past days these walls have rung with eulogies on liberty. A comparison between those times and the present is degrading to us." Opponents of manumission frankly acknowledged that they were abandoning the principles upon which the state and nation had been founded. Thomas B. Robertson argued that the bill proposed merely to renew an old prohibition, yet everyone knew that the long-standing prohibition of private manumission had given way, in 1782, to the impact of Revolutionary enthusiasm for liberty. No one knew this better than Robertson. All slave-holders, he declared, were offenders against principle: "The pro-posed measure is necessary. I advocate it from policy; and not because I am less friendly to the rights of men than those who oppose the bill." "Tell us not of principles," he cried; "Those principles have been annihilated by the existence of slavery among us."

Here precisely was Virginia's agony. The abandonment of the last vestige of emancipation was a stroke of realism, a confession of weakness, and a cruel confrontation with the damning fact that Virginia had failed to be true to herself. It was not, in 1806, an endorsement of slavery as a positive good. Restriction of manumission did not result, emphatically, from special fondness for slavery and the style of life it sustained. *That* variety of at-tachment to slavery was to come later as the sharp spike of guilt sank deeper and deeper into Virginia's social consciousness. In 1806, Virginians stood upon the corner of that development; but at the time they could only look back upon the generation of un-heeding acceptance, upon their great awakening, and now upon the wreckage of their hopes for their society's regeneration.

The evident source of Virginia's mounting determination to bring a halt to individual acts of emancipation was fear of in-crease in the free Negro population. More correctly, it was fear of *free* Negroes *as such*. By the 1790's, free Negroes were being repetitiously characterized as lazy nuisances, harborers of run-aways, and notorious thieves. They were further commonly de-scribed as potential instigators of slave rebellion, as they had been described occasionally for more than a century. The arrest-ing aspect of these accusations was, as always before, that they had little or no basis in fact. No free Negro had been deeply im-plicated in the Gabriel or any other plot, despite the widespread disposition to suspect them on the slightest provocation; yet Vir-ginians for some reason seemed intent on regarding free Negroes as dangerous incendiaries.

Given these circumstances, one is virtually compelled to regard the reaction against free Negroes as functioning primarily on a symbolic level. Most directly, free Negroes stood as perpetual representatives of the freedom for which slaves had actually struggled and were thought avidly to yearn. In this sense, especially in the wake of a slave rebellion, the free Negro embodied all too effectively the failure of white Americans to remain true to Nature and the corollary principles of liberty. From guilt concerning this failure to animosity toward the free Negro was an easy, perhaps a necessary, step. Still more compellingly, the free Negro was feared as an insurrectionary because his status was eminently suggestive of the equality which white men half-consciously feared would result from insurrection. Put another way, the free Negro and the slave revolt both served as symbols of the loss of white dominion; as such they were so inseparably linked to each other in the white man's mind as to warp his perception of the external facts. Functionally, free Negroes and insurrection were interchangeable manifestations of, and hence synonymous expressions for, the loss of white control over the Negro. In this sense, then, free Negroes *had* to be insurrectionaries.

It was in much the same sense, also, that the continued growth of the free Negro population *had* (mentally, for the white man) to result in physical intermixture. Proponents of the bills curtailing manumission were as fervently insistent on the inevitability of this development as were Jefferson and his fellow antislavery advocates for Negro colonization. Indeed the opponents of emancipation were considerably more explicit on the subject, not merely because a complete airing told to their tactical advantage but because intermixture stood in such intimate relation with free Negroes and slave insurrection.

If these latter twin manifestations of Negro freedom implied the loss of the white man's control, then physical amalgamation doubly jeopardized his security by implying not only that blacks were out of control but that whites were too. Long accustomed to relying upon slavery for the maintenance of social and personal controls, white men tended to view its termination (pacific or violent, little matter) as a total disintegration of indispensable restraints. Perhaps white men sensed how tightly the institution had controlled the pattern of sexual relationships between the races, how handsomely it had afforded them a sexual license and privilege which could be indulged without destroying their most vital institution of cultural integrity, the family. The controls of slavery were essential not only for curbing the licentiousness of Negroes, but, as the "swarms" of mulattoes so eloquently testified, for limiting the license of white men. For if the white man's sexual license were not prudently defined and circumscribed, might he not discover that it was he, as much or more than the Negro after all, who was licentious? Above all, the white man had to sustain his feeling of control; in restraining the Negro he was at the same time restraining and thereby reassuring himself.

The necessity of retaining control was the mediating and binding factor in the equation of free Negroes with intermixture and insurrection. And the character of the terms in the equation makes evident how desperately white men felt that necessity. For in advancing as the principal reasons for curbing the free Negro the twin dangers of intermixture and insurrection, white Americans were expressing—in the language in which such things are expressed—how greatly they feared the unrestrained exercise of their most basic impulses. Neither danger existed in anything like the proportions they saw; the proportions were much more theirs than the Negro's. In this sense, white men were attempting to destroy the living image of primitive aggressions which they said was the Negro but was really their own. Their very lives as social beings were at stake. Intermixture and insurrection, violent sex and sexual violence, creation and destruction, life and death—the stuff of animal existence was rumbling at the gates of rational and moral judgment. If the gates fell, so did humanness; they could not fall; indeed there could be no possibility of their falling, else man was not man and his civilization not civilized. We, therefore, we do not lust and destroy; it is someone else. We are not great black bucks of the fields. But a buck *is* loose, his great horns menacing to gore into us with life and destruction. Chain him, either chain him or expel his black shape from our midst, before we realize that he is ourselves.

To chain the free Negro, to re-enslave him, was an intolerable offense to conscience; the urge to do so was sufficiently eased by threatening newly freed Negroes with re-enslavement if they did

not remove themselves. Preventing their increase was all that conscience would allow, since the intellectual and moral imperatives
of Christianity, Revolutionary ideology, and "humanity"—taken
collectively, the cultural conscience—placed effective, if somewhat
indefinite, limits on what the white man could do to the free Negro. In other words, communal conscience sought to prohibit extreme, overt manifestations of aggression against him. On the
other hand, this same demand by the accretions of civilization
that aggressions be restrained, also urged that the Negro be controlled because he was aggressive, that is, because he had been
made to embody the white man's aggressions.

The supreme and tragic irony was that the white man's conflicting urges to liberate the Negro and to restrain him both derived from the same allegiance to his own higher self. Of the two
inner necessities, the urge to curb projected aggressions was certainly the more complex and perhaps in the long run the more
powerful; certainly in 1806 circumstances lent themselves to its
expression. By then, the failure to implement the principles of
the Revolution, the Gabriel insurrection and its reverberations,
and the diffuse but very real sense of insecurity characteristic of a
young nation had combined to generate a heavy charge of anxiety concerning maintenance of American physical and cultural
identity. Release was possible through the restriction of manumission—an admirable outlet indeed, for it conveyed precisely the
pent-up impulses without producing excessive shock to self-
respect. To restrict the free Negro and thereby intermixture and
insurrection was to fight the good fight for civilization and its restraints, for whiteness and the inner purity it signified. Failure in
this struggle would mean for the white man betrayal of the values
of his culture and loss of those things most precious to him, self-
esteem and his sense of who he was and where he was going.

All this was as clear in the debates on the bills restricting manumission as irrational phenomena are ever likely to be in the context of rational discussion. The white man's strong sense of racial
identity and solidarity found reflection in the frequent assertions
that all Negroes possessed this sense. Thomas B. Robertson made
this presumed feeling of solidarity among blacks an argument for

controlling them all by slavery. "For if the blacks see all of their color slaves, it will seem to them a disposition of Providence, and they will be content." This was to say that white men would be content too. "But if they see others like themselves free," he continued, still talking as much about white men as black, "and enjoying rights, they are deprived of, they will repine. Those blacks who are free, obtain some education; they obtain a knowledge of facts, by passing from place to place in society; they can thus organize insurrection. They will, no doubt, unite with the slaves." Robertson was certain that "it is the free blacks who instill into the slaves ideas hostile to our peace." It would have been more in agreement with the facts to say that it was the white man who instilled into others ideas hostile to his own peace of mind.

Another delegate, Alexander Smyth, was more troubled by the complementary term in the equation of black aggression. He opposed emancipation, he declared, because he assumed no one wanted "blacks indiscriminately blended with our descendants" nor America inhabited by "a blended and homogenous race." If blacks were accorded equal political rights or even simple freedom, he argued, inevitably they would struggle for complete equality and then for mastery. Proof lay in St. Domingo. Smyth had no doubt what equality meant: "I presume . . . that no white man will look forward with any complacency to that condition of society, in which the two races will be blended together: when the distinctions of colour shall be obliterated. . . . If this state of society, then, is so disagreeable to our feelings, surely we will not encourage the policy, which is fitted to introduce it." That white Americans must be allowed to remain white was precisely the point. The people of a new nation had at all cost to prevent loss of nationality. Another delegate, thrusting home the case against emancipation, concluded with a poignantly explicit restatement of these most inner fears. "There are now 20,000 free blacks among us. When they shall become more numerous, they will furnish the officers and soldiers around whom the slaves will rally. We cannot now avoid the evils of slavery. Partial emancipation is not the proper remedy. If it proceeds, and they continue to mix with the whites as they have already done, as we daily see,

I know not what kind of people the Virginians will be in one hundred years."

The dilemma was apparent. Virginia's distress was then America's writ large. The white American wanted, indeed *had,* to remain faithful to himself and to his great experiment. In doing so he was caught between the necessity, on the one hand, of maintaining his identity as the fruit of England's and Europe's loins and as the good seed of civilization planted in the wilderness, and on the other, the necessity of remaining faithful to his own image as the world's exemplar of liberty and equalitarianism, as the best hope of the civilization which he cherished. Whichever path he took he seemed to abandon part of himself, so that neither could be taken with assurance or good conscience. Individual Americans divided according to their private necessities, while at the same time the nation divided in response to pressures generated by economic, demographic, and cultural differences, but no American and no section of America could rest at ease with the decision. For Virginians especially, for many Americans, and for the nation as a whole it was impossible to make a clearcut choice.

Within every white American who stood confronted by the Negro, there had arisen a perpetual duel between his higher and lower natures. His cultural conscience—his Christianity, his humanitarianism, his ideology of liberty and equality—demanded that he regard and treat the Negro as his brother and his countryman, as his equal. At the same moment, however, many of his most profound urges, especially his yearning to maintain the identity of his folk, his passion for domination, his sheer avarice, and his sexual desire, impelled him toward conceiving and treating the Negro as inferior to himself, as an American leper. At closer view, though, the duel appears more complex than a conflict between the best and worst in the white man's nature, for in a variety of ways the white man translated his "worst" into his "best." Raw sexual aggression became retention of purity, and brutal domination became faithful maintenance of civilized restraints. These translations, so necessary to the white man's peace of mind, were achieved at devastating cost to another people. But the enormous toll of human wreckage was by no means paid *exclusively* by the Negro, for the subtle translation of basic urges in the white man necessitated his treating the Negro in a fashion which tortured his own conscience, that very quality in his being which necessitated those translations. So the peace of mind the white man sought by denying his profound inexorable drives toward creation and destruction (a denial accomplished by affirmations of virtue in himself and depravity in the Negro) was denied the white man; he sought his own peace at the cost of others and found none. In fearfully hoping to escape the animal within himself the white man debased the Negro, surely, but at the same time he debased himself.

Conceivably there was a way out from the vicious cycle of degradation, an opening of better hope demanding an unprecedented and perhaps impossible measure of courage, honesty, and sheer nerve. If the white man turned to stare at the animal within him, if he once admitted unashamedly that the beast was there, he might see that the old foe was a friend as well, that his best and his worst derived from the same deep well of energy. If he once fully acknowledged the powerful forces which drove his being, the necessity of imputing them to others would drastically diminish. If he came to recognize what had happened and was still happening with himself and the African in America, if he faced the unpalatable realities of the tragedy unflinchingly, if he were willing to call the beast no more the Negro's than his own, then conceivably he might set foot on a better road. Common charity and his special faith demanded that he make the attempt. But there was little in his historical experience to indicate that he would succeed.

Suggestions for Further Reading
(Books marked * are available in paperback editions.)

The information upon which this study relies is almost entirely derived from what people long ago were writing down. This is to say that what historians call "primary," as opposed to "secondary," sources constitute the basis of this book. By "primary" is meant those writings of long ago which were intended as commentary on matters of that moment, not as discussions of matters long since past. No thorough investigation of the distant past is possible without at least some knowledge, and understanding, of what men and women were then "saying," though of course prior to the invention of the phonograph and tape recorder we can learn only about what people wrote down on paper. By way of distinction, books and articles written later (usually much later) *about* what happened in the past are customarily called "secondary."

The following suggestions for further investigation consist of readily available secondary works, which if pursued will yield both further information and guidance into the world of the past—letters, newspaper and magazine articles, official reports, laws, accounts, speculations, and inquiries, written by people long ago. These secondary works have, of course, their points of view, and they should be judged accordingly. As this book should be too.

A great work which focuses on racism in the twentieth century is by a Swedish scholar, Gunnar Myrdal, *An American Dilemma: The Negro Problem and Modern Democracy* (New York, 1944).* A more historically oriented book deals in wide-ranging fashion with a specific matter from ancient times through to about 1760: David Brion Davis, *The Problem of Slavery in Western Culture* (Ithaca, N.Y., 1966).* A psychoanalytical approach is offered by Joel Kovel, *White Racism: A*

Psychohistory (New York, 1970).* More traditionally historical in approach is an essay by Gary B. Nash, "Red, White, and Black: The Origins of Racism in Colonial America," in Gary B. Nash and Richard Weiss, eds., *The Great Fear: Race in the Mind of America* (New York, 1970),* pp. 1-26. An important forthcoming book by Nash will deal with the contacts between Indians, Africans, and colonial Englishmen in early America.

A number of more specifically aimed studies have important bearing upon early Anglo-American racial attitudes. For England, Eldred Jones, *Othello's Countrymen: The African in English Renaissance Drama* (London, 1965) deals with a crucial period. The only book broadly covering blacks in England prior to recent times is James Walvin, *Black and White: The Negro and English Society* (London, 1973). There are a number of articles which bear on the early debasement of Africans in English America: one which takes a different view from that offered in this book is by George M. Fredrickson, "Toward a Social Interpretation of the Development of American Racism," in Nathan I. Huggins, Martin Kilson, and Daniel M. Fox, eds., *Key Issues in the Afro-American Experiences,* 2 vols. (New York, 1971),* vol. I, pp. 240-54. Two recent articles shed still more light on those crucial early years: Alden T. Vaughan, "Blacks in Virginia: A Note on the First Decade," *William and Mary Quarterly,* 3d ser., XXIX (July 1972), 469-78; and Warren M. Billings, "The Cases of Fernando and Elizabeth Key: A Note on the Status of Blacks in Seventeenth-Century Virginia," *William and Mary Quarterly,* 3d ser., XXX (July 1973), 467-74. While the origins of slavery have received much attention, the fifty years prior to the Revolution when the proportion of Africans in the total population was at its highest in our history have been relatively neglected. The three most useful studies are Gerald W. Mullin, *Flight and Rebellion: Slave Resistance in Eighteenth-Century Virginia* (New York, 1972)*; Thad W. Tate, Jr., *The Negro in Eighteenth-Century Williamsburg* (Charlottesville, Va., 1965)*; and Lorenzo J. Greene, *The Negro in Colonial New England* (New York, 1942).* Though all three focus on blacks directly, they have a good deal to say about the views of Anglo-Americans.

The same may be said of several of the larger number of works which deal with immediately post-Revolutionary America. The most revealing is Arthur Zilversmit, *The First Emancipation: The Abolition of Slavery in the North* (Chicago, 1967).* Slavery as an institution is emphasized in Donald L. Robinson, *Slavery in the Structure of American Politics, 1765-1820* (New York, 1971). Some of the scientific debate is covered in John C. Greene, "The American Debate on the Negro's Place in Nature, 1780-1815," *Journal of the History of Ideas,* XV (June 1954), 384-96. And Robert McColley, *Slavery and Jeffersonian Virginia* (Urbana, Ill., 1964) emphasizes the contributions of evangelical Christians to antislavery while questioning the motives of rationalist Virginia gentlemen. See also Fredrika Teute Schmidt and Barbara Ripel Wilhelm, "Early Proslavery Petitions in Virginia," *William and Mary Quarterly,* 3d ser., XXX (Jan. 1973), 133-46.

Unfortunately, the tendency among historians has been to separate ideas about Indians from ideas about Afro-Americans, the works by Gary B. Nash, mentioned above, being conspicuous exceptions. It is suggestive that writings about Indians and about European attitudes toward Indians are more easily separable from each other than writings about Afro-Americans and writings about European attitudes toward them. Of books falling into the second of these four categories the most important are Roy Harvey Pearce, *The Savages of America: A Study of the Indian and the Idea of Civilization* (Baltimore, 1953)*; and Bernard W. Sheehan, *Seeds of Extinction: Jeffersonian Philanthropy and the American Indian* (Chapel Hill, N.C., 1973). See also Gary B. Nash, "The Image of the Indian in the Southern Colonial Mind," *William and Mary Quarterly,* 3d ser., XXIX (April 1972), 197-230.

For anyone wishing to pursue this matter further, the most readily available and one of the very best bibliographies is James M. McPherson and others, *Blacks in America: Bibliographical Essays* (Garden City, N.Y., 1971).

Finally, let me reiterate that the best route to understanding of the origins of racism in the United States is through primary sources. They must be read with eyes and ears wide open and with the question always in mind (as with all reading), why did he write that?